Working with the Grain

Working with the Grain

Integrating Governance and Growth in Development Strategies

BRIAN LEVY

OXFORD
UNIVERSITY PRESS

OXFORD
UNIVERSITY PRESS

Oxford University Press is a department of the University of Oxford.
It furthers the University's objective of excellence in research, scholarship,
and education by publishing worldwide.

Oxford New York
Auckland Cape Town Dar es Salaam Hong Kong Karachi
Kuala Lumpur Madrid Melbourne Mexico City Nairobi
New Delhi Shanghai Taipei Toronto

With offices in
Argentina Austria Brazil Chile Czech Republic France Greece
Guatemala Hungary Italy Japan Poland Portugal Singapore
South Korea Switzerland Thailand Turkey Ukraine Vietnam

Oxford is a registered trade mark of Oxford University Press
in the UK and certain other countries.

Published in the United States of America by
Oxford University Press
198 Madison Avenue, New York, NY 10016

Library of Congress Cataloging-in-Publication Data
Levy, Brian, 1954–
 Working with the grain : integrating governance and growth in development strategies / Brian Levy.
   p.   cm.
 Includes bibliographical references and index.
 ISBN 978–0–19–936380–3 (alk. paper) — ISBN 978–0–19–936381–0 (alk. paper)
 1. Economic development. 2. Democratization. I. Title.
 HD75.L483 2014
 338.9—dc23
                2014006785

9 8 7 6 5 4 3 2 1

Printed in the United States of America on acid-free paper

To
Issy, Ray, and Larry
who, each in his own way, taught
me the power of a curious mind

CONTENTS

ACKNOWLEDGMENTS

This book explores the meeting of theory and action. I have explored this interplay in many, many conversations; over many, many decades; over many, many cups of coffee; in many, many settings—too many to acknowledge individually the hundreds of people from whom I have learned so much. So first and foremost, I want to acknowledge collectively the colleagues with whom I worked at the World Bank for almost a quarter-century. Contrary to the usual stereotypes, the large majority came to work each day dedicated to trying to make the world a better place and open-eyed about the complexities and ambiguities of the challenge. I especially want to acknowledge everyone with whom I worked closely in the following teams: the "anchor" public-sector reform group (including Sanjay Pradhan, Cheryl Gray, Mary Shirley, Randi Ryterman, and Graham Teskey); the Southern African Department (including Ataman Aksoy, Alan Gelb, and Yvonne Tsikata); the Bank-wide team tasked with implementing the Governance and Anti-Corruption strategy (including Ariel Fiszbein, Helene Grandvoinnet, and Anand Rajaram); the participants in the Bank-wide political economy community of practice (including Phil Keefer, for patiently injecting analytical rigor into our conversations for almost two decades); and all of the dedicated and committed staff who put up with me as their manager in the Africa public-sector reform and capacity-building unit.

A special thanks to Francis Fukuyama who, by inviting me in 2005 to co-teach an early-morning course with him at Johns Hopkins University School of Advanced International Studies (SAIS), set in motion my return to the university world. In the ongoing effort to build a bridge between institutional economics and development practice, thanks to Douglass North and Barry Weingast for engagement both early (as advisers in a 1991 joint research project with Pablo Spiller) and recent. In that recent engagement, thanks to the superb team that worked on the edited volume In the Shadow of Violence (especially to Mushtaq Khan, John Wallis, and Steve Webb).

For feedback on the ideas in this book and on earlier drafts, I am grateful to my students at SAIS and the University of Cape Town, to the Effective States and Inclusive Development research team at the University of Manchester; to Deborah Brautigam, Ishac Diwan, Bill Douglas, Cliff Gaddy, Sam Hickey, Alan Hirsch, Steve Knack, and Mike Walton; and to five anonymous reviewers and Scott Parris, my always-supportive editor at Oxford University Press. Finally, special thanks to my wife Lo Dagerman—for her wise, thoughtful, and encouraging comments on early drafts . . . and as a truly wonderful partner these past three decades in our shared journey through life.

PRELUDE

May 2012: I have been living in Cape Town for the first time in many years, and the drumbeat of dispiriting daily headlines tests my resolve not to be flooded with emotion and judgment but to begin where things actually are.

And where things are, I remind myself, is remarkable. Each morning, riding down the elevator of my ocean-facing Green Point apartment and hearing the chime that signals it is about to stop, I wait with anticipation to see who will join me. It could be the elderly Jewish woman who lives on the floor below; or it could be my friend Serge, from Bukavu in Eastern Congo, trying to make his way in Cape Town as a travel agent and tour guide. It could be Dakaro, the Venda physician who chose to ignore all the talk that Cape Town has retained its racist ways and moved to the city with his wife and infant daughter to take a position at Somerset Hospital (where my father occasionally used to do physicians' rounds). Or perhaps it's Shevin, who would have been classified as "colored" in the apartheid days and would have been forbidden to rent or own property in this "white" group area—and now is chair of our building's body corporate.

Indeed, South Africa's democracy has wrought remarkable change. But it also is passing through a period of stress. It's not only the many longstanding challenges that have not gone away: the desperate poverty and deep inequality; an economy that fails to create jobs, leaving more than half of young people under the age of thirty without work. There are emerging new elites, seeking political outlet for their ambitions, and unrestrained in their use of muscle power and racial populism to push their way forward. There are leaders who view the checks on abuse of power written into the country's democratic constitution as little more than a political compromise. And perhaps most distressingly of all for the long run, there's the stark reality that the country's schools are failing its young: that a noxious combination of past legacies and present politicization of teaching positions have resulted in 80 percent of

South Africa's children lagging their sub-Saharan African neighbors in educational performance, and this despite spending that is more than ten times higher per student.

South Africa is hardly alone in its journey along this arc from the exuberance of democratization in the early 1990s to the stark challenges of 2012. In the wake of the fall of the Berlin Wall in 1989, the 1990s saw a wave of democratization sweep the world. Globally, the number of democracies doubled, from 60 in 1984 to 120 fifteen years later. In Africa alone, the number of countries in which elections decided who would rule went from single digits in the 1980s to upward of forty by the latter 1990s.[1]

The 1990s was the era when liberal democracy seemed ascendant, and Francis Fukuyama could title a book The End of History to mark its presumed certain triumph. All that remained was the seemingly straightforward task of providing the facilitating framework that would enable humanity to realize its political, economic, and social fruits. The presumption was that there is a "best practice" out there that, once identified could—given "political will"—be adopted the world over, cookie-cutter-like, as the solution to the development problem.

If only it were that simple.

*   *   *   *

When I joined the World Bank in 1989, it was unimaginable how profoundly the world would change within a few short years—and how profoundly these changes would affect the discourse between development agencies and developing countries.

The World Bank was established in the immediate aftermath of the Second World War. For the first quarter-century of its existence, development economics had been a vibrant field—with heated debates between proponents of balanced versus unbalanced growth strategies and between theorists championing the cumulative power of modernization and more radical critics who focused on the ways in which the dependency of "peripheral" countries on the "metropolitan" core undercut development.[2] But by the 1980s, the subject seemingly had become little more than an applied branch of macro- and microeconomics. Reflecting that emphasis, the focus of development practitioners had turned to "structural adjustment" policies, which were preoccupied with addressing macro-imbalances and with liberalizing markets.

All of this changed with the fall of the Berlin Wall, the end of the Cold War, and the resulting (temporary) triumphalism of the dominant Western liberal democratic powers. These momentous political events coincided with an increasing emphasis in the academic literature on the ways in which good policies, and a well-performing economy, rest on a foundation of governance institutions—and the ways in which weaknesses in this institutional foundation could short-circuit efforts at policy change. The result was that the quest for good governance—a strong rule of law, capable bureaucracies, low corruption, and accountability of politicians and public officials to citizens—came to center stage in the discourse of development reform.

Over the long run, good governance may indeed be a destination to which, as countries develop, they converge. However, the ability to describe well-governed states does not conjure them into existence out of thin air. Best practices approaches assume that all policies and institutions are potentially movable and can be aligned to fit some prespecified blueprint. But the central issues for governance reform have less to do with the end point than with the journey of getting from here to there. The principal purpose of this book is to provide for policymakers, donors, civil society activists, and other development practitioners a practical, analytically grounded guide for making this journey—as an alternative to the "best practices" approach to governance reform (and development policymaking more broadly) that, in recent decades, has dominated the development discourse.

The approach to development policy laid out in this book is anchored in recent important conceptual breakthroughs in understanding how institutions, politics, and economic policy interact with one another.[3] But those conceptual breakthroughs generally have been used to analyze governance and growth from the Olympian heights of long-term history. By contrast, the focus here is less on the very long run than on how governance–growth interactions play out over a decade or so—a time horizon that is of more immediate practical relevance for policymakers. What types of actions might one take now that can provide a stronger platform a decade hence? What developmental gains can be achieved over the course of a decade? What actions can lead to a more attractive set of opportunities at the end of the period than at the outset? And how might the answers vary across different types of country settings?

To address these questions, the book lays out a "with-the-grain" approach to governance reform and development policymaking. A with-the-grain approach conceives of change in evolutionary rather than engineering terms and so directs attention away from the search for "optimal" policies and toward the challenges of initiating and sustaining forward development momentum. Its point of departure is that a country's economy, polity, and society—and the institutions that underpin each of these—are embedded in a complex network of interdependencies. To be successful, reforms cannot be reengineered from scratch but need to be aligned with these realities. They need to be compatible with the incentives of a critical mass of influential actors, so that they have a stake in the reforms and are willing to champion them in the face of opposition from those who benefit from the preexisting arrangements. The aim is to nudge things along, seeking gains that, though useful, often are initially likely to seem quite modest but can, sometimes, give rise to a cascading sequence of change for the better.

The book explores the implications of this with-the-grain approach from both a comparative, cross-country perspective and from the dynamic perspective of how governance and development interact over time within specific countries. The cross-country perspective takes the form of a "good fit" approach to development strategy—a middle ground between "one-size-fits-all" best practices and the view that every country is unique so needs an entirely unique set of policies.

Parts I and II develop a comparative typology that distinguishes among countries along two dimensions of governance: whether their polities are dominant or competitive and, within each of these, whether the rules of the game center around personalized deal-making or the impersonal application of the rule of law. It uses this analytical platform as a basis for exploring development from a dynamic perspective—specifically how each of the dominant and competitive trajectories potentially might evolve from personalized to impersonal rules of the game. Part III distinguishes among two broad sets of options for governance reform. One set is hierarchical and focuses on strengthening the chain of principal–agent relationships that govern the public bureaucracy. The other set focuses on strengthening horizontal peer-to-peer (principal-to-principal) micro-level relationships among multiple stakeholders as platforms for the emergence of "islands of effectiveness" within a broader sea of institutional dysfunction.

Dominant and competitive political orders each bring distinctive strengths and weaknesses, which affect the efficacy of hierarchical and horizontal approaches to reform. In early stages along the dominant trajectory, the constraints on political leaders can be few. While all too often the result can be predation and continuing dysfunction, on occasion leadership can emerge that is both developmentally oriented and has a firm hold on power. In such settings, hierarchical reforms that depend for their effectiveness on robust principal–agent governance may have good prospects for moving development forward.

By contrast, in early-stage personalized-competitive settings power often is fragmented, leaders are constrained, and public bureaucracies are weak. In these settings, time horizons can be short, maintaining political stability can be a challenge—and the deal-making through which stability is sustained can fall way short of any idealized notion of good governance. In such settings, a useful focus of reform efforts might be on establishing "islands of effectiveness." While an "islands" approach is incremental by definition, its cumulative consequences can be powerful.

To explore the dynamic implications of a with-the-grain approach, the book examines the potential for "virtuous circles"—focusing especially on interactions that link inclusive growth, positive expectations, and ongoing institutional improvement. Forward movement in some of these dimensions brings with it the possibility (though not the certainty) of gains in the others. For example, with continuing forward momentum, the private sector, civil society, and middle-class actors all are likely to strengthen. In turn, the growing strength of these actors can bring to the forefront a new set of institutional considerations. Actors who in earlier stages might have thrived on personalized arrangements might now seek something different—better public services, more contractual certainty, and greater openness.

Incremental, working-with-the-grain reforms thus offer a path of progress with the potential to cumulatively achieve progressively more far-reaching gains over time—and where, from the perspective of a decadal time horizon, the appropriate point of departure for devising a development strategy is agnosticism as to which specific reforms offer the better way forward. Sometimes the binding constraint to forward movement can be institutional, making governance reform the priority. At other times, the priority can better be on inclusive growth as the engine that provides momentum for a cascading chain of economic, social, institutional, and political changes. And some countries may have long been mired in stasis, with no prospect that with-the-grain entry points for initiating and sustaining momentum could take hold. In such settings, discontinuous policy and institutional reforms—perhaps even discontinuous political change—may be necessary.

This dynamic perspective offers some useful insights into the challenge of locking in sustainable democracies. Sustainable democracies are characterized not just by competitive elections but also by complementary, impersonal checks and balances institutions that constrain the unchecked, personalized exercise of power. As this book shows, with continued forward momentum, institutions can strengthen incrementally, gradually transforming personalized into more impersonal arrangements.

But getting to impersonality is only part of the story. Even if (as in South Africa) a country is able to establish a seemingly stable constitutional platform of electoral competition and impersonal checks and balances, stability over the longer run depends on broad-based commitment of its populace to the institutional order. And this, in turn, depends on inclusion—both in the narrow sense that the benefits of growth are reasonably broadly shared and, more broadly, in positive expectations that a country's trajectory of change is one that offers hope for the future. If momentum stops too soon, virtuous circles can all too easily go into reverse, wiping out hard-won gains.

The chapters that follow drill down deeply into the details of what a with-the-grain approach can bring to the development discourse. The approach is intended as an orienting framework—a guide for helping to identify which of a broader array of alternative interventions potentially are most relevant as points of departure for shaping development strategies in specific country settings. The intent is not to prescribe hard-and-fast rules. The approach thus contrasts starkly with maximalist assertions that the full set of "good governance" reforms is necessary for development. If the only available actions and outcomes are "all" or "nothing," then efforts at change will almost certainly fall short, leading to disillusion and despair. This book, by contrast, aims to encourage the exploration of possibilities that respond creatively to the governance ambiguities of our early twenty-first-century world. In so doing, it draws in spirit on the earlier generation of development economists—the spirit of "a bias for hope."[4]

Working with the Grain

I

CONCEPTS—A DYNAMIC TYPOLOGY

Part I introduces the dynamic typology around which the book is organized. The typology comprises a parsimonious set of divergent trajectories through which countries evolve from low to high incomes and from weaker to stronger governance institutions. It distinguishes among countries along two dimensions of governance: whether their polities are dominant or competitive and, within each of these, whether the rules of the game center around personalized deal-making or the impersonal application of the rule of law.

The resulting framework can be put to work in two ways. One way is to view each of the country types as a world unto itself—each comprising a distinctive platform for development, with distinctive incentives for the participants, distinctive constraints and risks, and distinctive frontier challenges. Careful attention to these incentives and constraints provides a platform for identifying specific "good fit" policy actions that are both worthwhile and feasible, given country-specific institutional realities.

A complementary approach is to view the framework from a dynamic perspective—with the focus less on distinctive governance patterns of incentive and constraint and more on how governance and growth interact. This longer-run perspective can usefully be framed in terms of three phases of a virtuous circle: initiating change, building momentum, and sustaining momentum over time. While virtuous circles unfold differently along each of the dominant and competitive trajectories, the interactions between governance and growth that propel forward movement are akin to a snowball that builds in size as it rolls down a hill. As long as momentum can be sustained, by the time the snowball gets to the bottom of the hill it will have built formidable power, irrespective of where it started.

CHAPTER 1

The Search for a Useful Development Paradigm

They were to arrive within the hour—and it was not the usual suspects. Six months earlier, I had been asked to lead a team to better understand why a decade-long reform effort in Zambia seemed repeatedly to disappoint. The difficulty was that, though there had been lots of action, very little seemed to have changed on the ground. As an internal 2005 review of the World Bank's program in the country put it:

> By and large, agreeing on policies and programs was the easy part of the Bank's relations with the government. The really difficult part was and continues to be implementation.[1]

The problem, everyone knew, was governance. But what exactly did that mean?

"This is going to be interesting," said the external affairs officer in the World Bank's Lusaka office, rubbing his hands together excitedly, a nervous smile on his face. "The World Bank making a briefing on governance, to government and its critics in civil society. The sparks are going to fly."

"Let's see," I replied.

For the past decade, I had been part of a group championing the integration of governance into the World Bank's development practice—but my disquiet at the way mainstreaming was going had been rising. Meanwhile, there was a ferment of new ideas among researchers and practitioners at the cutting edge. The Zambian work was an early opportunity to try a new approach. I was hopeful that something very different could happen—less predictable but potentially far more constructive than my colleague expected.

Good Governance and Its Discontents

Certainly the external affairs officer's nervous intuition reflected the emerging track record. Back in 1996, then-Bank president Jim Wolfensohn brought governance to center stage with a speech that decried the "cancer of corruption." Corruption was the "C" word, the one that, until that speech, could not speak its name in the polite company of the endless flow of meetings, diagnostic studies, memoranda of understanding—and lending—that comprised government-donor dialogue on the allocation of aid.

In 1997, the Bank produced a widely publicized "man-bites-dog" flagship World Development Report on *The State in a Changing World*. What made the report noteworthy was its central message—that an effective state is key for development. This was seemingly a 180-degree turnaround for the World Bank which, hitherto, had been perceived as an unrelenting champion of market liberalization, of a small state, and of the dismantling or privatization of a broad swathe of public-sector organizations.

Post-1997, the profile of the "good governance" agenda continued to rise. Good governance had become central (at least rhetorically) not only to the World Bank and other development agencies but to the Western foreign policy establishment more broadly. But, ten years on, the challenge of integrating governance into development strategy was proving to be more difficult than expected.

Rather than becoming a powerful tool for increasing the effectiveness of development practice, the new focus on governance and institutions seemed to be embroiling development practitioners and donor agencies in endless new cycles of conflict—often with countries and governments that, from a more traditional development perspective, seemed to be model performers. Zambia was hardly the only example. Consider:

- In 2000, Ethiopia's prime minister, Meles Zenawi, had been feted globally for his efforts to turn around what had long seemed one of the world's development basket cases. Donor aid was flooding into the country; Meles had been appointed cochair, with British Prime Minister Tony Blair, of the Millennium Commission for Africa. But in 2005, in the wake of an election that turned violent, many donors were considering withholding their support.
- Bangladesh had been one of the most successful countries in the world in meeting the millennium development goals for poverty reduction. Infant mortality, for example, had fallen from 145 per 1,000 children in 1970 to 46 per 1,000 in 2003. But in 2005, Bangladesh also had the dubious distinction of being rated by Transparency International as the most corrupt of all 150 + countries surveyed.

- Then there were the many countries—from Albania to Cambodia, from India to Kenya, plus many, many more—where rapid gains in poverty reduction were being overshadowed by a seemingly endless flow of corruption scandals that threatened to undermine the legitimacy of the aid endeavor itself.

Meanwhile, a new set of conflicts emerged as to how financial transfers could most effectively be integrated into development work. These were conflicts over competing first principles; they went to the heart of the professional identities—indeed, of deeply held values and life commitments—of the protagonists.

- There was conflict between governance advisers who saw the strengthening of "country systems" within the public sector as key to effectiveness and protagonists who gave priority to more bottom-up, community-based approaches to development work. Protagonists of working with communities derided government as the enemy to be avoided at all costs. And, in a mirror image of virulence, public management types often derided their community-oriented counterparts as short-sighted romantics.
- There was a parallel conflict between protagonists of strengthening public management systems on the one hand and champions of more innovative globalization-linked initiatives on the other. The latter ranged from "vertical global programs" to improve health (often funded generously by the Gates Foundation); to global anticorruption and transparency codes; to the use of sustainability standards to combat the degradation of forests, fisheries, and other natural resources; to the use of "fair trade" principles to combat child labor. Viewed from the perspective of country systems, these vertical programs undercut country ownership and, indeed, added new difficulties to the challenge of strengthening country systems.

How had the high hopes of those of us who, from early on, had embraced the governance agenda led us into such a seeming impasse? What was the way out? This book addresses these questions.

*   *   *   *

The governance agenda that took shape post-1997 was nothing if not ambitious. It generally incorporated the following:

- Provide an enabling environment that protects human rights, as well as rights to property, via the rule of law.
- Have capable bureaucracies, staffed with public officials committed to the achievement of social goals, with well-defined roles and responsibilities and transparent and predictable decision making—plus robust internal arrangements for monitoring how effectively resources are used.

- Allocate resources on the basis of priorities determined by political leaders and the citizens who elect them.
- Help assure accountability of public officials and politicians to the citizens that they are intended to serve through electoral and other oversight arrangements—at national and local levels and at the service-provision frontline.
- Keep corruption to a minimum—and, when it is discovered, meet it with the sanction of law.
- Most broadly, assure that the overall public order is broadly accepted as "legitimate" by the vast majority of society.

Taken together, these elements comprise the institutional characteristics of well-functioning, democratic states in affluent societies. To put it a bit more sweepingly (but hopefully not inaccurately): Good governance is nothing less than an institutional embodiment of the values of the Western enlightenment!

The rise of good governance as a focus for development reform can be linked to the fall of the Berlin Wall, the end of the Cold War, and the resulting (temporary) triumphalism of the dominant Western liberal democratic powers. These momentous political events coincided with an increasing emphasis in the academic literature on the ways in which good policies, and a well-performing economy, rest on a foundation of governance institutions—and the ways in which weaknesses in this institutional foundation could short-circuit efforts at policy change.

In response, a new subspecialty of academics, consultants, and staff in development agencies emerged—protagonists of public sector governance reform. At first, these governance reformers (a group of which I was, and am, a part) took the reform challenge to be the engineering-like one of putting in place "good governance," through a comprehensive redesign of the governance system in all facets, on the principle that the different parts of the system were mutually reinforcing. "A chain is only as strong as its weakest link" became the reigning metaphor.

For some, getting governance on the development agenda in this comprehensive way was a matter of deep conviction. Democracy and human-rights advocates have long been passionate about their causes; they viewed them less as a means to a development end than as ends in themselves. They had long chafed at the seeming dismissiveness of development agencies, so they—though remaining suspicious of what they still perceived as a half-hearted embrace of the agenda by these agencies—were supportive of this new direction.

There were also some darker reasons for the rise of the good governance agenda. There is a deeply rooted tendency for people to find ways of thinking well of ourselves by setting standards, viewing ourselves without much self-critical reflection as worthy exemplars of those standards—and then judging others for their supposed shortcomings. This is part of what happened on the governance front. Somehow, the discourse of democracy and human rights became a tool of hubris, part of the rationale for the US invasion of Iraq.

As a growing number of scholars were pointing out,[2] there was something truly extraordinary about coming up with a comprehensive governance reform program for low-income countries by describing the characteristics of the world's most affluent and most open societies and then reverse engineering them. Consider the realities that prevailed in these self-same countries in the mid-nineteenth century, when their levels of development were broadly similar to those prevailing in many of today's lower and middle-income countries. In parts of Europe, rule was absolutist; in much of the rest, the right to vote was severely restricted. Japan was feudal, with the modernizing Meiji reformation still a few decades away. In the United States, it was taken for granted by the great emancipator, Abraham Lincoln—at the time the country was in the throes of devastating conflict, complete with secession and civil war— that public appointments were sinecures, favors granted at the discretion of political leaders.

Vast sweeps of history brought these countries from there to here— no smooth arc of progress but a history that includes war, revolution, and economic depression. Ignoring this long sweep, and instead turning the outcome into a blueprint for immediate action, seems like a breathtaking combination of naivete and amnesia.

Working with the Grain—Development as an Evolving, Interdependent System

Yet for all of the risks of over-reach, for many of us in the development profession the rise of the governance agenda came as a relief and an opportunity. The conventional development discourse was coming to seem increasingly unreal—its "best practice" economic prescriptions labored under a set of assumptions as to what shaped policy and its implementation, which bore little relation to the realities on the ground.

Contra the assumptions of the conventional discourse, economic policies are not made in a vacuum. Engaging effectively with policy meant understanding better the incentives that shaped the behavior of policymakers—and this, in turn, directed attention to institutions and politics. The governance discourse provided an opportunity to address the challenges associated with institutions and politics more systematically. But how to do so was deeply contested.

Over the long run, good governance may indeed be a destination to which, as countries develop, their governance systems converge. But the ability to describe the characteristics of effective states does not conjure them into existence out of thin air. Best-practices approaches assume that all policies and institutions are potentially movable and can be aligned to fit some prespecified blueprint. But they cannot. The central questions (of both the governance and economic variety) had less to do with the end point than with the journey of getting from here to there.

But there is also a risk at the opposite end of the spectrum from the hubris of the good governance agenda. Leaving behind both narrowly economistic thinking and one-size-fits-all best-practice prescriptions laid those of us probing a new path vulnerable to reaching a dispiriting conclusion—that every country is unique and that there is little to be learned in one setting that can be helpful in another.[3] The challenge is to find an orienting framework that is capable of filling the gap between hubris on the one hand and despair disguised as humility on the other.

At the center of the approach laid out in this book is a sustained focus on how governance and economic development interact—the ways in which they are interdependent, and potentially mutually supportive, the leads and lags in their interplay. Both governance and growth have, of course, been analyzed in great depth, and a series of path-breaking new contributions have focused on interactions between the two. What distinguishes the approach laid out here is its time horizon.

The recent contributions consider governance–growth interactions from the Olympian heights of long-term history.[4] By contrast, the principal purpose of this book is less to provide a grand unified theory that explains everything than it is to provide practical guidance to policymakers, donors, civil society activists, and other development practitioners. Its focus thus is less on the very long run than on how governance–growth interactions play out over a time horizon of, say, a decade. Given the way governance and growth interact, what types of actions might one take now that can provide a stronger platform a decade hence? What developmental gains can be achieved over the course of a decade? What actions can lead to a more attractive set of opportunities at the end of the period than at the outset? And how might the answers vary across different types of country settings?

To preview the analysis, consider the development process as an example of a complex system. A country's economy, polity, and society—and the institutions that underpin each of these—are embedded in a complex network of interdependencies. Politics (stakeholders, and their power, incentives, skill, capacity to organize, and constraints) inevitably constrains and shapes the dynamics of reform. Three empirically robust propositions as to how complex systems can evolve in a way that yields ongoing, cumulative gains in performance, turn out to be especially relevant for the approach to development adopted in this volume.[5]

- First, change is cumulative.

Beginning from a specific point of departure, complex, interdependent systems evolve one step at a time. But because the different parts of the system are causally connected with one another, change in any one part has knock-on effects on others. Over time, the system as a whole can thus become fundamentally transformed—via the cumulative consequence of many small shifts.

Thinking about development as an ongoing, cumulative process was a central theme of two of the greatest development thinkers of the past half century, Albert Hirschman and Douglass North. As each underscored in his different way, a country's policies, rules of the game, and organizational capabilities are mutually reinforcing. Changes in policies and the institutional rules of the game evoke complementary investments in the capabilities of organizations that operate within that specific environment. And these organizations are likely, in turn, to generate pressure for a further round of supportive policy and institutional reforms. The result is a cumulative process of change.[6] Effective action will seek to work with rather than against a country's grain in order to nudge forward this interdependent, dynamic process.

- Second, cumulative change can, over long periods of time, generate a very wide dispersion of patterns.

As countries move from low to middling levels of income, their patterns of institutional change can diverge rather than converge—and actions that can nudge the system forward along one trajectory need have no effect (or could even be counterproductive) along another. A "with-the-grain" approach aims to better identify a variety of potential trajectories—and then to seek out actions that are a "good fit" within a given trajectory—nudging the system forward so that, say ten years on, it performs better in at least some (not all) domains. There is no formula that can straightforwardly be applied across all countries and over time.

- Third, as countries move from low to high levels of income, previously divergent patterns of institutional change may increasingly converge.

Why? Because as a country's economy grows—and as its citizenry becomes wealthier and more empowered—pressure is likely to grow for institutions that can undergird more sophisticated economic interactions, a more open civic realm, and enhanced economic and political competition. But note that, while pressure to adapt is likely to build, it will not necessarily be met successfully. And note further that the possibility of convergence is less a call for good governance than it is a call for taking a long view. Except for a small number of settings where the opportunities are ripe, the time horizons are too long for the prospect of convergence over time to be the basis for advocacy in the short term. On the contrary, the corollary of taking a long run with-the-grain approach to development is—over, say, a decade—a principled rather than a merely tactical agnosticism about what to do next.[7]

To incorporate the above three features into thinking about development, the book introduces and uses a typology—a parsimonious set of divergent trajectories through which groups of countries have evolved from low to high incomes and from weaker to stronger governance institutions. Any typology is, by definition, a conceptual construct; typologies use "ideal types" to bring analytical order to messy, multifaceted reality. The intent of the typology laid out in this book is thus not to suggest that by grouping countries into categories one can summarize (let alone capture) the whole of any single country's development path. Rather, the aim is to highlight some key characteristics that are shared in common among some subgroups of countries—and can be directly contrasted with other subgroups that share a different set of characteristics—and to use these features to facilitate more effective comparison of "like with like" and thereby be more targeted and effective in identifying feasible options for moving forward.

The aim is to find feasible entry points—seemingly modest changes in one part of the system that can evoke adaptations in other parts, in an ongoing, cumulative process. Country-specific realities imply that many seemingly desirable policies may not be implementable. Their effectiveness might depend on complementary institutions and capacities that are absent; they may breach political "red lines" that a country's leaders deem essential to their hold on power, or to stability more broadly.

For all of the ambition of the endeavor, an important limitation must be noted up front: The focus of this book is almost entirely on country-level dynamics, with very little attention to the broader global context. This is not to imply that patterns of global change are unimportant. The acceleration of globalization, the rise of China, global booms and busts in demand for natural resources—all of these profoundly alter the opportunities and challenges confronting developing countries. Countries with domestic institutions capable of capitalizing on global changes potentially have unprecedented opportunities to thrive; countries with weaker institutions potentially are even more at risk than they would be in a less vibrant and volatile world. Even so, an exploration of these global dynamics, and their interaction with country-level institutions, goes beyond the scope of this book.

A Roadmap

The argument is laid out in twelve chapters that group loosely into four distinct parts. Part I—this chapter and the next two—provides a broad conceptual overview of the "typologies approach" to development strategy.

Part II uses country-level experiences to illustrate how the typology can help us understand and address the challenges of economic growth and governance reform. Chapters 4 and 5 are organized around the diverse experiences of four countries—South Korea, Ethiopia, Bangladesh, and Zambia—each of which has enjoyed at least some development success (in varying degrees and much more sustained for some than for others) but via very different pathways. Chapter 6 takes a longer-run view of how governance evolves, drawing on the experiences of Korea (again), South Africa, and the late-nineteenth-century United States. Chapter 7 uses descriptive statistics to map the patterns of governance and growth for a larger group of low- and middle-income countries.

Part III shifts the focus from the broad macro-dynamics of how governance and growth interact to the specifics of micro-level governance initiatives—less as ends in themselves than as means to address binding constraints on development. It examines a variety of different approaches, each better adapted to some country circumstances than to others. Chapter 8 explores the conditions needed for top-down public-sector reform to succeed—and also, for settings where top-down approaches are unlikely to succeed, the potential of multistakeholder approaches to establish islands of development effectiveness within a broader sea of institutional dysfunction. Chapters 9 and 10 explore multistakeholder approaches empirically. Chapter 9 uses the examples of basic education and community-driven development to assess the potential of transparency and participation initiatives to address weaknesses in top-down public-service provision. Chapter 10 focuses on the private sector; it explores whether and how multistakeholder approaches can provide a platform of commitment needed to foster private investment and govern markets in ways which support positive development outcomes in settings where conventional prescriptions for improving the business environment cannot gain traction.

Finally, Part IV explores how the effort to build governance institutions capable of supporting ongoing development momentum might be approached strategically: how to identify an initial round of actions that opens up the path for later stages of the journey, how to assess constraints that might inhibit this initial round of actions, and, as needed, how to identify alternative pathways that get around those constraints. It aims to help clarify what is to be done, how, and by whom.

CHAPTER 2

Constructing a Typology

I learned up close how difficult it was to reform governance when, between 1999 and 2003, I headed the World Bank's team charged with supporting public-sector governance reform across Africa. From one perspective, the field was wide open. There was strong demand to incorporate governance into many of the World Bank's programs of country-level support. And many of the staff in my group had superb skills and vast experience in public finance, administrative management, and the operation of a variety of checks and balances systems—and were enormously eager to give of their expertise. The difficulty was that having skills to offer, and a demand for those skills, did not translate into a coherent, workable program.

Worldwide, Bank teams, working with counterparts in government, designed ambitious programs to address weaknesses in the operation of the public sector. Sometimes the initiative would be successful and lead to sustained reform. But all too often, initially high expectations would be dashed: Governments would embrace the initiative in principle, and a lending operation would go to the Bank's board for approval—but once the loan was approved, things would bog down. In many countries, the game was played over and over, with a similar outcome each time. Even so, I was assured by the staff working on the not-yet-implemented reform program, it was worth continuing the effort. Next time would be different.

Why this continued appetite for action in the face of such meager returns? Part of the reason is surely that the players involved have much to lose and little to gain from calling a halt to an ambitious—on paper—project to improve governance. For the technical staff involved, calling a halt would amount to a difficult defeat—not merely in narrowly careerist terms but in having to recognize the deep practical limitations of their hard-acquired specialist skills. One of the criticisms often made of technical specialists in the development profession is that "because they have a hammer, they see nails everywhere." Recognizing the limitations of one's own hammer is not easy.

For in-country political leaders (and also for senior managers in development agencies) the potential loss from scaling back the ambition of a governance reform agenda is a different one. Even when a reform program works well, it can take up to a decade to begin to show practical results. So, from the perspective of political leaders, one of the consequent "virtues" is that an embrace of ambitious reform can provide the appearance of commitment and momentum over a long period of time even if the effort is, in fact, going nowhere.

In an effort to break through this preoccupation with a normatively driven agenda that often was yielding meager results, I asked each of the staff in my team to review the African experience in their area of specialty—and pressed each of them not to reiterate their prescriptions of what should be done but instead to explore what actually happened with efforts to implement reform and why. The results—which were published in 2004 as a book, *Building State Capacity in Africa*[1]—were illuminating: Table 2.1, adapted from one of the chapters in the book, captures the essence of what we learned.

The table reports on progress and results for an unbiased sample[2] of fifteen public-sector reform initiatives that had been supported by the World Bank subsequent to 1995 and for which sufficient time had elapsed to gauge progress. The table makes two sets of distinctions: between countries with a limited commitment to reform and countries where reform commitment was strong, and between comprehensive and narrow reform initiatives. Three findings are noteworthy:

- First, comprehensive reform initiatives appeared to progress well in countries where the commitment to the reform process was relatively strong. (The three positive examples of comprehensive reform were from Cape Verde, Tanzania, and Uganda.)
- Second, there was indeed a repeated tendency to push for comprehensive reform in countries where reform commitment was limited—with unsuccessful, or mixed, results. Indeed, four of the seven comprehensive reform programs were in such countries. (Along with Zambia, the other countries in this category were Kenya, Guinea, and Ghana.)
- Third, more narrowly focused reforms quite often seemed to get traction, even in more difficult governance environments.

While I felt confident at that time that the distinctions in the table were real, and not simply an ex post rationalization of the observed patterns, the research approach was a bottom-up bootstrapping one, which raised obvious methodological questions. We did not have an analytically robust framework for differentiating among the types of countries, nor was the analytical distinction between "comprehensive" and "narrow" reform well articulated.

Table 2.1 **Reform Design, Country Characteristics, and Project Performance**

Project Scope	Project Performance	Country Commitment to Public Sector Governance Reform	
		Limited	Strong
Comprehensive	Satisfactory	0	3
	Unsatisfactory	2	0
	Mixed	2	0
Narrow	Satisfactory	5	–
	Unsatisfactory	1	–
	Mixed	2	–

Source: Poul Engberg-Pederson and Brian Levy, "Public Sector Reform: Patterns of Project Performance," in Levy and Kpundeh, *Building State Capacity in Africa.*

Over the next few years, I became increasingly preoccupied with the challenge of how to fill this analytical gap. There is, of course, a rich academic literature on comparative political economy. But I came at the issues from a somewhat different angle than my university-based research colleagues. My goal was to distil, from the confrontation between experience on the ground and ongoing academic research with which I was involved, a practical guide for governance and development work at the front lines. The goal was a framework that could help clarify how policy priorities could usefully vary across different polities and how, within individual countries, policies might be better sequenced over time. I was after a typology along the lines which I lay out in this book.

A Preview

The principle of Occam's razor nicely captures the challenge of building a useful typology: What framework is both as simple as possible and capable of capturing the core complexities of the problem at hand? If the distinctions are made too finely, then the framework is more likely to obscure, to be weighed down by the burden of excess analytical complexity, than to shed light. But with too few distinctions, the effort to bring analytical order will end up with unhelpful, cartoonish oversimplifications. The aim is to delineate a small number of "ideal types" that are each very different from one another, with each capturing a distinctive set of characteristics that resonate with a subset of actual country cases—and that, considered together, delineate a spectrum of patterns along which most real-world examples could fairly straightforwardly be aligned. Like Goldilocks' search for porridge, a practically useful set of distinctions needs to have a very specific analytic temperature—not too many, not too few, but just right!

I begin with the familiar, almost clichéd distinction between democratic and authoritarian polities—but with an important difference. The conventional debate generally is intensely normative, combining widely divergent first principles as to the appropriate relationship between individuals and society, with a series of "gotchas."

I won't pretend to be impartial in this debate. Taking a very long-run perspective, I am deeply committed to a democratic, rights-based economic, political, and social order. In the short run, too, I'd much prefer to see struggling existing democracies find their way forward as democracies, rather than have them embrace an authoritarian alternative. Indeed, one of my purposes in writing the book is to try and help rescue democracy from some of its so-called champions. But these preferences cannot substitute for careful reflection.

For the purposes of building a useful typology, two of the "gotchas" used by champions of authoritarian approaches offer especially interesting food for thought. Why, they would point out, were the most successful development experiences of the past sixty years—the countries of the East Asian miracle— usually authoritarian? And why have so many of the democracies, whose creation was so celebrated in the wake of the fall of the Berlin wall—from Cambodia to Thailand, Mali to Ukraine—become poster children of corruption, conflict, and generally dysfunctional government?[3]

These questions point to a key gap in the popular discourse on authoritarianism versus democracy. Consistent with the approach introduced in chapter 1, perhaps it would be useful to distinguish between early-stage and later-stage democratic and authoritarian regimes? Perhaps much of the debate over the relative merits of democratic and authoritarian systems moves haphazardly in its arguments between early-stage and later-stage settings, blurring the distinction between them?

It is important to be explicit here: The aim is not to resuscitate the old modernization argument of "authoritarian first, then democratic"[4]. Rather, I'm asking a more neutral, analytic set of questions:

- First, without judging which is better, how do early-stage regimes with dominant political leadership and early-stage regimes where political leadership is selected competitively actually work? To answer this question, we need to look more closely at the character of "political settlements."
- Second, within each of the dominant and competitive categories, what distinguishes early- from later-stage regimes? One useful way to address this question is to look carefully at the characteristics of institutions and how they evolve.

We'll get to political settlements and institutions in a moment. But first it is useful to use Figure 2.1 to preview where these distinctions take us. The figure distinguishes among six very different country types. Two of the six—conflict (cell #1) and sustainable democracy (cell #6)—are not the focus of the present effort. The book is not about countries that are failing to develop because they are trapped in endemic, violent conflict—although for many countries how to escape the trap of such conflict is, of course, a central, ongoing challenge. And countries that have successfully built a platform of sustainable democracy generally will already have gotten beyond the development challenges with which we are concerned— although understanding the differences between democracies that are sustainable and those that are not will be a central concern throughout this volume.

The middle cells are of direct interest. These cells utilize distinctions between dominant and competitive political settlements and between person-alized and impersonal institutions to distinguish between four very different country-types:

- *Dominant discretionary* (cell #2), where strong political leadership (perhaps military, perhaps civilian; perhaps organized around a political party, perhaps a charismatic individual) has successfully consolidated its grip on power, but formal institutions remain weak, so rule is personalized.
- *Rule-by-law dominant* (cell #4), where institutions are more impersonal but political control remains monopolized.
- *Personalized-competitive* (cell #3), where politics is competitive, but the rules of the game governing both the polity and the economy remain personalized.
- *Rule-of-law competitive* (cell #5), where the political and economic rules have become more impersonal—though some other necessary aspects of democratic sustainability have not yet been achieved.

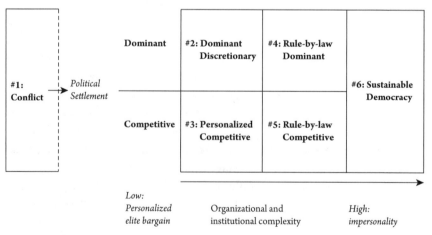

Figure 2.1 **A Development Typology**

As will become evident, each of these four country types comprises a distinctive platform for development, with distinctive incentives for the participants, distinctive constraints and risks, and distinctive frontier challenges. Careful attention to these incentives and constraints provides a way of identifying specific policy actions that are both worthwhile and feasible, given country-specific institutional realities. Chapter 4 will explore in depth the dominant-discretionary and rule-by-law dominance country types, using the experiences of Korea and Ethiopia. Chapter 5 and 6 will focus on the personalized and rule-of-law competitive types, drawing on the experiences of Bangladesh, Zambia, South Africa, and the late-nineteenth century United States. Of course, argument by anecdote has obvious limitations. So throughout the book we complement the case studies with data that map into the typology the patterns of governance and growth among almost the full universe of countries with per-capita incomes of under $10,000 as of the year 2000.

But we are getting ahead of ourselves. Before we can drill down into the different country types, there is more conceptual work to be done.

Political Settlements

Let us return to the distinction between early-stage dominant and early-stage competitive regimes work. Mushtaq Khan of London University's School of Oriental and African Studies provides an especially useful analysis. Khan defines a political settlement as the set of institutional arrangements through which a country addresses the most fundamental of governance challenges—restraining violence.[5] Two basic types of political settlement can be distinguished. The two have very different relationships between the rulers and the ruled and thus very different ways of assuring stability.

The first type of settlement concentrates power in the hands of a dominant party or political leader. Examples include monopoly control by communist parties in countries such as China, Vietnam, and Cambodia; military rule, as in Korea from 1961 to 1987, Spain and Portugal from the end of World War II to the 1970s, and much of Latin America over a similar period; and de facto "big man" rule in countries such as Tajikistan and Uganda. For settlements of this type, the disparity between the power of the rulers and the opponents is very large. The rulers' grasp on power is strong in the sense that it would take an extraordinary level of commitment by the opponents to mount a credible challenge to the status quo. Barring extreme levels of dissatisfaction—extremes that history shows us are, on occasion, reached—there is thus an "equilibrium" in which the political leadership can govern as a "principal" and engage others in the country as "agents" (or subjects). Annex 2.1 provides a somewhat more formal characterization of this pattern.

The second, contrasting settlement is "competitive"—organized around a "truce" in which rival forces agree on peaceful rules for political competition. Examples range from Bangladesh to Mozambique, to Nicaragua and Sierra Leone. Here, the disparity in violence potential between the rulers and their opponents is much narrower than in the dominant settlement. For example, the ruling party might be faction-ridden, and excluded factions might also be strong—so it would take a much lower level of commitment for opponents to mount a credible challenge to the status quo. To maintain stability, rulers would thus need to respect the '"rules of the game" that provided the basis for the competitive settlement. This settlement thus is less one between a principal and its agents and more in the nature of an agreement between principals. Again, Annex A2.1 provides the analytic logic.

Table 2.2 summarizes the overall empirical pattern; it shows the distribution of 119 countries for the year 2000 by per-capita income and by trajectory, using Polity IV data for the latter. Given the well-known imperfections of measures of governance, the table includes an intermediate category of countries for which the data do not permit their straightforward classification into one or the other of the two behaviorally relevant trajectories. As the table shows, the full range of per-capita incomes are represented within each governance category—though with disproportionately large shares of low-income countries in the dominant trajectory, and of higher income countries in its competitive counterpart. Annex Table A2.1 provides a detailed country-by-country listing.

Table 2.2 **Mapping 119 Countries into the Trajectories**

	Per-Capita Income, Year 2000			Total Number of Countries
	Low (Under $500)	Medium ($500–$1,500)	Higher ($1,500–$9,999)	
Dominant trajectory	25	16	10	51
Intermediate	17	10	12	39
Competitive trajectory	4	3	22	29

Note: For data sources and definitions, see Table A2.1 and Chapter 7.

Institutions

The distinction between "dominant" and "competitive" regimes takes us part of the way to where we want to go. But it needs to be complemented with insight into what, along either path, distinguishes early from later stages. This brings us to the analysis of institutions. While institutionalism has a long and sometimes distinguished history in the social sciences,[6] for much of the twentieth century it had gone into eclipse. But in recent decades, it has seen a major revival, under the rubric of the new institutional economics. Key contributors include five Nobel Prize winners: Douglass North, Elinor Ostrom, Herbert Simon, Ronald Coase, and Oliver Williamson.[7]

New institutional economics anchors the study of institutions in a rigorous, micro-analytic examination of the efforts to human beings to respond rationally to their environments (this is, of course, an approach especially beloved by economists). Drawing on this micro-economic reasoning, in his classic 1990 book, *Institutions, Institutional Change and Economic Performance,* North distinguishes between "actors" (individuals or organizations) and the institutional "rules of the game" that constrain their actions. Institutions incorporate the following three dimensions:

- *rules,* which clarify who the relevant participants are in a particular set of interactions, what their distinctive roles are, how they interact with one another, and what goals are to be achieved;
- *monitoring arrangements,* including what measures will be used to assess performance in relation to the goals, how the monitoring will be undertaken and by whom, and how information with respect to performance will be shared; and
- *enforcement arrangements,* including clarification as to what the consequences of noncompliance will be, who will adjudicate conflicts among the participants, and how penalties for noncompliance will be enforced.

From the start, the potential of the revival of institutional economics to shake up the field of development economics has been abundantly clear. It is functions that matter—not the specific forms in which they are embedded[8]—and institutional economics provides a framework for exploring diverse arrangements. How might such analysis be done?

In the early 1990s, I was part of a team that aimed to use the example of telecommunications regulation to demonstrate the practical relevance for development work of the new institutional economics—specifically, how different approaches to regulation might play out across diverse country environments.[9] Institutional arrangements that worked well in some settings might, we argued, be less effective in others—and in some settings seemingly inefficient arrangements might be the only workable options.

The research results highlighted the ways in which the quality of a country's judicial system determined which regulatory approaches were likely to be successful in specific country settings. Where the judiciary is strong, and is underpinned by broad constitutional protections, quite open-ended regulatory rules could support a thriving telecommunications sector. In less robust settings, the premium was on more precise rules, even at the cost of a loss of flexibility. Settings that were even weaker confronted an especially intractable problem, with recourse to international mechanisms likely to be needed to underpin the sector.

At the time, the approach and findings of the telecommunications study were viewed as something of a breakthrough.[10] Now, though, the way in which that study addressed institutional diversity seems to me to be strikingly incomplete. The limitation was not only that the study was narrowly preoccupied with one specific institution, the judicial system. More fundamentally, its approach was a static one—it did not explore how institutions might serve different functions at different stages in the development process.

In analyzing institutional change, a crucial distinction is between formal and informal institutions—or rather, to introduce the terms I use throughout this book, between impersonal and personalized institutions. In their 2009 book, *Violence and Social Orders,* Douglass North—plus coauthors John Wallis and Barry Weingast[11]—explored this distinction in depth. Both personalized and impersonal institutions, they underscore, are built around rules, monitoring, and enforcement. But where institutions are personalized, the rules— and their monitoring and enforcement arrangements—are built around the specific identities (and threat potential) of the parties involved. By contrast, impersonal institutions are codified in formal, written law, and responsibility for monitoring, adjudication, and enforcement is assigned to an impartial, formal, third-party organization dedicated to this task (e.g., the judiciary in constitutional democracies).

Impersonal institutions cannot be engineered on the basis of some prespecified blueprint. As North, Wallis, and Weingast put it:

> Societies do not jump directly from personal to impersonal relationships; rather, it is a long process of development.... On the one end of the spectrum, personal relationships are characterized by repeated and idiosyncratic interactions; on the other end, impersonal relations are characterized by intermittent and standardized interactions. In between the two extremes are relationships where the identity of the individuals is uniquely defined, but regularities in interactions between individuals arise....

Transplanting institutions and policies cannot produce economic development. Indeed, to the extent that these institutions are forced onto societies by international or domestic pressure but do not conform to existing beliefs about economic, political, social and cultural systems, the new institutions are likely to work less well than the ones they replace. Worse, if these institutions undermine the political arrangements maintaining political stability, these new institutions may unleash disorder, making the society significantly worse off. [12]

Looking across countries and over times, there is thus a spectrum encompassing the range of institutional forms—personalized, impersonal, and in-between. This spectrum is evident across a variety of specific sets of institutions and organizations. Five sets in particular, grouped into two broad categories, are especially relevant for work on governance. They are:

- The extent to which the *public bureaucracy*—both the "central bureaucracy" and front-line executive agencies—functions in an ad hoc, personalized way or according to impersonal rules.
- The extent to which impersonal *checks and balances* (sometimes described as nonexecutive institutions of accountability) constrain arbitrary action by the political leadership and the bureaucracies. Within this broad category are:
  - The extent to which *the rule of law* functions as an impartial, third-party mechanism for resolving disputes between public and private parties, within the state (or, for that matter, disputes among private parties);
  - The extent to which *political parties* become formalized and organized around programmatic platforms rather than the conferral of patronage to insider clients;
  - The quality of *elections*—that is, the extent to which they are competitive, free, and fair; and
  - The extent of *openness*—that is, the presence of rules (e.g., on freedom of information) and actors (such as the media) that ensure the open operation of civil society and the transparent flow of information.

Taken together, the functioning of these institutions shape the incentives and behavior of a country's political and economic actors.

The quality of elections and the extent of openness are, of course, intrinsic to the functioning of a competitive political settlement but less central (indeed often absent) in dominant settings. By contrast, there is wide scope within both the dominant and competitive trajectories for variations in the quality of the bureaucracy and, to a lesser extent, in the rule of law. The degree of formalization of political parties comprises an intermediate category: Generally (at least in the

Table 2.3 **Trajectory and Rule-Boundedness for 119 Countries**

	Extent of Formal Rule-Boundedness			Total
	Weak	*Intermediate*	*Better*	
Dominant trajectory	30	10	11	51
Intermediate	17	11	11	39
Competitive trajectory	5	7	17	29

Sources: Rule-boundedness is measured using the Worldwide Governance Indicators measure of Rule of Law. For further details, See Table A2.1 and chapter 7.

Note: "Weak" is defined as rule of law (ROL) < -0.75; intermediate as $-0.75 < \text{ROL} < -0.25$; better as $\text{ROL} > -0.25$.

West) rule-bound political parties are perceived to be a central element of democracy; in dominant settings too (China, for example), there is strong evidence of changes over time in the extent to which a dominant political party is led by individual strongmen or by leaders selected via an impersonal system of rules.

Table 2.3 provides an initial overview for 119 countries of the balance between personalized and impersonal institutions along each of the dominant and competitive trajectories, using a measure of the rule of law as a proxy (and, again, using intermediate categories in recognition of the limits of the data). Again, the full range of patterns of rule-boundedness is evident within each trajectory—but with a proportionately higher share of weaker countries in the dominant trajectory and of stronger countries in its competitive counterpart.

Rents

To see how these institutional differences translate into different patterns of incentives and constraints across the country types, it is helpful to turn to the economic concept of "rents." In different ways, both economists and political scientists have used a focus on rents to better understand the interactions between economics and politics. Economists brought their standard "best practices" lens to explore how "rent-seeking" can detract from economic efficiency.[13] The interest among political scientists came initially from those with a regional or country-specific orientation whose focus was on better understanding the interaction between contestation over rents and the way political power was exercised.[14] Mushtaq Khan made a pioneering effort to integrate the economic and political approaches to the analysis of rents.[15]

In all economic systems built around individual incentives, rents—defined as returns that exceed the opportunity cost of resources that might otherwise be deployed in a competitive market—are ubiquitous and are the driving motive force that moves economies forward. But the ways in which rents serve as a spur to action are very different depending on the prevailing institutional rules of the game. Specifically, as North, Wallis, and Weingast and other scholars highlight, the roles played by rents are very different in settings where institutions are personalized and settings where they are impersonal and the rules of the game are competitive.[16]

In settings where institutions are impersonal, rents are accessed on the basis of initiative and talent (and differential access to the human and financial capital, which can be key to transforming initiative and talent into action). The potential to earn returns to innovation spurs productivity—and then competition, as new actors seek to participate in markets that offer opportunities for high profit. Over the longer run, competition bids away the rents—this is the ongoing process of "creative destruction" that drives a market economy forward.[17] (Note that a parallel process of "creative destruction" can play out in the political realm—where returns come from innovative ideas for political action and the test of success is the ability to win votes.)

In personalized settings, by contrast, the discretionary allocation of rents comprises the currency of politics. Rents can take the form of the allocation of access to natural resources, of access to public jobs and procurement contracts, or of the conferral of privilege through restrictive economic policies. In settings where impersonal institutions have not yet taken hold, the discretionary conferral, and threat of withdrawal, of access to these rents is the glue around which the polity is organized.

In some settings, a personalized polity can be wholly predatory, with personal enrichment of the powerful the sole function of rent allocation. In other settings, though, the discretionary conferral and withdrawal of rents comprises the platform of stability on which development can move forward. In these latter settings, as North, Wallis, and Weingast emphasized in the earlier quotation, a premature effort to replace personalized arrangements with unworkable, impersonal rules of the game risks derailing the development endeavor as a whole.

Less can be More

Robert Kennedy's 1966 speech at my hometown university, the University of Cape Town, was one of the inspirational moments of my youth. His visit to Cape Town came a quarter century before Nelson Mandela, then imprisoned on Robben Island, just offshore from the city, would be released from jail. The idea that Mandela would one day be South Africa's president seemed entirely implausible. So I can see that there is wisdom in Kennedy's vision that "some men see things as they are and say 'why?' I dream things that never were and say 'why not'?"[18]

But my many years spent wrestling with the challenges of governance reform have made me wary of sweeping high-mindedness. It has come to feel too much like a rhetorical sugar high: exhilarating for a short while but with a certain crash to come. Nowadays, when seeking inspiration, I take refuge in a more sober-seeming Jewish proverb: "It is not for us to complete the work; but neither is it for us to desist from it."[19]

For staff working at the World Bank and other donor agencies, development advising can be a lot like a sugar high. There is the self-important exhilaration of engaging with Very Important People. There is the certainty, buttressed by an in-house echo chamber, that one's prescriptions will solve the problems of the country, which is the object of the advice. And then there is the let-down and blame-shifting when it becomes apparent that implementation will fall far short of the "best practices" vision one had been advocating.

This pattern plays out over and over again. It was what lay behind the example of Zambia with which I began this book: It took fifteen years of repeated examples of ambitious programs and dashed expectations before a different approach to engagement was considered. Indeed, the pattern repeats itself so often, with seemingly so little learning, that it's easy to conclude that the whole process is cynical and opportunistic, that both donor staff and recipients of donor largesse have much to lose and little to gain, from calling a halt to their policy minuet. The fact that the music sometimes stops only after donor financial support has been provided adds weight to more cynical interpretations.

But I am not a cynic. I continue to think of the large majority of my (former) colleagues at the World Bank as sincerely, often passionately, committed to what they do. The willingness to keep playing the same game over and over comes not so much from opportunism as from a more deeply rooted desire to have clarion calls to respond to. It is much harder to rally behind an approach to engagement that deliberately keeps expectations more modest, gets results— and then, hopefully, sees momentum build cumulatively. But this latter is the approach advocated in this book.

Consider again the typology in Figure 2.1. Here is an obvious example of how specific institutional configurations shape incentives and constraints: Dominant political leaders are unlikely to be enthusiastic to take on reforms that constrain their authority and subject them to competition (although, for reasons we will explore in subsequent chapters, the pressure on them to do so is likely to grow as development proceeds). And here is a second, perhaps less obvious one: The ability to describe impersonal institutions does not mean that personalized arrangements can straightforwardly be reengineered; institutional change needs to be underpinned by stakeholders with the incentive and influence to see reform enacted. As a result, and as we will explore in depth, the transition from personalized to impersonal rules of the game tends to be cumulative, incremental.

The practical implications of clarifying where a particular country might be located within "typology space" are thus profound. The difficulties of implementation that led to my involvement in Zambia included a failure to follow through on transparent, competitive processes to involve the private sector; the absence of a level playing field business environment; and a failure to build a capable, rule-bound public sector. Each of these can be traced back to personalized decision making—and, as chapter 5 will explore in detail, Zambia is a classic example of a personalized-competitive country.

The aim of the Zambian work was to take seriously this personalized-competitive reality. The goal was to seek out practical ways forward on a variety of policy fronts—infrastructure reform, support for local government, rural land management—which were compatible with the incentives and constraints within which decision makers functioned.

Subsequent chapters will provide more detail on some of the specific recommendations. For now, I'll simply note some of the immediate consequences. Sparks did not fly at the report-back meeting to government and civil society (described in chapter 1). Instead, shifting the focus from the "shoulds" of the usual governance dialogue to "why do things work the way they do—and with what implications for policy?" turned out to illuminate constraints on decision making that provided a constructive practical platform for dialogue. The governance work was not the expected harsh critique delivered by outsiders critique but a useful mirror.

This new platform was embraced by the Bank's Zambia country team in its 2008 country assistance strategy. Here is how the 2008 document described the political economy exercise and its influence:

> *The Bank has reassessed its strategic position in Zambia to determine where it should be active, passive, or disengaged, based on its strategy, resources, and comparative advantage. . . . The Bank has undertaken a separate analysis that illuminates issues related to the political economy of reform. The analysis concludes that the World Bank's engagement in Zambia has been characterized by repeated attempts to promote far-reaching reforms, derived from first-best principles. It recommends that this country assistance strategy focus its engagement more narrowly. . . . The new strategy gives priority to very specific interventions in which the beneficiaries are clear, with goals that unequivocally are supported by the political authorities.* [20]

Initially, senior management at the Bank was critical of the lack of ambition of the proposed approach. But five years later, as some of the results became apparent, the repositioned country program increasingly has been recognized as a model of how to build forward momentum in an environment where things are more complicated than they might superficially seem.

Annex A2.1: Distinguishing Among Political Settlements

Figure A2.1 depicts graphically the distinction between dominant and competitive political settlements. For simplicity, the figure presumes that there are two sets of actors in society, the rulers (A) and their opponents (B). The horizontal axis measures the violence potential of each actor. The vertical axis measures the level of commitment of the opponents to oppose the rulers (C); C can be interpreted variously as the extent of ideological opposition, or of anger at perceived oppression, or (looked at from an opposite perspective) as the extent to which the rulers lack legitimacy. To further simplify, assume also that B and C are additive. A political settlement is thus stable (in the sense that the rulers cannot be overthrown violently) as long as:

$$A_i > B_j + C_j$$

In Figure 2.1, the violence potential of the rulers is set at A1. Given this level of violence potential, stability will be sustained at all points where the combination of the violence potential and commitment to oppose of those out of power is below and to the left of the 45-degree line that connects the horizontal and vertical axis. To illustrate, consider the two alternative levels of violence potential of the opponents, B1 and B2, depicted in Figure 2.1. Each is associated with a very different type of political settlement.

A dominant political settlement can be characterized as an A1–B1 combination. In this combination, the disparity between the violence potential of the rulers and the opponents is very large. The rulers' grasp on power is strong in the sense that it would take an extraordinary level of commitment by the opponents (depicted as C1 in the figure) to mount a credible challenge to the status quo. There is thus an "equilibrium" in which the political leadership can govern as a "principal" and engage others in the country as "agents" (or subjects).

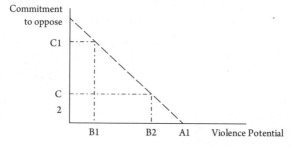

Figure A2.1 **Violence Potential, Legitimacy, and the Character of Political Settlements**

A competitive political settlement can be characterized by the A1–B2 combination. In this combination, the disparity in violence potential between the rulers and their opponents is much narrower. For example, the ruling party might be faction-ridden, and excluded factions also might be strong. With this combination, it would take a much lower level of commitment (C2) by the opponents to mount a credible challenge to the status quo. To maintain a stable equilibrium, the rulers would thus need to respect the rules of the game that provided the basis for the competitive settlement. This settlement thus is more in the nature of an agreement between principals.

Annex Table A2.1 **Distribution of 119 Countries by Trajectory and Per Capita Income, 2000**

	Dominant (51)		Intermediate (39)		Competitive (29)	
Per-capita income $1,501–$10,000	Tunisia	Iran	Russia	Peru	Lithuania	Romania
	Egypt	Oman	Colombia	Turkey	Slovakia	Poland
	Malaysia	Algeria	Botswana	Macedonia	Panama	Uruguay
	Libya	Gabon	Bulgaria	Latvia	Estonia	Czech
	Jordan	Saudi Arabia	Croatia	Namibia	Thailand	Argentina
			Guyana	Lebanon	Mauritius	South Africa
					Dominican Republic	Hungary
					Chile	Mexico
					Brazil	Venezuela
					Costa Rica	Jamaica
					El Salvador	Guatemala
Per capita income $500–$1,500	Eqt. Guinea	Azerbaijan	Armenia	Georgia	Bolivia	Philippines
	Angola	China	Ukraine	Albania		Honduras
	Turkmenistan	Belarus	Sri Lanka	Indonesia		
	Kazakhstan	Uzbekistan	Ecuador	Paraguay		
	Bhutan	Pakistan	Cote d'Ivoire	Papua New Guinea		
	Syria	Congo-B				
	Swaziland	Yemen				
	Cameroon					
	Morocco					

28

Annex Table A2.1 (continued)

	Dominant (51)		Intermediate (39)		Competitive (29)	
Per-capita income under $500	Myanmar	Cambodia	Nigeria	Mozambique	(a) India	Mongolia
	Tajikistan	Vietnam	Moldova	Bangladesh	(b) Senegal	Madagascar
	Rwanda	Ethiopia	Niger	Zambia		
	Sudan	Laos	Malawi	Nepal		
	Mauritania	Kyrgyzstan	Kenya	Lesotho		
	Burundi	Gambia	Ghana	Guinea		
	DRCongo	Guinea	Benin	Bissau		
	Somalia	Afghanistan	Nicaragua	Mali		
	Haiti	Togo	Central African	Sierra Leone		
	Liberia	Zimbabwe	Republic			
	Eritrea	Uganda				
	Burkina Faso	Tanzania				
		Chad				

Notes: The list comprises all countries with year 2000 per capita incomes below $10,000—excluding countries with populations below 1 million and some countries in conflict. Income data are from the International Monetary Fund, International Financial Statistics. Polity IV data for 2000 are used to classify the countries along the intermediate-competitive spectrum. Construction of the variable is as specified in chapter 7, with a minor adjustment for seven countries (Ghana, Kenya, Lebanon, Lesotho, Peru, Sierra Leone, and Zambia). All seven are rated "intermediate" in the table above, even though their 2000 Polity IV scores either were "in conflict" or (temporarily) "dominant." All experienced almost immediate subsequent changes and for the remainder of the decade rated intermediate or competitive.

CHAPTER 3

The Edge of Chaos

The reign of the "Washington Consensus" began in the early 1980s.[1] It comprised, at its core, the canon of the mainstream economics profession as to how to engineer development, and incorporated three distinct sets of policy prescriptions:

- some largely uncontroversial micro- and macroeconomic nostrums as to the benefits of markets and the importance of avoiding excessive inflation, excessive budget deficits, and overvalued exchange rates (although, of course, clarity as to what constitutes "excessive" remains a work in progress);
- a much broader "neoliberal" agenda of economic reform—of, beyond the provision of basic public goods (again a category where the devil continues to be in the details), scaling back the role of government so that the twin miracles of market incentives and private entrepreneurship could work their development magic; and
- in an "expanded" version, the full panoply of good governance reforms detailed in chapter 1.

When it first began to shape the development discourse, the Washington Consensus seemed to many to be a welcome corrective to an economic policymaking (and aid-giving) environment that, in many countries, had lost almost all discipline. Indeed, the economic turnarounds enjoyed by many developing countries over the past two decades can be linked directly to structural reforms "imposed" by the World Bank, the International Monetary Fund and other donors that helped restore macro-economic balances, and facilitated greater market-based micro-economic flexibility.[2] But over time, the Washington Consensus lost its allure, as its agenda became increasingly expansive—and as its limitations were exposed by the complexity of the transitions of post-Communist societies, and then by misguided hard-line economic prescriptions in the wake of the 1997 Asian financial crisis.

In 2006, Dani Rodrik of Harvard University's Kennedy School published a landmark article, "Goodbye Washington Consensus, Hello Washington Confusion."[3] In that article, he famously described Washington Consensus prescriptions as tantamount to throwing spaghetti against a wall to see what sticks. The result can be a mess: failed implementation; frustration on all sides; sometimes a downward spiral of deteriorating relations between government and donors; perhaps even civic discontent as raised expectations are dashed.

How to do better?

One way, introduced in chapter 2, is to give careful attention to how country institutions shape the incentives and constraints of decision makers—and to prioritize those policy reforms that seem both worthwhile and feasible, given country-specific institutional realities. But what about those parts of the governance and development agenda that remain unaddressed in this more incremental approach? Does the strengthening of democratic institutions have no place in Ethiopia's development strategy? Should Bangladesh not attend to the challenge of building an honest, results-oriented public sector?

"It is all a matter of sequencing" is the easy, but ultimately trite answer to these questions. Yes—but what should be the sequence? What should be done sooner, and what later? How might this vary from country to country? This chapter explores these questions conceptually. Chapters 4, 5 and 6 use the examples of Korea, Ethiopia, Bangladesh, Zambia, South Africa, and the late-nineteenth-century United States to show how these dynamic processes play out in practice.

To begin, consider Figure 3.1. Visually, it is the same figure as the typology introduced in the previous chapter, with arrows added to link the cells. But in chapter 2 each of the cells was introduced as a world unto itself, with distinctive incentives, constraints, and frontier challenges—each a distinctive platform for development, with distinctive policy options. Now, though, the

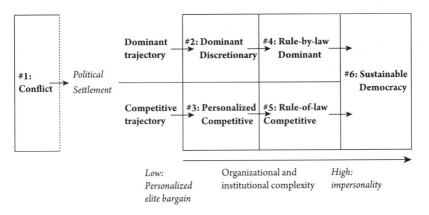

Figure 3.1 **Development Trajectories—Moving Forward**

cells are considered from a dynamic perspective as encompassing two principal trajectories of change—a dominant and a competitive trajectory—with
(not shown in the figure, but explored later in the chapter) the potential for
zig-zagging between them, and (also not shown) the potential for backward as
well as forward movement.

Pictorially, the sequences are straightforward:

- As countries develop along the dominant trajectory, their institutions
  become less discretionary and more rule-bound—though, until the
  institutional arrangements cross the final chasm to become democratic, the
  incumbent leadership maintains the ultimate veto.
- As countries develop along the competitive trajectory, the basis for building political stability shifts from personalized relationships—a combination of bargaining among elites and patron-client relationships—to
  rule-constrained political competition. Since political incumbents are credibly at risk of electoral loss, this rule-boundedness is "rule-of-law" rather than
  "rule-by-law". But, as per the figure, rule of law competitiveness is not necessarily equivalent to sustainable democracy.

But what is it that drives the process forward? And how is forward momentum sustained? Throwing spaghetti at a wall to see what sticks is one approach.
Working with the grain is another.

To work with the grain is to look for entry points that can unleash an
ongoing, virtuous circle of cumulative change. Virtuous circles have been
studied across multiple disciplines: from economics, to biology, to physics
and mathematics. Across all of these, the key to forward momentum is to navigate the "edge of chaos," a frontier of continuing movement, exploration and
adaptation, where order endlessly threatens to dissolve into anarchy.[4] The idea
of development as an evolving, interdependent system, carried forward by
interactions between governance and growth was introduced in chapter 1.[5]
How is this virtuous circle initiated? How does its momentum build? How
is momentum sustained? This chapter and the next three examine these
questions in depth, beginning with an initial conceptual overview.[6]

Initiating a Virtuous Circle

The ways in which the cumulative process gets started are very different along
the dominant and competitive trajectory.

Getting development going along the dominant trajectory.   The dominant
trajectory is the trajectory of the top-down developmental state.[7] Along this

trajectory, rulers focus on strengthening their bureaucratic capability, without expanding the openness of the political or economic system. They base their claim to legitimacy on an implicit promise that their decisions will serve the broader long-run public interest.

Early-stage state discretionary dominance characterizes countries where strong political leadership (perhaps military, perhaps civilian; perhaps organized around a political party, perhaps a charismatic individual) has successfully consolidated its grip on power. In the first flush of authority, there can be a general sense of a country on the move—especially if the leadership has embraced systematically a coherent, and seemingly technically well-grounded, strategy for development.

Dominant leaders offer a springboard for accelerated development via a promise of coherence, and of action. A dominant ruling group does not need to tread cautiously, second-guessing its policies according to their impact on the ruling coalition. Rather, in the parlance of principal-agent economic theory, the political leadership comprises a well-defined "principal" that can set, monitor, and enforce very clear goals throughout government, and society more broadly. Rights—including the right to contest policy—may be constrained; but in return, so goes the promise, the country can finally be on the move; and in the long-run all things are possible.

Three distinct channels link better government and economic growth:

- Better policies, more efficient infrastructure, a transactionally more efficient bureaucracy, better service provision—all of these contribute to a better investment climate, creating new opportunities for profit and thus potentially for private investment and growth. Note, though, that improving infrastructure and the bureaucracy takes time, with little opportunity for 'quick wins—policy, though, can be turned around quite rapidly.
- Newly empowered dominant leaders often offer gains in credibility—via enhanced expectations that leadership has emerged with the "political will" to build state capacity. Even before public sector performance actually improves, confidence can rise among private investors as to the productive potential of the economy—with the credibility gain itself sometimes sufficient to attract private investment, and an acceleration of growth. (one common way to secure such credibility has been to move rapidly to adopt far-reaching "stroke of the pen" economic reforms.)
- Leaders sometimes assert a broader commitment to "fairness"—to inclusive growth with broadly shared benefits. Insofar as citizens believe this commitment, state legitimacy and stability will both be enhanced—contributing more broadly to improvements in the investment climate, and hence to growth.

Chapter 4 explores further how development along the dominant trajectory might succeed, using the examples of Korea and Ethiopia as illustrations. Yet the dark side of these promises must always also be kept in mind. Action aimed at accelerating development is possible—but so, too, is action in service of the private ends of the rulers, with kleptocratic predation an all too common outcome. Indeed, the empirical track record suggests that failure along the dominant trajectory is at least as likely as success. A dominant party might increasingly focus only on its own narrow interests; personalized leadership might become increasingly self-seeking and predatory. The former Zaire and the Philippines during the Marcos era are only two of many post World War Two examples (with the catastrophic histories of Nazism and Stalinism reminders from an earlier age of how badly things can go wrong along this path).

The top row of Table 3.1 summarizes the patterns of growth between 2000 and 2010 among the fifty-three countries that fall into the dominant trajectory. (Annex Table A3.1 provides country-specific information.) As the table shows, countries within the dominant trajectory are disproportionately clustered in the high-growth or low-growth tails of the overall distribution. Chapter 7 provides some descriptive statistics on patterns of institutional change for the eighteen countries on the dominant trajectory that grew in excess of 50 percent between 2000 and 2010.

Getting development going along the competitive trajectory.   The competitive trajectory is characterized by agreement among elites on a political settlement that has peaceful rules for political competition, generally via elections. Where public institutions are already strong—normally in middle- and high-income countries—elections can be organized around competing political platforms, each of which lays out a distinctive programmatic vision for public action.

Table 3.1 **Growth Performance Along the Trajectories for 119 Countries**

	Real Economic Growth, 2000–2010			
	Low Growth (Under 25%)	Medium Growth (25–50%)	High Growth (Above 50%)	Total Number of Countries
Dominant Trajectory	21	12	18	51
Intermediate	12	14	13	39
Competitive Trajectory	11	11	7	29

Sources: See Annex Table A3.1 and chapter 7.

But where public institutions are weak, the basis for political competition—indeed the platform for political stability—is very different. Contending elites need to address two challenges. First, they need to strike bargains that are sufficiently attractive so that a critical mass prefers to keep the peace than to resort to violence. Such bargains often involve personalized deals that use state authority to capture rents, and allocate the rents among elite groups in rough proportion to their potential to be disruptive. Second, they need to assure acquiescence among nonelites to the arrangements. This is often achieved via networks that bind nonelite "clients" to their elite patrons. To sustain these networks, elites may, in return for continuing support, promise to direct public resources to favored clients rather than commit to governing for the public good.

Personalized competition is likely to be the prevalent pattern in those settings where an initial political settlement centers around a "founding" election. In such settings, after the flush of electoral enthusiasm has worn off, formal institutions capable of supporting continuing competition are unlikely to be in place. The result can be a polity in which the rules of the game are personalized, which teeters, seemingly indefinitely, on the edge of chaos, and in which opportunities for systematic strengthening of a country's policy or institutional platform will be limited. Why?

One reason is that a competitive political settlement is based on a credible prospect of alternation, so whichever faction is in power is likely to have a short time horizon. Further, because the institutional arrangements that provide a basis for political order are personalized, political elites continually must maneuver to sustain stability within the ruling coalition, and to assure the continuing loyalty of clients. For both tasks, as per chapter 2, the crucial political currency is the discretionary allocation of rents: market privileges; patronage public employment; single-sourced procurement contracts; preferential access to natural resources. In such settings, far-reaching policy reforms to improve the business environment, or to strengthen public sector governance will be low on the agenda.

That's the bad news. The better news is that this edge of chaos can be compatible with significant economic dynamism. Empirical work by Ricardo Hausmann, Lant Pritchett and Dani Rodrik on "growth accelerations" has demonstrated that far-reaching reforms—either institutional or economic—are not necessary to kick-start growth. They identified over 80 growth acceleration episodes worldwide between 1950 and 1990. A careful analysis of the determinants of these accelerations led them to conclude that:

> *The onset of economic growth does not require deep and extensive institutional reform ... Moderate changes in country-specific circumstances (policies and institutional arrangements, often interacting with the external*

*environment), can produce discontinuous changes in economic perfor-
mance ... Once growth is set into motion it becomes easier to maintain a
virtuous cycle with high growth and institutional transformation feeding
on each other.*[8]

Chapter 5 explores further how modest changes in circumstances can
produce large gains, using Bangladesh and Zambia as examples.

The second and third rows of Table 3.1 provide an overview of growth rates
for 29 countries in the competitive trajectory—plus 39 for which the data are
too limited to classify them unequivocally into either of the two behaviorally
relevant trajectories. Twenty countries enjoyed decadal growth between 2000
and 2010 in excess of 50 percent—and another 25 grew at a decadal rate of
25 percent or more. (Annex Table A3.1 lists the individual countries.) Chapter 7
presents some descriptive statistics on patterns of institutional change for this
group of rapidly-growing countries.

Building Momentum

Interactions between governance reform and economic growth (or, more
specifically, inclusive growth, which distributes gains—and more importantly
hope for a better future—widely across society[9]) are akin to a snowball that
builds in size as it rolls down a hill. By the time the snowball gets to the bottom
of the hill, it can be big—and it doesn't much matter where it started. Similarly,
as Figure 3.2 illustrates, once growth is underway it can set in motion a cascading chain of economic, social, institutional and political changes.[10] Multiple
links move the process forward.

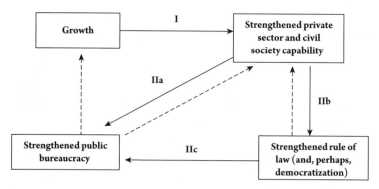

Figure 3.2 **Interactions Between Governance and Growth**

First (as illustrated by link I in Figure 3.2), growth can set in motion profound social transformation. As has been recognized at least since the publication in the eighteenth century of Adam Smith's the *Wealth of Nations,* sustained growth strengthens the private sector, the middle class, and civil society more broadly. It brings new economic complexity. New social and economic classes come onto the scene, accompanied by new organizations— civil society activists, trade unions, business associations. Traditional forms of authority increasingly are undermined.

Second, strengthened private sector and civil society organizations can, in turn, generate pressures for knock-on improvements in a variety of organizations and institutions. Multiple causal linkages connect growth, changes in the private sector and social structure more broadly, and improvements in the rule of law and in the quality of the public bureaucracy. Chapter 7 reviews some of the statistical evidence on these inter-relations. For now, it will suffice to highlight some of the key patterns:

- Strengthened private and civil society organizations potentially can generate new pressures on the public sector bureaucracy to improve its performance (link IIa)—with the late nineteenth century shift in the United States from patronage to meritocratic public employment, discussed in chapter 6, an especially powerful example.
- Growth and the rule of law are interdependent—with evidence of two-way causality.[11] A stronger private sector and a rapidly growing middle class bring new pressures for a strengthened rule of law (link IIb)—and a stronger rule of law creates, in turn, new momentum for growth. Sometimes this argument is made in a quite fundamentalist way via the suggestion that a strong rule of law is necessary for growth. However, as chapters 4 through 7 explore, in many countries growth has gotten underway even where the rule of law is weak.
- A stronger rule of law creates in turn an impersonal platform of rules that can be an impetus for further strengthening of organizational capabilities in both the public and private sectors—potentially providing a platform for organizing the civil service along more meritocratic lines (link IIc), and facilitating more complex contracting within and between private firms.[12]

Most far-reaching of all are the propositions concerning the relationship between democracy and growth. Modernization theorists from Samuel Huntington to Fareed Zakaria have asserted that economic modernization can provide a platform for subsequent democratization.[13] Here the evidence is mixed, as we shall discuss further in chapter 7. Democratic transitions, it turns out, are equally likely to happen at all levels of per capita income; but there is some (although ambiguous) support for the proposition that higher per capita incomes make democracies more robust to the risk of reversal.[14] There also is quite strong evidence that democracies produce greater short-term stability, and yield more predictable long-run growth rates and more equitable outcomes than their authoritarian counterparts.[15]

For all of the potential cumulative power of the array of growth-governance interactions, it is important to underscore that there is no inevitability that governance improvements will accompany growth. Incentives may indeed shift in favor of governance reform, but powerful interests supportive of the status quo remain in place. All reform, including institutional reform, requires effort. Indeed, virtuous spirals notwithstanding, there is no teleology. As we examine further below and in chapter 6, countries can stagnate, can zig-zag from one trajectory to another, or can suffer development reversals.

How Institutions Transform—A Closer Look

If the momentum of the governance-growth snowball can be sustained, governance increasingly becomes less personalized, and more rule-bound. This will be true for both the bureaucracy and for checks and balances—the two broad categories of institutions that we highlighted in chapter 2. However, as Figure 3.3 highlights, the patterns of leads and lags will be different along the dominant and competitive trajectories. (An intermediate case is also included in the figure as a reminder that the trajectories are ideal types, and that the actual trajectory of institutional change in many countries will lie somewhere between them.)

Consider first the evolution of checks and balances institutions. Overall, as Figure 3.3 illustrates, gains will come earlier along the competitive trajectory, but there are some intriguing nuances:

- For openness (and also the quality of elections)—it is almost definitionally true that the two trajectories will differ from one another in the timing of institutional improvement: dominance is defined by tight top-down

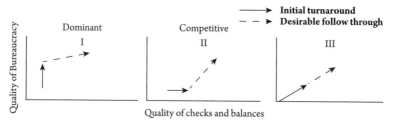

Figure 3.3 **Divergent Governance Trajectories**

control; competitiveness by the provision of space by those outside of government to contend for power at some future stage. Note though that, as per the figure, as rule-by-law authoritarianism takes root, dominant leaders can open up space for more critical discussion, albeit in carefully controlled ways. Ethiopia's use of bottom-up monitoring of service quality, discussed in chapter 4, provides one example. China's increasing openness to investigative reporting and activism around environmental issues provides another.

- For political parties, while a priori one might expect that political competition would accelerate the emergence of more programmatic political parties, the evolution of governance within China's communist party offers a striking example of how, even where one political party remains dominant, its internal governance arrangements can become increasingly formalized, and organized around programmatic platforms rather than the conferral of patronage to insider clients.[16]
- Rule of law institutions will almost surely provide greater protection to citizens against arbitrary government action sooner along the competitive trajectory—but business-related restraints potentially can strengthen incrementally on both the dominant and competitive trajectories, as economic growth and the emergence of a more sophisticated private sector and civil society create a demand for better rules and impartial enforcement mechanisms capable of underpinning more complex private contracting, and restraining arbitrary decision making by government actors. Along both trajectories, the timing of these gains will depend on country-specific drivers of the relative strength of interests favoring impersonality, and of interests that remain committed to the status quo.

The timing of improvement in the quality of bureaucracy also can vary sharply across the two trajectories—and the reasons can be traced back to the different ways in which the bureaucratic and political realms interact along each trajectory.[17] In dominant settings, especially at the early stage, bureaucratic performance will depend on the goals of the dominant political leader. Performance is likely to be poor where these goals are predatory and/or short-term. But on occasion, dominant political leaders can emerge with a strong developmental orientation. In such settings, as per the Figure 3.3 illustration (and as per the examples in chapter 4 of Korea and Ethiopia) even at an earlier stage of the broader transition from personalized to impersonal institutions, the potential may be high for unexpectedly strong bureaucratic performance.

Politics is also the key determinant of the performance of the bureaucracy along the competitive trajectory. But whereas along the dominant trajectory there exists the possibility (though by no means the certainty) of the early emergence of a political leader committed to strong public sector performance, in early stage competitive settings the centrality of politics makes it less likely that the bureaucracy's performance will improve. Political time horizons are likely to be short, so there is little incentive for political leaders to invest in the long-term task of building bureaucratic capability. Moreover, with no one faction having a clear monopoly of power, there are unlikely to be clear signals as to how to deploy whatever bureaucratic capability may be available. But as growth builds momentum, the potential grows for the bureaucracy to improve; chapter 6 explores this further, using the example of the United States.

Sustaining Momentum at the Edge of Chaos

A "with-the-grain" approach to reform builds on strengths, works around constraints, and leverages the momentum of governance-growth interactions to keep the process moving forward. Sustaining forward momentum is something of a high-wire act, with ever-present risks of reversal.

It is tautological that reversals are bad for development. But the magnitude of their effect goes beyond the obvious. Table 3.2 groups 180 countries into six categories according to their per capita incomes. Over the half-century plus from 1950 to 2004, there turns out to be little difference in the rates of growth during thriving periods between the higher and lower per capita income country groups. The big difference is in vulnerability to a loss of momentum. On average, countries in the high-income group grew for forty-five of the fifty-four years—and their economies declined at an average annual rate of 2.3 percent during the down years. By contrast, the lowest income group grew in only thirty of the fifty-four years, and their declines—in excess of 5 percent per annum—generally wiped out most of the gains from the good years.

Table 3.2 **Growth in Good and Bad Years, 1950–2004**

Per Capita Income, 2000	Number of Countries	Percentage Positive Years	Average Positive Growth Rate	Average Negative Growth Rate
Above $20,000 (non-oil)	27	84%	3.9%	−2.3%
$15–20,000	12	76	5.6	−4.3
$10–15,000	14	71	5.3	−4.1
$5–10,000	37	73	5.3	−4.6
$2–5,000	46	66	5.4	−4.8
$300–2,000	44	56	5.4	−5.4

Source: North, Wallis, and Weingast (2009) Table 1.2, p. 5.

Viewed from this long-run perspective, understanding what drives development forward is thus only half the battle. As important is being able to anticipate, and forestall, reversals. Sometimes the source of these reversals may be in shifts in the global economy (and so fall outside the scope of this study). But at other times the roots of reversal may be found in country-level governance dynamics—and these risks play out very differently for countries on the dominant and the competitive trajectories.

Along the competitive trajectory, a "truce" between contending elites can provide an initial platform of stability sufficient for the governance-growth virtuous circle to get moving. But as the chapter 5 example of Bangladesh will underscore, risks of reversal can seem to be everywhere. As described earlier, decision making is constantly contested; narrow interest-seeking and individual corruption are ubiquitous; political incentives to supply public goods are limited. Corruption and conflict continually threaten to spiral out of control.

Whether an early-stage competitive country can sustain its high-wire act for a sufficiently long time for the gains to be consolidated, or whether the "edge of chaos" is a prelude to backsliding—or perhaps the embrace of a dominant political leadership promising to bring order and direction—is uncertain. Continually, one or another constraint threatens to short-circuit expansion—perhaps weaknesses in the delivery of infrastructure or public services to the most dynamic parts of the economy, perhaps a rise in corruption as public officials seek their share of the growing economic pie, perhaps rising social alienation with a growing sense on the part of citizens that government doesn't care about their everyday problems, perhaps, the need for more sophisticated laws and institutions to underpin an increasingly sophisticated economy. Yet until quite late along the competitive trajectory, the public sector institutions capable of addressing these constraints in a comprehensive and systematic way are unlikely to be in place.

For these early -stage competitive settings, rather than anticipating and addressing in advance all possible institutional constraints, this book explores an approach that builds on the "binding constraints" framework for growth diagnostics laid out by Ricardo Hausmann, Dani Rodrik, and Andres Velasco.[18] The emphasis is on addressing specific capacity and institutional constraints as and when they become binding. Sustaining growth involves continual crisis management, endlessly putting out fires in an environment that to the casual observer seems quite dysfunctional, but nonetheless defies the odds by sustaining continuing dynamism. Chapter 5 provides further detail—highlighting the ways in which the binding constraints framework might be extended to incorporate more explicitly the governance dimensions.

Readers familiar with India will surely find much to recognize in the above three paragraphs. India's endemic corruption, and continuing difficulty in providing infrastructure and public goods, signal that it is only part-way along the trajectory from personalized- to rule-of-law competitiveness and then sustainable democracy. It is troublingly difficult to find twentieth century examples of countries that have managed a sustained, incremental evolution along the trajectory, open throughout. An intriguing earlier example, which chapter 6 explores, is the 1880s–1920s Progressive Era in the United States.

Turning to the dominant trajectory, here a principal early risk is that discretion might degenerate into tyranny and predation. Subsequently, if early-stage discretionary dominance is successfully traversed, then a new set of frontier challenges will come to the fore. The middle class is likely to grow, bringing with it rising civic demands for greater openness. The result could be a relatively smooth transition to democracy—as in Korea where, as chapter 4 details, rule -by-law authoritarianism evolved fairly seamlessly into sustainable democracy.

But the embrace of electoral competition in a hitherto dominant setting could also unleash previously suppressed conflicts, setting in motion a new generation of governance challenges. The result, notwithstanding substantially higher levels of per-capita income, and a strong rule -of -law platform could be a set of challenges uncomfortably similar to those confronting countries in the earlier stage competitive category. South Africa, discussed in chapter 6, provides a vivid example of a politically fraught zig-zag pattern, and highlights how difficult it can be to sustain forward momentum in the face of deep-seated structural inequalities. Egypt and Thailand offer other contemporary examples.

Policy Leapfrogs, Policy Incrementalism

Here is the central policy lesson from this chapter's exploration of how governance and growth interact: To be sustainable, institutions (the "rules of the game") need to be aligned with the incentives of a critical mass of political, civil society and private sector stakeholders. The realm of institutions and institutional development is not separate from the economic, social and political realms.

As development takes hold, new stakeholders come onto the scene with incentives to support the emergence of more impersonal rules of the game. The process of change is not automatic—many powerful actors will continue to have a strong stake in the more personalized status quo. But the combination of pressure for change from new players, support from insiders within government committed to moving development forward, and useful knowledge as to what is needed can provide a potent platform for sustaining momentum on both governance reform and inclusive growth.

Attention to interdependence between governance and growth suggests a key shift in how institutional reform might be approached. Specifically, in stark contrast to the Washington Consensus prescriptions with which we began this chapter, institutions are not "exogenous" vis-à-vis other dimensions of development, and so cannot be super-imposed on the basis of some "best practices" blueprint. Leapfrogging by re-engineering is unlikely to be successful.

To be sure, on rare occasions and in the very short -run a combination of external pressure and a powerful national champion may result in startlingly rapid institutional improvement. Georgia under Mikhail Saakashvili and Rwanda under Paul Kagame stand out as leading recent examples of rapid gains in the multicountry descriptive statistics presented in chapter 7. But without a critical mass of influential stakeholders supportive of more impersonal institutions, "good governance" reform is unlikely to be sustainable. Success is far more likely to come incrementally—from step-by-step approaches that work to strengthen institutional capabilities by building on the incentives of emerging players with a stake in less personalized ways of doing things, and with sufficient influence to make a difference. Chapter 6 explores further, taking a long-run perspective, how institutional evolution can unfold, using the example of the late-nineteenth-century United States. Chapters 8 through 10 lay out in detail some policy options for reformers in settings where incremental approaches to institutional reform are likely to be the practical way forward.

Attention to interdependence also shifts how we understand and assess progress. In the exuberant early years following the fall of the Berlin Wall, democratic transitions were accompanied by high expectations that well-functioning institutions could rapidly be put in place, and that open markets and competing, programmatic political parties could quickly become the norm. But by the early 2000s, we had come to what Tom Carothers called "the end of the transition paradigm."[19] As he documented, rather than sustainable democracy, the far more common result was one of two more ambiguous patterns:

> *"Dominant-power politics" . . . (where) countries have limited but still real political space, some contestation by opposition groups, and most of the basic institutional forms of democracy. Yet one political grouping dominates the system in such a way that there appears to be little prospect of alternation of power.*

Or:

> *"Feckless pluralism" . . . (where) countries enjoy alternation of power between genuinely different groupings . . . but the alternation of power seems only to trade the country's problems back and forth from one hapless side to the other.*

Certainly, the results of governance reform have fallen far short of initial, ambitious hopes. But, contrary to Carothers' depiction, the trajectories framework suggests that it is too negative to describe the results as dysfunctional. Rather, the transitions analyzed by Carothers and others might better be conceived as important "reset" moments along a continuing evolutionary path.

Perhaps everywhere—in the historical experience of contemporary high-income sustainable democracies; more recently for today's emerging economies—the development path is a profoundly discomfiting one. As we'll explore in the next two chapters, the strengths of one trajectory are mirrored as the weaknesses of the other: The dominant state trajectory is top-down, tightly controlled and—insofar as it is implemented effectively—exceedingly orderly. The personalized-competitive trajectory is haphazard, and seemingly chaotic—but can also be a "good enough" platform for accelerated economic growth, and incremental improvements in governance. As long as inclusive economic growth is rapid, perhaps a seeming excess of order or a seeming excess of chaos may be less a signal that a country is off-track than part of the (medium-term) nature of things.

Annex Table A3.1 **Distribution of Countries by Trajectory and 2000–2010 Real Growth Rates**

	Dominant (51)			Intermediate (39)			Competitive (29)		
Per capita income $1,501–$10,000	*Growth > 50%*			*Growth > 50%*			*Growth >50%*		
				Russia	63%	Bulgaria 62%	Lithuania	63%	Romania 56%
				Latvia	52%		Slovakia	59%	Panama 53%
							Estonia	51%	
	Growth 25–50%			*Growth 25–50%*			*Growth 25–50%*		
	Tunisia	40%	Jordan 46%	Botswana	34%	Lebanon 49%	Thailand	48%	Poland 48%
	Egypt	32%	Iran 42%	Namibia	34%	Peru 48%	Dominican Republic	40%	Argentina 39%
	Malaysia	29%	Oman 25%	Colombia	32%	Turkey 35%	Mauritius	36%	Uruguay 37%
				Croatia	29%	Macedonia 25%	Chile	28%	Czech 34%
									SouthAfrica 26%
									Brazil 26%
	Growth <25%			*Growth <25%*			*Growth <25%*		
	Libya	20%	Algeria 22%	Guyana	22%		Costa Rica	24%	Hungary 23%
	Gabon	0%	Saudi Arabia 2%				ElSalvador	13%	Guatemala 9%
							Venezuela	13%	Mexico 6%
							Jamaica	2%	

continued

Annex Table A3.1 **(continued)**

Per capita income / Growth	Dominant (51)	Intermediate (39)	Competitive (29)
$500–$1,500 — Growth > 50%	Eqt. Guinea 245%, Turkmenistan 196%, Angola 120%, Kazakhstan 100%, Bhutan 78%, Azerbaijan 241%, China 156%, Belarus 115%, Uzbekistan 72%	Armenia 110%, Ukraine 63%, Sri Lanka 51%, Georgia 83%, Albania 63%	
Growth 25–50%	Morocco 45%, Pakistan 28%	Indonesia 44%, Ecuador 33%	Philippines 30%
Growth < 25%	Syria 22%, Swaziland 14%, Cameroon 4%, Congo-B 18%, Yemen 12%	Paraguay 23%, Cote d'Ivoire –15%, Papua New Guinea 16%	Bolivia 18%, Honduras 18%
Per capita income under $500 — Growth > 50%	Myanmar 118%, Tajikistan 75%, Rwanda 70%, Chad 67%, Cambodia 88%, Vietnam 77%, Ethiopia 71%, Laos 67%, Tanzania 59%	Nigeria 80%, Sierra Leone 79%, Moldova 68%, Mozambique 77%, Bangladesh 52%	India 76%, Mongolia 73%

Annex Table A3.1 **(continued)**

Dominant (51)				*Intermediate (39)*				*Competitive (29)*	
Growth 25–50%				*Growth 25–50%*				*Growth 25–50%*	
Sudan	45%	Kyrgyzstan	32%	Ghana	37%	Zambia	36%	Madagascar	–1%
Uganda	47%					Nepal	28%		
Burkina Faso	34%			Mali	36%				
Growth < 25%				*Growth < 25%*				*Growth < 25%*	
Mauritania	16%	Gambia	12%	Niger	23%	Lesotho	16%	Senegal	17%
Burundi	6%	Guinea	4%	Malawi	20%	Benin	9%		
DR Congo	0%	Afghanistan	0%	Kenya	16%	Nicaragua	0%		
Somalia	0%	Togo	–5%	Central African Republic	–11%	Guinea Bissau	1%		
Haiti	–12%	Eritrea	–24%						
Liberia	–21%	Zimbabwe	–40%						

Sources: See Annex Table A2.1.

47

COUNTRIES—THE TYPOLOGY IN ACTION

Part II uses in-depth country examples and multicountry descriptive statistics to explore the typology introduced in Part I. As the examples underscore, each country type identified by the typology is aligned with a specific set of political realities, and is supported by a critical mass of influential actors with a stake in the prevailing institutional arrangements. All good things need not come together—rather, the strengths of one country type can be mirrored as the weaknesses of the other.

Along the dominant trajectory, leaders championing development promise that they can "make government work," and that this can, in turn, unlock private investment and thereby accelerate economic growth. Chapter 4 explores how top-down dominance can set development in motion, using the examples of South Korea and Ethiopia. The discussion of Korea focuses on the quarter century from the early 1960s to the mid-1980s, an era of hyper-rapid growth under authoritarian rule, with strong state intervention in the economy. For Ethiopia, the relevant period began with Meles Zenawi's accession to power in 1991. In both countries, top-down hierarchical rule has been associated with major gains in growth and poverty reduction. But the gap between dominant trajectory rhetoric and reality can be very large, with very high risks of capture and predation by dominant leaders. Notwithstanding the risks, many countries continue to pursue the dominant path.

Along the competitive trajectory, early stages of development can be characterized by a paradoxical combination of rapid growth and open, but seemingly dysfunctional, governance: The time horizons of political leaders are shorter; their hold on power is more fragile; political elites within the ruling coalition continually maneuver to sustain stability and to assure the continuing loyalty of clients. Yet, as chapter 5 explores using the examples of Bangladesh and Zambia, personalized competition can, sometimes, provide a workable platform for economic development. Continually, one or another constraint might threaten to short-circuit the process, but incremental reforms can do "just enough" to keep things moving, addressing specific capacity and institutional constraints as and when they become binding, somehow defying the odds and sustaining continuing dynamism.

Chapter 6 explores the typology from a dynamic perspective, using country examples, and drawing on a voluminous conceptual and empirical literature. Its focus is less on distinctive patterns of incentive and constraint, and more on how the momentum of virtuous circles that link governance and growth can be sustained. Two points are highlighted:

- First, institutions can evolve incrementally—as the historical experience of the United States illustrates. For most of the nineteenth century, the American government was rife with patronage and corruption. But the country's institutions also provided a framework within which a century later, as the economy and society changed and pressures for better government grew, a progressive movement for fostering public sector reform could emerge.
- Second, over the long run, stable democratic institutions rest on a platform of broad-based economic and political inclusion. A contrast between patterns of institutional change in South Africa and Korea, subsequent to each country's democratization, underscores the centrality of inclusion for democratic sustainability.

Chapter 7 uses descriptive statistics to map a variety of patterns of institutional change among forty-one countries that grew rapidly between 2000 and 2010 along the dominant, intermediate and competitive trajectories.

The importance of sustaining forward momentum emerges as a central policy implication of a long view of governance. For many countries, resilience to shocks builds through cumulative interactions between governance and growth. In such settings, if momentum stops too soon, virtuous circles can all too easily go into reverse, wiping out hard-won gains. But the practical implications of this conclusion cannot be derived mechanistically. The process of development is a knife edge: Too much pressure for change risks derailing the positive momentum of virtuous circles, but with insufficient attention to things that need to be changed, the process risks grinding to a halt. In crafting a way forward, no simple reform dictum can substitute for in-depth, country-specific knowledge and informed judgment.

CHAPTER 4

The Dominant Trajectory in Action

In 2004, Ethiopia's then prime minister, Meles Zenawi, seemed in an unassailably strong position. He had put the difficult and contentious border war with Eritrea behind him and, as cochair with the British Prime Minister Tony Blair of the millennium Commission for Africa, was feted as one of the new generation of leaders ushering in an African renaissance. It was more than a dozen years since he had taken the reins of power, and a decade since the promulgation of a new constitution. His economic team had put together a bold new program of public investments, totaling over $38 billion, no small sum for a country of over 70 million people whose annual GDP at the turn of the millennium was under $10 billion.

How could Ethiopia finance its ambitious agenda? The key, it seemed, was to deepen the confidence of the international donor community, and so get them to further intensify their already substantial financial support—and the way to do this was to win an incontrovertible electoral mandate. Such a mandate seemed within Meles' grasp: His victory against Eritrea had helped cement his nationalist credentials; he had given new authority to Ethiopia's diverse regions and, for the first time in the country's long and storied history, had put in place a development strategy that promised new opportunities to this overwhelmingly rural country's smallholder farmers. Meles embarked on a new round of multiparty elections, with unprecedentedly open campaigning, complete with a televised debate with his leading opponent for the presidency.

But an incontrovertible mandate was not to be. Within a few hours of the polls closing, the head of the European Parliament's electoral observer mission began doing the rounds of the capital city Addis Ababa's foreign missions, spreading the disturbing report that Meles and his Ethiopian People's Revolutionary Democratic Front (EPRDF) had lost the election. That such a conclusion could be reached so quickly is astonishing to the point of incredulity. It was always inevitable that Meles, never popular with the urban residents of

Addis Ababa who were disproportionately made up of the ethnically Amhara ruling elite who he had displaced, would lose the vote in the capital city. But, with a population that was 85 percent rural, the votes that counted were in the countryside and, given the country's woeful infrastructure, the tally of these votes would not be known for days.

Regardless, the damage was done. The story took hold that Meles had stolen the election, and mass protests broke out in Addis Ababa. Over the next few months, hundreds of people were killed by government forces, and upwards of ten thousand opposition supporters jailed. The reverberations were felt throughout the donor capitals, not least in Washington, DC., where the always vociferous expatriate Ethiopian community expressed their displeasure through loud, angry demonstrations outside the World Bank buildings. The clamor arose to withdraw from the country; dictators who killed their own citizens, it was argued, should not be supported.

The Ethiopian crisis and its aftermath decisively marked an end to any exuberant optimism I might have felt as to the ease with which Africa would turn the corner in its millennial renaissance, with all good things coming together. I had been engaged on and off in Ethiopia for the previous half-dozen years. In 1999, I had led a day-long small group workshop on potential capacity building strategies for Ethiopia, organized at prime minister Meles' request, in which he was an active participant throughout the day. Like many in the donor community before me, I was struck by his zeal, commitment, and intellectual incisiveness. (There cannot be many prime ministers who, upon acceding to office, decide that they need to engage the cutting edge of development thinking and so, even as they wrestle by day with the challenges of governing a country, enroll for a distance-learning master's degree; Meles earned an MBA from Britain's Open University in 1994, and by many accounts was one of the best students they had ever had.)

I also could not help but interpret Meles' development strategy for Ethiopia through the lens of South Korea's experience. At the time of the workshop with Meles and his team, I had been researching and writing about Korea's developmental authoritarianism for over fifteen years, including a sabbatical period at the Korea Development Institute in 1987, with a focus on the country's approach to industrial policy (as it happened, I was in Korea at the moment Korea's quarter century of authoritarian rule came to an end—but more on that later). Over the course of an intensive lunch conversation with prime minister Meles, I had been struck by the depth of his knowledge of the East Asian experience, and his eagerness to take a leaf out of its book by actively promoting new export industries. He described for me some of his ideas for building an Ethiopian leather and footwear export sector, and I shared with him my view that this seemed premature.

Even in the democratizing 1990s, I did not feel especially ambivalent about praising Korea's developmental model. The country was a demonstrable success, both economically and in its successful democratic transition. The hard edge of General Park's rule in the 1960s and 1970s had receded into the distance. But in 2005, as the World Bank team working in Ethiopia polarized into sharp disputes over what to do next, the realities of Ethiopia's "hard" state confronted me directly.

I knew all too well that authoritarianism was more often an excuse for rapacity than a platform for development. In 1987, en route to Korea, I had spent a few months in the Philippines, in the immediate wake of the collapse of Ferdinand Marcos's corrupt authoritarian rule. And in the 1990s, from my perch in the World Bank's Africa region, I had witnessed that continent's transition to democracy as one corrupt African dictator after another had fallen. Daniel Arap Moi in Kenya, Hastings Banda in Malawi, Sekou Toure in Guinea, and Generals Amin in Uganda, Mobutu in Zaire, and Babangida in Nigeria comprise only a few of the long litany of names. And, of course, I had thrilled at my own country, South Africa's, seemingly miraculous transition from authoritarian apartheid to majority democratic rule.

At the heart of a "working with the grain" approach to development strategy, however, is a recognition that all good things do not come together; that countries have different strengths and weaknesses, and that an approach that aims to build on strengths often is the key to forward momentum. For both Korea and Ethiopia, one important set of strengths was a legacy of top-down, hierarchical rule.

This chapter explores how these strengths translated into an unprecedentedly successful era of broad-based growth in Korea, and, in the contemporary period, may be providing a platform for an acceleration of broad-based growth in Ethiopia. The chapter also begins to explore the implications of this type of growth path for governance reform, in the short, medium, and long run.

Does laying out the logic of these experiences make me an apologist for authoritarianism? Such a conclusion would be a misreading of what I am trying to argue. Central to the typologies approach is the idea that the "dominant trajectory" is a potentially viable option only for a small subset of countries where the relevant enabling conditions are in place, and only for a limited period of time; that in countries that lack these conditions the result is likely to be disastrous; and that (as per chapter 5) there exists an alternative approach along the competitive trajectory that, for many countries, may yield better results (on the growth as well as governance fronts). The full argument only comes into view when the argument in the book is considered as a whole, so I ask for forbearance: Prejudging would risk throwing out the baby with the bathwater.

Growth along the Dominant Trajectory

Let us briefly review the logic of the dominant trajectory laid out in chapter 3. A classic promise by leaders championing development along the dominant trajectory is that they can "make government work"—and that this can, in turn, unlock private investment and thereby accelerate economic growth.[1] In the short and medium run, the gains from development along the dominant trajectory may principally be economic, but over the longer-run they potentially are way more far-reaching. Figure 4.1 (a variant of Figure 3.2) depicts how an initial focus on strengthening bureaucratic capability potentially could set in motion a virtuous development circle.

Transmission channel I in the figure illustrates the links between enhanced bureaucratic capability and accelerated growth. In turn, transmission channel II suggests how sustained, market-driven economic growth can have powerful knock-on effects. Almost by definition, it will result in a strengthened private sector (channel II). In time, a strengthened private sector can generate pressure for yet stronger performance by service-providing public agencies, and for a system of law capable of supporting increasingly complex private contracting. Insofar as growth is broad-based, it is likely also to be accompanied by the rise of a middle class. This, in turn, generally is associated with increased civil society activity, giving added impetus to pressures for better government and a stronger rule of law.

As noted earlier, the risks are high of capture and predation by dominant leaders; so the gap between the rhetoric and the reality of developmental states can be very large. Yet, notwithstanding the risks, many countries have gone down this route. The dominant model—the logic of the "developmental state"—underlay East Asian development. It was an aspiration of many Latin American countries (including Brazil and Mexico) prior to the 1980s. The former centrally planned economies offered a (failed) radical variant for much of the twentieth century. Aspirations of progress via the development state model persisted, in countries as disparate as Rwanda and Uganda in Africa, to Azerbaijan in Central Asia, and Vietnam in Southeast Asia. Today, drawn by

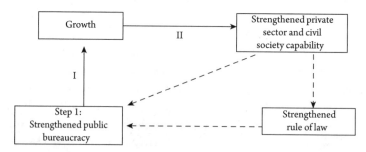

Figure 4.1 **The Dominant Trajectory's Virtuous Spiral**

the example (and influence) of China's spectacular success, there is renewed interest in a "state capitalist" model.[2]

Whether the optimistic vision of what the dominant trajectory can bring indeed plays out this way is an empirical matter. Questions arise for each step along the path:

- Does the dominant political leadership indeed follow through on its promise to strengthen bureaucratic capability?
- Does this enhanced capability translate in turn into accelerated economic growth?
- And, insofar as growth accelerates, does the resulting economic transformation result in stronger institutions, a more engaged civil society and, at the limit, democratization?

Clearly, the answers to these questions will vary from country to country. Chapter 7 uses cross-country data to examine how broadly applicable the dominant model might be in practice. Here we take a more in-depth focus, using the examples of South Korea (henceforth "Korea") and Ethiopia to illustrate how top-down dominance can play out in practice.

For Korea, the key relevant period is the quarter century from the early 1960s to the mid-1980s, an era of hyper-rapid growth under authoritarian rule. For Ethiopia, the contemporary period, beginning with Meles Zenawi's accession to power in 1991 is the most relevant. As will become evident, there are large differences in the way in which the dominant trajectory has been implemented in each country, although this may in part be a result of their different levels of development during the relevant period.

Korea's Development Miracle

In the late 1950s, in a classic case of "famous last words," an American aid official proclaimed that Korea was a development basket case, with no prospect of improvement. Over the subsequent quarter century, Korea became one of the great development success stories, of the contemporary, or any other, era. Between 1961 and 1987 (the year of transition from military dictatorship to democracy), Korea grew at an average real annual rate of over 6 percent per annum. In the early 1960s, over half the population lived below a minimum threshold of absolute poverty; by the mid-1990s, the proportion had fallen below 4 percent.[3]

The policies championed by the Korean authorities over the 1961–1986 quarter century of the country's "dominant trajectory" growth miracle cannot be easily reconciled with orthodox prescriptions. Not only was government unabashedly authoritarian, it used its top-down political levers to override markets and private decisions in highly targeted discretionary ways.

Korea's embrace of the "dominant" trajectory is very deeply rooted historically. A classic political history of the country, *The Politics of the Vortex*, describes the five-centuries long monarchical centralization of the Korean state;[4] indeed Korea has been described as having been for many centuries the most relentlessly and hierarchically Confucian of all East Asian societies. In the early twentieth century, Japan became Korea's colonial occupier, supplanting the local feudal, and increasingly dysfunctional, monarchy; like all colonial powers everywhere, its rule was relentlessly top-down.

In the aftermath of World War II, and the withdrawal of Japan from Korea, an effort was made by the occupying American power to implant democracy. However, in the absence of either supportive formal institutions or a legacy of strong horizontal social capital, the democratic seed failed to take root. Instead, within a very few years of acceding to power, strongman Syngman Rhee embraced authoritarian rule; government became increasingly corrupt.

Rhee's regime was brought down in early 1960 by a civilian/student uprising. Political chaos in the immediate aftermath resulted in a military coup in 1961, led by General Park Chung-Hee. General Park dominated Korean politics over the next eighteen years (until his assassination in 1979), governing the country as a top-down "developmental state." The Park era ushered in a period of rapid growth and poverty reduction, and far-reaching economic and social transformation.

At the heart of Korea's development success was the relationship between a dominant leader, General Park Chung Hee and the country's leading private firms, the "*chaebol.*" In a classic book written in the 1980s, Leroy Jones and Sakong Il contrasted the relationship between business and government in Korea with that of Japan:

> *In the notion of "Japan, Inc.," economic growth policies have been jointly decided and jointly executed by politicians and appointed officials jointly with representatives of private business . . . [though], there is some difference of opinion as to where dominance lies: some would have government dominating business, others the reverse. . . In Korea, the dominant partner is unequivocally the government. . . . The success of government requires the success of business . . . [but] the Korean government can ensure the failure of any businessman, should it care to do so . . . the government's wishes are tantamount to commands, and business dare not take them lightly.[5]*

Jones and Sakong describe the relationship between business and government in Korea as one of "partial mutuality"—where one participant (i.e. business) undertakes an action in order either to win goodwill, or to forestall an action by the other participant (i.e., government) that would inflict an even greater loss.[6]

The tone was set almost immediately General Park came to power, with the passage of a "Law for Dealing with Illicit Wealth Accumulation." Under the provisions of the law, most of the country's leading businessmen were arrested. Soon thereafter, a deal was struck whereby the government would exempt most businessmen from criminal prosecution, in return for which they would work closely with General Park to identify and make investments that would help accelerate economic growth.

The dominant role of government in this dance of "partial mutuality" was sustained, Jones and Sakong argue,[7] by government's control over credit. Control over credit was an especially powerful lever because Korean growth was fuelled by borrowing: The ratio of debt to equity among the country's private corporate sector rose from 1.2 in 1966 to 3.9 in 1971; between 1963 and 1974, two-thirds of private corporate finance was sourced through debt. Throughout this period, all of Korea's major banks either were wholly publicly owned, or had a mix of public and private ownership; but even for the latter, shareholder voting provisions ensured that government had ultimate control over decision making. Control over credit was thus the *"fulcrum . . . the knowledge that the government can cut off the credit tap at any time is sufficient for the operation of partial mutuality. The threat need only be carried out occasionally".*[8]

The implementation of Korea's manufacturer's export-led development strategy illustrates powerfully the central role of "partial mutuality" and government discretion in the country's development success.[9] The example of television manufacture illustrates. Korea's entry into TV production began in the 1960s, with the introduction of a local station with television programming, and a simultaneous ban on the importation of black and white TV sets. A few years later, it followed a similar path with color TV: initiating color-TV broadcasts, and banning imported color sets. Numerous failed experiments with import substitution the world over confirm that, much of the time, the liberal use of protection against imports is the recipe for a dead-end: It locks in high prices, high-cost production, and the absence of pressure on local producers to improve performance. It becomes part of a syndrome of a cozy, rent-sharing, low-performing alliance between business and government elites. This is not what happened in Korea. Today, Samsung and other Korean companies, the same companies (or their direct descendants, after rounds of corporate restructuring) who went into the production of black-and-white TVs in the 1960s behind the shelter of an import ban, are world leaders in the manufacture of high-end TVs.

Korea avoided the fate of other failed import substituters by combining domestic protection with strong, top-down pressures on companies to export. The organizational infrastructure put in place to achieve this combination was remarkably robust.[10] Monthly, product-specific export targets were negotiated and agreed with individual firms. These targets were closely monitored by government in an export "war-room," and were reviewed at monthly meetings chaired by the President, and attended by both government officials and private executives. A key focus of these meetings was on obstacles to achieving the targets, and on what action could be taken (especially by the public sector) to help meet them. Problems were surfaced, agreements made to address them, and follow-up on progress reviewed at subsequent meetings. It was all in the spirit of "partial mutuality," but with government firmly in the driver's seat.

The origins of Korea's ship-building industry offers an especially vivid example of partial mutuality in action:

> One of the more impressive entrepreneurial feats in Korea was the creation of a world-class shipbuilding firm by Hyundai. This venture seemed quixotic to most Koreans.... Not only had Hyundai had no previous experience in shipbuilding, but Korea itself had never produced a vessel larger than 10,000 tons.... International financiers and shipbuilder were not doubt bemused at the pretensions of someone soliciting funds with little more to show than a picture of a lovely sandy beach where the proposed Hyundai dry dock was to be built.... Hyundai Chairman Chong persevered only because of the urgings of President Park [who encouraged him by saying "if you only want to do what is easy you'll get no help from me...."].
>
> Finally in April 1972, an agreement was reached with a Greek shipowner whereby two vessels—of 240,000 and 260,000 tons—were to be delivered in two-and-a-half years.... A dry dock was built, workers trained, supplementary facilities completed... the first vessel was delivered in November 1974.... When the 1975 world shipbuilding slump led to the cancellation of orders for three virtually completed tankers... the government decided that it would be a good idea if Korean oil refineries started to ship crude from the Middle East in Korean-owned bottoms.[11]

As of 2012, Korea was (after Ukraine) the second largest builder of deep-sea supertankers in the world.

Ethiopia—Escaping a "Poverty Trap"

Compared with Korea, Ethiopia's development strategy has so far been somewhat less directly contrary to the mainstream, market-friendly development paradigm. But, like Korea, the impetus has been overwhelmingly top-down.

For many decades, Ethiopia was associated with famine, destitution, and desperation. The proximate cause of famine usually is drought; a deeper cause often is governance failure. In Ethiopia, one manifestation of very long-term failures in governance comprised the extraordinary shortfalls in the country's infrastructure:[12]

- As of the late 1990s, Ethiopia had less than 40 kilometers of roads per square kilometer, as compared with close to 100 kilometers per square kilometer for Tanzania and 140 kilometers per square kilometer for Uganda. Even controlling for both population density and per capita incomes, Ethiopia's actual road network was less than a fifth of its predicted levels.
- Ethiopia's electricity supply was similarly underdeveloped: After controlling for per capita income, urban population shares, and surface areas, electricity consumption was just one-thirtieth of the predicted level.
- Although the headwaters of the Nile are in Ethiopia, and the country's mountainous terrain makes it well suited for dams (and hence irrigation and hydropower). As of the early 1990s, Ethiopian dams had the capacity for less than 10 cubic meters of managed water per capita, as compared with about 200 cubic meter per capita in South Africa, and over 900 cubic meter per capita in the United States. Just 2 percent of Ethiopia's 3.7 million hectares of potentially irrigable land was irrigated.

In the face of infrastructural shortfalls of the magnitude described above, market reforms alone can do little to break out of the development dead-end. Meles Zenawi, in a paper titled "African Development: Dead Ends and New Beginnings," makes the case vis-à-vis agricultural growth. While this requires a shift, he notes, from subsistence to market-based production, creating an integrated market needs much more than price liberalization:

> Investments in infrastructure and market support institutions are needed.... The dead-end can be broken only if government invests in rural physical infrastructure, in institutions for technological capability accumulation and in [rural credit].... The fundamentals of the neo-liberal paradigm go against the grain of what is needed to bring about rapid and sustained growth in African agriculture.[13] (Section 17.1)

An infrastructure-oriented development strategy is hardly outside of economic orthodoxy. Recognition that there exist classes of public goods, such as infrastructure, for which returns cannot be internalized by private investors (i.e., for which social benefits are in excess of private benefits) and that this creates a case for public action is a central tenet of conventional economics. But an economic prescription focused on major infrastructural investment presupposes a government committed to development, a relatively long-term horizon, and "good-enough" bureaucracy.

While in many low-income developing countries this level of state capacity cannot be taken for granted, in Meles' Ethiopia, it was present. Why? Part of the answer has to do with political leadership, the authority Meles enjoyed, and the way in which he governed. But another, perhaps even more fundamental part is rooted in the logic of "path dependence," in history. As with Korea, top-down hierarchical rule is deeply rooted in Ethiopian society.

Never systematically colonized, Ethiopia (or, more precisely, Ethiopia's Amharic-speaking population) was ruled continually, since the thirteenth century, by an emperor (the imperial family claimed direct descent from the Solomonic era Queen of Sheba). In point of fact, for long portions of this history, the grip on power of "imperial" rule was tenuous, sustained by the emperor and his retinue continually touring their territories in their tent caravan. But, beginning in the mid-nineteenth century, the Amharic overlords began to modernize and extend the reach of their state. Modern Ethiopia can be dated as starting from a series of military victories (against Egyptian invaders, the Sudanese dervishes, and putative Italian colonizers) of King Yohannes in the latter-nineteenth century. Over the subsequent century, Ethiopia's territory continually expanded, encompassing an ever-widening, multi-ethnic territory under Amharic imperial rule, and with political authority heavily centralized in Addis Ababa.[14]

Consistent with this long history of hierarchical, centralized rule, the traditional Amharic social order was organized around rigid superior-subordinate relationships. A 1972 study described the pattern as follows:

> *Subservience to, and respect for, persons of higher authority is a fundamental lesson taught to the Ethiopian child. Authority figures are subject to highly elaborate expressions of praise, and it is expected that, at least in appearance, there will be compliance to the wishes of any authority figure . . . any act of initiative on the part of the subordinate is, in a sense, a rejection of this show of dependency demanded by the big man . . . there does not appear to be a word in Amharic equal to the notion of "public servant" in English; the terminology used for government officials is translated as "employee of the government."*[15]

For much of the twentieth century, Ethiopia was ruled by the emperor Haile Selassie. His cautious efforts at modernization built the platform of a modern bureaucracy, one that subsequently has stood the test of time. But, while not providing any institutional framework for post-imperial rule, it did produce a new elite that chafed under imperial authority. After Haile Selassie was overthrown in 1974, power was consolidated under an increasingly totalitarian (and increasingly unpopular) military regime, the Derg. In 1990, in the aftermath of the collapse of the Soviet Union, the Derg, too, was forced from power.

Meles, then leader of the Tigray People's Liberation Front (which later was transformed into the EPRDF) filled the subsequent vacuum. Even before the 2005 election and its difficult aftermath, he was ambivalent as to what democratic rule would bring in many low-income countries. Here's how he put it in *Dead Ends And New Beginnings:*

> *Even if a developmental state was to be solely concerned about accelerating growth, it would have to build the high social capital that is vital for its endeavors. It would have to stamp out patronage and rent-seeking. There is a catch, however. When a developmental state is established it is unlikely to find a situation where rent-seeking has been stamped out, social capital accumulated etc.... Initially therefore the risk of democratic politics becoming riddled with patronage and rent-seeking will be there. How can the developmental state clean-up the mess of patronage and rent-seeking in the initial stages of its establishment by anything other than undemocratic means?*

This ambivalence is evident in the two parallel tracks through which he addressed the challenges of political governance.[16] On one track, Meles championed far-reaching constitutional reform. In 1994, the country adopted what seemed like a democratic constitution, complete with separation of powers between the legislature, executive, and judiciary, multiparty electoral competition, plus a radical devolution of authority to each of the country's nine regions. Meanwhile, on the parallel track, he invested heavily in strengthening the reach and authority of the EPRDF. Party cadres play a central role at all levels of government; "party-statal" enterprises are active in many sectors in the economy. So in practice, notwithstanding the democratic forms, Ethiopian governance since the early 1990s has continued along classic dominant leader/party lines.

Meles successfully utilized the country's top down capacities to deliver on his infrastructure-led development strategy:

- The country's core road network doubled from 26,500 kilometers in 1997 to over 50,000 by 2010 and is scheduled to increase by a further 30-plus percent between 2011 and 2015—with major complementary investments in local roads.
- Between 2005 and 2010, power generation capacity increased from 714 megawatts to 2,000 megawatts, with plans to ramp capacity up within the decade to 10,000 megawatts, and provide electricity to about 75 percent of villages.

- Alongside infrastructural development, education also has expanded rapidly, with the gross primary school enrollment rate rising from 32 percent in 1990 to 96 percent by 2011. Moreover, unlike in some other countries, where new opportunities were provided for educational access without a complementary investment in teachers, along with increasing enrolment, Ethiopia has managed to bring down student-teacher ratios, from 69 to 1 in 2004 to 62 to 1 in 2010 for primary education.
- The death rate of children under the age of five has been dramatically reduced, from 204 per 1,000 births in 1990, to 68 per 1,000 in 2012.

Real economic growth has continually been rising, at an average annual rate in excess of 10 percent between 2000 and 2010. This growth has been broad-based: Agriculture and related activities are reported to have grown at an average rate of 8 percent per annum over the period. Poverty rates are falling the proportion of people living below the country's poverty line declined from 45 percent in 1995 to 30 percent in 2011.

These growth rates have been contested. Based on inconsistencies across different sources of data, there has been some speculation that, in the context of a strong "dominant" pattern of rule, local officials have inflated performance results as a way of remaining in favor. There also has been continuing criticism of the Ethiopian authorities over the country's sometimes restrictive and unwelcoming policies in some sectors, and in relation to some private firms. Yet for all of the controversy, there is general consensus that growth over the most recent five-year period has been in excess of 7 percent per annum, and that the pattern of growth has been broad-based. Against the backdrop of Ethiopia's long having been among the poorest countries in the world, these economic achievements are impressive.

Taming Leviathan

As the Ethiopian and Korean successes suggest, the dominant trajectory is seductive: Combine strong leadership and a capable bureaucracy, and development seems there for the taking. But rhetoric to the contrary, "dominant" is not a synonym for "developmental." In practice, sustained success via the dominant route remains more the exception than the rule: Many countries with dominant political leaders fail to grow, and, among those that do, only for a subset is that growth accompanied by sustained improvement in the quality of formal public institutions. Annex Table A4.1 provides further detail for the fifty-one dominant countries, including both decadal growth rates and estimates of the quality of the rule of law.

History is replete with leaders who have touted themselves as "developmental," concentrated authority on the basis of its necessity for their achieving developmental goals, and been showered with largesse from a supportive donor community, only to have their reigns end in recrimination, corruption, and disgrace. As we saw in chapter 3, between 2000 and 2010, only eighteen of the fifty-one countries in the dominant trajectory grew rapidly, and almost half barely grew at all.

Chapter 7 examines how governance patterns changed over the decade for these eighteen countries. As it shows, some align well with the dominant leadership model described above, others are more ambiguous, and yet others are oil-exporting countries that show striking weaknesses in governance. The patterns of control over corruption within the dominant group are especially striking. Even the otherwise better performers score worse on this dimension than their competitive counterparts, a reminder of one of the hidden costs of a lack of accountability.

In interesting recent work, Tim Kelsall and David Booth introduce the notion of "developmental patrimonialism."[17] From the perspective of the framework laid out here, it is a hybrid category, similar to the dominant trajectory in its degree of centralization, and similar to the competitive trajectory in the use of clientelism as a tool for building alliances. Kelsall and Booth argue that the combination of centralization of authority and patrimonialism sometimes can provide a good enough platform for development to proceed. The poor record on control of corruption for most of even the better performing countries on the dominant trajectory suggests that developmental patrimonialism may indeed have some empirical traction, but that the line that distinguishes developmental patrimonialism from predatory, destructive growth may be a thin one.

What makes the track record of growth along the dominant trajectory so mixed? In his classic seventeenth century treatise, *Leviathan*, the political philosopher Thomas Hobbes identified the central puzzle: Political order requires, he argued, a leader with sufficient power and authority to quell revolt. However, such dominant authority leaves much (for good or ill) to the discretion of leaders. A dismal outcome is not inevitable: On occasion, as Korea and (though it is too early to tell) perhaps Ethiopia illustrate, the promise of the dominant trajectory turns out to be real. But the risks are all too high, and things are all too likely to work out badly. It's somewhat like playing a game where the aim is to get a high score, but one is playing with unusually loaded dice: There's one six but five ones.

Might there be a way of improving the odds? As subsequent chapters explore, one central question concerns how the balance between top-down dominance and bottom-up inclusiveness evolves over time. But in advance of this broader discussion, the Korean and Ethiopian cases suggest that, even in these quintessentially hierarchical settings, the disconnect between top-down dominance and bottom-up accountability need not be total, and that dominance need not be forever.

Inclusiveness and democratization in Korea.   When my wife, our eighteen-month-old toddler, and I arrived in Seoul, Korea in January 1987, we hadn't expected that we would spend a good part of the next few months planning our movements so as to bypass street clashes between students and police, or keeping our windows closed on warm afternoons to protect ourselves from the effects of tear gas. I had experienced some of these things as a student in South Africa in the mid-1970s, but I'd come to Korea to learn more about its economic miracle, not for another rude lesson about the hard edge of governance. Life, however, brings what it brings.

In point of fact, Korea has a long and storied history of student protest. There were protests in the early twentieth century, as Japanese rule was taking root. There were sustained protests during the corrupt years of the Rhee regime, which culminated in the rise to power of General Park. There were repeated protests in the 1970s and 1980s, including a round of protests in 1979 in the city of Kwangju, which turned violent and resulted in a massacre of hundreds by government forces.

Indeed, springtime in Seoul was often a season of protest, almost an annual ritual. Red bandana-ed students voiced their displeasure at the failures of their elders; they confronted fearsome-looking, riot-gear-clad police, complete with batons and crowd control shields who came to "keep the peace"; rough street clashes ensued. Usually, after a few weeks of disruption and many bruises, things returned to normal, and the country went back to its (high-productivity) business.

But 1987 was different. This time, the students didn't simply return to their dormitories. This time, Seoul's white-collar middle class came out in support of the students. This time, with the Seoul Olympics intended to showcase to the world an emerging, modern Korea just a year away, the momentum of events kept building. General Chun (the successor to General Park, and President at the time of the Kwangju massacre) stepped down, and his successor, General Roh Tae Woo, committed to hold elections and usher civilian, democratic rule. Elections were held and won by Roh after rival opposition candidates split their vote. Then in 1992, the long-time dissident Kim Young Sam was elected president, to be succeeded in 1997 by the election of a second, even more vociferous dissident, Kim Dae Jung. By 2012, power had alternated multiple times; Korea had become a mature democracy.

At first glance, then, Korea's transition to democracy is a remarkably clear affirmation of the virtuous spiral laid out in Figure 4.1: Growth produced a sophisticated private sector, the complex impersonal institutions needed to support it, and a thriving middle class. And this middle class, in turn, had become large and powerful enough to be the decisive influence in bringing down the military regime. All of this is true, but there is more to the story.

As we shall explore further in chapter 6, what made Korea's transition to democracy relatively seamless was an underpinning of equity.[18] This broad base of social equity meant that the country's rulers were not acting for, and protecting the interests of, a narrow elite. They could govern with relative autonomy, with less to lose, and thus less to defend, when the social pressures for institutional transformation became compelling.

Additionally, and paradoxically for a society that on the surface was highly hierarchical, Korea's equity also, it seemed to me, had a cultural dimension. This is evident in the way in which the "partial mutuality" described earlier was implemented. Consider the monthly meetings between government and the private sector. The country's president was in the chair, and called the shots. But there was also mutuality in these meetings, and in the many other joint fora involving the public and the private sectors. The private sector was not only being held to account, implicitly it was also holding government to account for delivering on its side of the bargain.[19]

I also had a more personal sense of this cultural dimension. Each morning, I would be fetched by a driver from the Korea Development Institute (the car was an early model, nowhere-near-yet ready-for-export sub-compact) to be taken to my office. As we drove through the gates of the Korea Development Institute, the guard would salute, as he did to all the arriving scholars. But the meaning of the salute felt very different to me than the crude acknowledgement of hierarchy that I knew well from South Africa and elsewhere. Korea was simultaneously hierarchical and egalitarian, an embodiment of a Confucian culture of well-defined roles, complemented by well-defined mutual obligations. A working class guard would salute a white-collar scholar, but the salute was not unconditional. In that deference, there seemed also to be a reminder: that the other side of the coin was an obligation on the part of the scholar/bureaucrat/soldier/leader to act to the best of his ability on behalf of the collective good. Were this obligation ever to be ignored, the willingness to defer also would be withdrawn.

Ethiopia—Planting seeds of bottom-up accountability. A sense of mutuality also is key to the global aid endeavor that has played a central role in Ethiopia's efforts to escape its poverty trap. Between 2000 and 2010, aid inflows averaged about 5–8 percent of total annual income (in the range of $1 billion annually), and accounted for about one-third of public expenditures.[20] But when it comes to aid, mutuality often plays out in a troublingly superficial way: political support from citizens of donor countries depends importantly on the aid effort's ability to evoke among "Northern" taxpayers a warm feeling of doing the right thing.

Prior to the 2005 election, Ethiopia had become a poster-child of "good" aid. Back in the 1970s, along with Bangladesh, it had been the country where images of starving children had evoked a rash of "live aid" rock concerts and feel-good donations. For a while, the brutality of the repressive military Derg regime undercut the narrative. But finally, with the emergence in Meles Zenawi of a new generation leader committed to development, the narrative could come together. The strength of commitment by donors to Meles Zenawi's government was evident both in the amount of aid, and in the form in which it was given. Ethiopia became a leading example of new, cutting edge approaches to development aid.

A common criticism of aid is that it supports gold-plated enclaves (complete with the donor country nameplate) in the form of initiatives that destroy the capacity of national governments by undercutting the recipient government's ability and willingness to make choices, and by luring the most talented people away from the public sector. In response to this criticism, in countries where governments seemed committed and capable, donors increasingly were moving to provide aid as annual "budget support" for the country's expressed priorities. (This isn't quite the blank check it seems. It provides a platform for in-depth dialogue between donors and recipient governments as to priorities and performance. As champions of budget support pointed out, having some influence over all of government spending was surely likely to do more to combat poverty than having direct control over what rarely amounted to more than 5–10 percent of the total spend.) Meles' commitment to development, plus the country's track record of managing resources prudently, had made Ethiopia a major recipient of budget support.

But in the violent aftermath of the 2005 election, the positive story came undone. It became politically impossible to write an annual budget support check; that would signal seemingly unqualified support for the Meles regime. Instead, the clamor arose for donors to withdraw support entirely from Ethiopia. What was to be done? Donors adopted a two-part response.

One part was a fig leaf of sorts. In place of budget support, and without cutting aggregate levels, donors embraced a new aid model for Ethiopia: the protection of basic services. Formally, there were two large differences between the old and new models. Aid no longer was made available for general purposes: It was specifically targeted to support a scaling-up of social sectors by paying the costs of teachers and health workers. Better yet, in Ethiopia's radically devolved formal constitutional arrangements, education and health were the functions of regional governments; the support provided was no longer going directly to Meles. In practice, though, budget revenues that aren't used for one thing can be used for another. Provincial levels had no independent revenue-raising capabilities, and teachers and health workers were already being paid indirectly by the center through intergovernmental transfers. But budget fungibility is an argument for technicians. Viewed through a more political lens, the advantages are large vis-à-vis donor country electorates of reframing aid in terms of direct support for teachers, nurses, and doctors.

The second part of the donor response also might initially have seemed symbolic, though it was especially difficult to negotiate with the Ethiopian government. In return for large-scale continuing aid support for the provision of basic services, donors pressed hard for the introduction of a variety of bottom-up mechanisms to enable citizens and civil society organizations to monitor whether public resources indeed were delivering on their intended purposes (chapters 9 and 10 explore in more detail the global experience with initiatives along these lines).

Implementation was a long, slow process; for four years, there were repeated disagreements between donors and government, and associated delays. But, remarkably, the Ethiopian authorities themselves increasingly have embraced the bottom-up approach. As of 2012, over 3,000 officials from across the country have been trained in how to design and implement good practices in local level financial transparency and accountability; over 50,000 local leaders have been sensitized as to how they can proactively monitor public spending; over 90 percent of all local governments were posting budgets.[21]

To be sure, no one would confuse contemporary Ethiopia with a vibrant, multiparty democracy along the lines of contemporary Korea. Meles' regime was not one to make the same mistake twice. Going into elections in 2010, there was little doubt as to the outcome. In the event, the EPRDF won close to two-thirds of the vote, and 99 percent of the seats in national and regional parliaments. But the journey of development along the dominant trajectory can be a long and surprising one. In the early 1960s, no one would have predicted that forty years later Korea would be a thriving multiparty democracy. Whether Ethiopia can sustain a further two decades of stability and broad-based, inclusive economic growth is enormously uncertain, and Meles' untimely death only underscores the risks. But if Ethiopia is able to remain on its current trajectory, the seeds of better governance that have been planted over the past two decades, a de jure democratic constitution with strong formal checks and balances, and a de facto willingness to explore how bottom-up transparency can help hold public officials accountable for performance could yet be early harbingers of a profoundly transformed polity and society.

A discomfiting journey.   For those of us steeped in the values of the Western enlightenment, the dominant trajectory is profoundly discomfiting. Even as we acknowledge its potential, cognitive dissonance can set in, making the trajectory difficult to embrace as a way forward. As two postscripts illustrate, the difficulty seems to go beyond a wise recognition that the odds of success are long.

The first postscript concerns Korea, or at least the way in which the mainstream development paradigm has engaged with the Korean experience. Denial of the disconnect between Korean reality and laissez-faire ideology was, for a long time, the principal response. Gradually, though, through the painstaking efforts of many committed people who knew that the reality was different, the paradigm began to move: In 1994, the World Bank issued a widely read report on *The East Asian Miracle.* For all its flaws,[22] the report went further than the organization had previously gone in coming to grips with the reality of policies whose success was attributable, in part, to the ways in which they overrode markets. But then came the financial crisis of 1997, which engulfed Korea along with other East Asian economies. As it happened, the Korean economy turned around very rapidly, continuing its rapid growth. But the damage had been done. Market triumphalism enjoyed a renewed reign; it was as if a tidal wave had washed away the efforts to bring complexity and nuance to the discourse on the interactions between the private sector and development. The resilience of an ideologically comfortable paradigm in the face of compelling evidence to the contrary was both startling and dispiriting to behold.

The second postscript concerns Ethiopia's leather and footwear industry, the one for which I had confidently advised prime minister Meles during our 1998 lunch conversation to avoid premature activism.[23] This unsolicited advice was entirely ignored. Over the subsequent decade, the Ethiopian government made major investments in the sector:

- It established a Leather and Leather Products Technology Institute which, as the first training institute in the sector in the country, is facilitating a rapid upgrading of skills of a rapidly growing workforce.
- It worked together with foreign donors (UNIDO, USAID, and others) to foster co-operation among the country's hundreds of small and medium leather firms to jointly address challenges of production space, access to finance, and market linkages.
- More controversially, it restricted the export of raw animal hides, thereby mobilizing a wave of new investment in leatherfinishing equipment by the country's 21 large-scale tanneries.

These investments have paid off – culminating in January 2012 in the opening by the Chinese company, Huajian, in the first large-scale investment of its kind, of a new footwear factory, employing 600 workers and targeting export markets. Huajian's ambitious goal was to invest up to $2 billion (with funding coming from the China-Africa Development Fund) to establish a light manufacturing special economic zone in Ethiopia, creating employment for close to 100,000 Ethiopians. And in 2013 a Taiwanese company, with a strong global presence in the sector, committed to construct three additional factories, at an outlay of $50 million.[24] As a reader of this chapter will surely concur, I am hardly one of the die-hard critics of dominant-led development. Even so, Ethiopia's unexpectedly strong export achievements in the sector, and, more broadly, the transformative potential of the dominant trajectory, took me by surprise, and left me feeling impressed. But I also found myself feeling uncomfortably ambivalent, given how easily the case for discretionary dominance can be distorted to support predatory and personalized ends.

Annex Table A4.1 **Countries in Dominant Trajectory, by Rule of Law, Income, and 2000–2010 Real Growth Rates**

	Per Capita Income, 2000			Total number of countries
	Low (under $500)	Medium ($500–$1,500)	Higher ($1,501–$10,000)	
Quality of the Rule of Law, 2000				
High (ROL > 0.45)			Oman 25%	1
Medium Higher (−0.25 < ROL < 0.45)	Gambia 12%	Bhutan 78% Morocco 45%	Jordan 46% Tunisia 40% Egypt 32% Malaysia 29% Saudi Arabia 2% Gabon 0%	9
Medium Low (−0.75 < ROL < −0.25)	Vietnam 77% Tanzania 59% BurkinaFaso 34% Mauritania 16% Togo −5% Eritrea −24%	China 156% Syria 22% Swaziland 14%	Iran 42%	10
Low (ROL < −0.75)	Myanmar 118% Cambodia 88% Tajikistan 75% Ethiopia 71%	Eqt. Guinea 245% Azerbaijan 241% Turkmenistan 196% Angola 120%	Algeria 22% Libya 20%	30

continued

Annex Table A4.1 (continued)

	Per Capita Income, 2000			Total number of countries
	Low (under $500)	Medium ($500–$1,500)	Higher ($1,501–$10,000)	
Low (continued) (ROL < –0.75)	Rwanda 70%	Belarus 115%		
	Laos 67%	Kazakhstan 100%		
	Chad 67%	Uzbekistan 72%		
	Sudan 45%	Pakistan 28%		
	Kyrgyzstan 32%	Congo–B 18%		
	Burundi 6%	Yemen 12%		
	Guinea 4%	Cameroon 4%		
	Afghanistan 0%			
	DR Congo 0%			
	Somalia 0%			
	Haiti –12%			
	Liberia –21%			
	Zimbabwe –40%			
Number of countries	24	16	10	51

Source: See Table A2.1 and chapter 7.

CHAPTER 5

Personalized Competition in Action

It was monsoon season when I visited Dhaka in 2005, and the city's drainage didn't work. Everywhere was hot and humid and often flooded as well. One of the perks of working in the World Bank's Bangladesh office was an air-conditioned car pool, complete with driver, giving staffers the opportunity to chat, catch up with work, or snatch a few moments of calm during the interminable downtown traffic jam. We were a target for traffic in human suffering: the deformed, the filthy street children, the abandoned aged, the emaciated mothers and their hungry children; wet, sweaty, dressed in rags, crowding around the stationary vehicle (still stuck in traffic), oblivious of the pouring rain, challenging us to respond. But we also were a target for traffic in street commerce: cigarettes, fruit, individual household items, books, and magazines, including $3 knock-off paperback versions of the latest Harry Potter saga, available on the Dhaka streets just two days after the global hardcover launch of this children's book phenomenon.

Bangladesh boggles the mind and confounds development orthodoxies. Its population of over 150 million people is crowded into an area the size of the American states of Maryland and Virginia. The country is a floodplain, directly on the path taken by some of the world's major rivers—the Ganges, the Brahmaputra, and the Meghna—as they wend their way from the Himalayan mountains to the Bay of Bengal. A normal year is one where 20 percent of the country is underwater during the wet season; a drought year is one where only 10 percent of the country becomes waterlogged.

Dhaka's overwhelming, endless flood of human suffering is, of course, a classic Bangladesh stereotype. Economic vibrancy is not part of the stereotype, but commerce was everywhere; not just on the street but also in the enthusiasm with which the country's nascent industry of computer software entrepreneurs shared their experiences, plans, and dreams with me. Indeed, Bangladesh has the best of records and the worst of development records.

Consider the best: Over the past few decades, Bangladesh has grown rapidly and has done so in a way that has yielded major gains in poverty reduction:[1]

- Between 1995 and 2008, real GDP grew at an average annual rate of 5.5 percent.
- Gross primary school enrollment rates rose from 72 percent in 1970 to 77 percent in 1980 and 98 percent by 2001.
- The mortality rate of children under five has fallen by over three-quarters— from 235 per thousand in 1970, to 151 in 1990, 100 in 2000, and 52 per thousand by 2009. Infant mortality declines have been almost as dramatic—from 145 per thousand in 1970, to 92 in 1990, and 46 per thousand in 2003.

But then there is the worst of records. This is not so much the fact of continuing poverty; poverty reduction, even at Bangladesh's exceptionally rapid rate, takes time. What is difficult to stomach is the impunity that pervades parts of the society. Indeed, impunity helped account in small part for some of the worst flooding I saw during my trip to the country. Blocking up drainage worsens flooding, and when the flooding gets too bad, even people with nowhere to go must leave. That creates the opportunity for property development: for fencing off the land, reopening the drainage, and selling off parcels to the rapidly growing middle class, ever on the lookout for relief from relentless overcrowding. One especially unscrupulous property developer had gone further. To signal that he had no intent of easing the flooding until the poor had permanently left, he had ostentatiously established a fish farm on some abandoned land. He was connected, had money to bribe and access to thugs to back him up. He'd wait them out, then cash in.

This was no isolated example: In 2001 and 2005, Bangladesh had the dubious distinction of being rated by Transparency International as the most corrupt of all 150 + countries surveyed. Though its rating has improved, it continues to be ranked within the bottom quarter of all countries in perceptions of corruption.

Bangladeshi democracy also reflects the best and the worst of records. On the one hand, the country has met a crucial test of democracy: Power has alternated three times between rival parties; in 1996, 2001, and 2008. But on the other hand, as the aborted election of 2006 underscored, the country's electoral system is crisis-prone.

This combination of solid economic performance and repeated disappointment on the governance front is hardly unique to Bangladesh. The 1990s saw a surge of democratization worldwide: across the post-Soviet bloc, from Eastern European countries seeking to align themselves with the

European Union, to Mongolia, and to the Kyrgyz Republic that aspired to become the Switzerland of Central Asia; across Latin America where military governments were decisively on the retreat; and across Africa, where a wave of political opening lifted the number of democracies from single figures to upward of forty.

Many of these countries have enjoyed rapid economic growth, as we saw in Table 3.1. In the decade since 2000, for example, the average growth performance across sub-Saharan Africa has exceeded 5 percent annually, second globally only to emerging Asia. Even so, the early democratic euphoria is long gone, as wave after wave of corruption crisis and electoral scandal threatens to wash away the earlier gains. (The US invasion of Iraq, and the enormous difficulties of consolidating democratic stability in Afghanistan, have not helped buttress the reputation of democracy; but that's another story.)

Chapter 7 summarizes the patterns of governance and growth between 2000 and 2010 for twenty competitive and intermediate countries that enjoyed decadal growth in excess of 50 percent, plus an additional three with decadal growth in the 30 to 50 percent range. As those data underscore, the combination of political openness, rapid growth, and weak formal governance institutions is quite ubiquitous.

How does this combination of continuing growth and open but seemingly dysfunctional governance hang together? It's not only puzzling when viewed through the lens of a "good governance" template; it's also puzzling from the perspective of a private, market-led view of how growth happens. A thriving private economy is built on a platform of confidence, of entrepreneurial energy evoked by the conviction that the future offers opportunity rather than threat. Viewed through a conventional development lens, it is difficult to understand where confidence can come from in the midst of seeming chaos.

But the combination is less puzzling when considered through the lens of the analytic framework laid out in chapter 3. Viewed through that lens, the seemingly chaotic patterns of governance—a combination of political competition, personalized bargaining among elites, and clientelism—are precisely what one would expect in the early stages of the competitive trajectory. What is intriguing and encouraging about the experience of Bangladesh and other countries is the possibility that personalized competition can, sometimes, provide a platform for economic development.

This chapter uses the experiences of two countries, Bangladesh and Zambia, to explore how this platform might work. Bangladesh is a natural case to consider; it's the poster child of the phenomenon. Zambia stands out among African countries, not only for being the first on the continent to participate in the 1990s wave of democratization and for having stayed the democratic course over the subsequent two decades but also for having long been a bastion of peace and political stability in conflict-ridden central and southern Africa. In addition to being competitive and personalized, both countries have also been enjoying quite rapid economic growth (Bangladesh more so, and for longer, than Zambia).

Of course, the fact that these two countries have grown should not be taken to suggest that all countries characterized by personalized competition do so. As Annex Tables A5.1 and A5.2 underscore with data from sixty-eight competitive and intermediate countries, there are large cross-country variations in growth rates, per capita incomes, and the quality of the rule-of-law. What we are looking to understand here is how and why, sometimes (not always), personalized political competition on the one hand, and growth on the other, can come together.

But the goal is more ambitious than simply to understand. A central aim throughout the book is to offer pointers for development practitioners, and the early stage of the competitive trajectory offers some especially large challenges. With so much seemingly unsatisfying, especially on the governance front, what are the risks to the stability of the development platform? How can they be managed? What room is there for improvement? What changes can help accelerate development, and what changes might risk killing the goose that is laying if not gold then silver eggs? Both countries offer some powerful and cautionary answers to these questions.

Governance and Growth Along the Competitive Trajectory

While it takes a certain arrogance to write a book like this one, it is arrogance of an unusual type: it's not the arrogance of certainty in a fixed view but rather the arrogance of determination to puncture fixed views. It's the arrogance of certainty that a fixed view, whatever it is—and the triumphalism that often accompanies it—is surely wrong.

As democrats, we can easily see how triumphalism is a trap when it comes to dictators. The self-parodying farce of their strutting power is an especially ghoulish form of black humor. We chill at the knowledge of the destruction they can wreak, but we also take a modicum of cold comfort in the knowledge that, in time, they will self-destruct.

But we democrats have our own triumphalist trap. It comes when we confuse our visions of what is good, noble, just, and true with what is actually real. This confusion can lead to a willful unwillingness to see, not only the glory and potential of our vision but also its limits. So when we are finally confronted with these limits, we recoil. Instead of recognizing the reality, the necessity of the long, difficult journey ahead, we overreach and set perfection as our standard. Even if we do not destroy, through our overreach, all that we have worked for, we end up succumbing to disappointment, to cynicism. Bangladesh and Zambia, our two examples of personalized competition, bring this lesson into sharp relief. As this chapter details, both countries have combined some seemingly dysfunctional governance practices with gains on the economic front.

Figure 5.1 delineates a development sequence that is compatible with this ambiguous personalized competitive trajectory. The focus is directly on growth and, consistent with the incentives and constraints of governments in personalized competitive settings, the reform agenda is incremental: do "just enough" to sustain it.

The dotted lines in the figure illustrate how a "just enough" development strategy might work. As growth proceeds, one or another constraint might threaten to short-circuit expansion: perhaps weaknesses in the delivery of infrastructure or public services to the most dynamic parts of the economy; perhaps a rise in corruption as public officials seek their share of the grow- ing economic pie; perhaps rising social alienation with a growing sense on the part of citizens that government doesn't care about their everyday problems; perhaps, as the change process deepens, the need for more so- phisticated laws and institutions to underpin an increasingly sophisticated economy.

With a "just enough" strategy, the goal is not to anticipate and address in advance all possible institutional constraints. Rather, as chapter 3 suggested and the figure highlights, the emphasis is on addressing specific capacity and institutional constraints as and when they become binding. Sustaining growth thus becomes something of a "high-wire" act—continual crisis management, endlessly putting out fires in a seemingly dysfunctional environment, but one that defies the odds by sustaining continuing dynamism—which brings us back to Bangladesh.

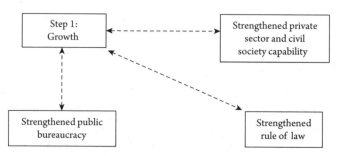

Figure 5.1 **Growth Along the Competitive Trajectory**

Explaining the Bangladesh Paradox[2]

Bangladesh's development track record since independence illustrates vividly both sides of the personalized competitive coin: weak formal institutions on one side and islands of effectiveness that can move the economy forward on the other. How did these come to coexist?

Institutional improvisation. The first quarter century of existence of the Bangladeshi state saw repeated institutional improvisation. This improvisation was necessitated by the unusual way in which the country came into being and the near vacuum of state institutions that resulted.

In 1947, its territory (then East Pakistan) was separated from India as part of the partition that accompanied the subcontinent's independence from Britain. Though East Pakistan comprised a majority of the population of Pakistan as a whole, prior to 1971 the country was governed from West Pakistan. Rule was top-down, reflecting both the feudal character of West Pakistani society and the fact that a disproportionate share of the rulers were outsiders: champions of the Muslim League, who left India at the time of partition and took political power in Pakistan. The precipitate exodus in 1971 of the (West) Pakistani ruling class following war, and the break-up of Pakistan, resulted in an institutional, organizational, and political vacuum.[3]

In the two decades following independence, Bangladesh struggled to shape a political order capable of containing conflicts among the country's many aspirants to power and resources, none of whom enjoyed clear dominance. In the first decade, the country lurched from independence to populist authoritarian rule to military control, with the process punctuated by the assassinations of both the civilian and military founding leaders of the country. Over time, though, a more inclusive equilibrium began to emerge. This inclusive equilibrium blurred the boundaries between insiders and outsiders, in a way that gave outsiders hope that a path was available through which they could, in time, become insiders themselves.

The inclusive model initially was constructed under the umbrella of military rule, but in 1991 the military was overthrown by a popular uprising, leaving a political vacuum. In an ad hoc improvisation, the chief justice was installed to head a caretaker government and to organize a free and fair election. Two parties, which have dominated Bangladeshi politics ever since, contested the election. Each of the parties is led by a charismatic daughter of a charismatic founder of the Bangladeshi nation: The Awami League is led by Sheikh Hasina, daughter of Sheikh Mujib Rahman, the politician who led the country to its independence; and the Bangladesh National Party (BNP) is led by Khaleda Zia, daughter of General Zia, the national hero who stabilized the country and provided a platform for the subsequent decades of growth and prosperity. Both parties are powerful electoral machines, and both are quite unrestrained in their use of the "street" to whip up support. The elections have something of a "winner take all" feel, so the stakes always are high.

The 1991 election was won by the BNP and, thanks to the impartial job done by the caretaker government, the result was accepted by all as fair. But this did not bring sustained political stability. In the run-up to the next election, there was again rising confrontation, partly as a reaction to efforts by the ruling party to use its incumbency to manipulate the elections and widespread civic resistance. To restore order, a constitutional amendment was passed that institutionalized the caretaker government arrangement used in 1991: ninety days before each election, the ruling party would step down in favor of the chief justice who guaranteed the impartiality of the electoral process. The system worked, at least for a while. The 1996 elections were won by the opposition Awami League; in 2001 the Awami League, in turn, ceded power back to the BNP. But it came unglued again in 2006 when the party in power (the BNP) found new ways to stack the deck. In the face of rising polarization and street violence, and with the prospect of a credible election diminishing by the day, the military stepped in and took power. We pick up the story of what happened next at the end of the chapter.

At first glance, the seeming excess of chaos of Bangladesh's improvised and personalized political competition could not be more different than the excess of order associated with Korea's development along the dominant trajectory. But there is a striking parallel: an underpinning of equity and associated civic engagement.

Perhaps the most deeply rooted basis for equity is the fact that Bangladesh, almost entirely Bengali, is unified ethnically, religiously, and linguistically; and Bengali culture is vibrant, deeply rooted, and egalitarian. Equity was further fostered in the aftermath of the 1947 partition of the subcontinent. The period following partition witnessed a gradual exodus to India of East Pakistan's Hindu population (the process was far more sudden, and far more turbulent, on the western border); since most of East Pakistan's large-scale landowners were Hindu, this exodus further reinforced the area's nonhierarchical character. A final contribution to an egalitarian ethos came via the manner of Bangladesh's independence from Pakistan. The resulting institutional vacuum was filled rapidly by Bangladesh's civil society, leading to the continuing expansion over time of an unusually powerful network of nongovernmental organizations (NGOs; precursors to the Grameen Foundation, BRAC, and other Bangladeshi NGOs that have been leaders in the NGO movement worldwide). These organizations became a powerful countervailing force to any propensity for top-down hierarchical control.

Inclusive economic development at the edge of chaos.   In Bangladesh, a political order that was personalized, competitive, and clientelistic provided not only a political roller coaster but also a surprisingly strong platform for broad-based economic development—both the provision of services to the poor and broad-based economic growth. How were these achieved?

Consider first how Bangladesh has met the challenge of service provision. A crucial contribution came from NGOs.[4] Bangladesh has a long history of civic engagement, rooted in local village-level institutions and Bengali traditions of religious charity and philanthropy. This spirit of voluntarism proved crucial in the devastating aftermath of the country's 1971 war of independence and a typhoon that same year.

Those experiences provided the platform for the emergence of an extraordinarily strong set of NGOs. Bangladesh's NGOs are best known for their successful promotion of microfinance: As of the early 2000s, the four largest microfinance NGOs (Grameen Bank, BRAC, ASA, and Proshika) were working with over 12 million active borrowers. But the role of NGOs goes way beyond the best known organizations, and way beyond microfinance. As of 2004, there were approximately 2,000 formalized, developmental NGOs in the country, plus tens of thousands smaller and less formal organizations. Eight percent of all primary schoolchildren (and one-fifth of children from the bottom quintiles of the income distribution) were enrolled in NGO-run schools. And NGOs accounted for approximately one-third of combined NGO-government spending on health (with NGO spending much better targeted toward the poorest quintiles). Evidence suggests that NGOs are more cost-efficient and achieve better results than their government counterparts. And increased collaboration with governmental providers has expanded their role in improving service provision beyond the reach of their frontline programs.

Now consider economic growth: Bangladeshi growth is a story of "islands"—of the emergence, and rapid expansion, of enclaves of dynamism within a broader sea of policy and institutional dysfunction. The garments sector comprises the best-known example.[5] The value of garments exports rose from nothing in 1980 to $2.5 billion in 1996, to $7.9 billion by 2006. As of that year, there were over 3,500 garment-exporting firms in the country, employing over 2 million people and accounting for 70 percent of the value of all Bangladeshi exports. The way in which this happened provides a powerful example of cumulative causation in action.

In 1979, the Korean *chaebol*, Daewoo, in an effort to find a way around import quotas on its garments production, initiated a partnership with a retired Bangladeshi civil servant, Nurul Quader, to establish a manufacturing company in Bangladesh, Desh Garments (the partnership had the explicit support of General Zia, then Bangladesh's president). While the role of Desh itself quickly receded into the background, the consequences of the initial effort were far-reaching. It provided the initial platform of skills: to kick-start its venture, Daewoo brought 130 workers for intensive training in its Korean factories. As important, drawing on the Korean experience, the Bangladeshi authorities put in place a series of targeted policy measures to work around obstacles to exporting: special purpose arrangements to enable garment exporters to finance inputs needed to meet confirmed export orders, plus bonded warehouses and duty drawback arrangements that enabled them to access imported inputs duty free. Within a few years almost all the 130 workers who had trained in Korea—having learned the business and figured out how to link with the global market—left Desh garments to start their own companies. Growth was explosive.

Though garments is the best-known example, there have also been other "islands" of market development that helped spur Bangladesh's growth:[6]

- Exports of shrimp grew at an annual average of over 10 percent per annum in the 1990s, with the sector's share of GDP rising over the period from 3 to 5 percent. Though shrimp exports subsequently stagnated as a result of phyto-sanitary challenges, aquaculture has continued to expand (e.g., via growth in exports of frozen fish).
- In agriculture, the liberalization of imports of diesel engines set in motion a large volume of investment in tubewell irrigation. The result was the trebling of a winter rice crop from 4,100 tons in the 1980s to upward of 12,500 tons by 2005, the major contributor to a doubling of rice production (which accounts for two-thirds of agricultural value added) over the period.
- Streamlining of the processes for temporary outward migration and financial transfers resulted in a surge in the number of Bangladeshis working abroad (up to 3 million, the equivalent of 6.5 percent of the country's workforce) and a trebling of the value of worker remittances from $1.5 billion in 1998 to $4.8 billion by 2006.[7]

One reason this "islands" route to growth succeeded is that it requires only narrow, focused institutional and policy reforms. In personalized-competitive settings such as Bangladesh, the overall political environment is too fragmented and contested for any effort at broad-based policy reforms to be effective. But "islands" do not need broad-based reforms. As long as the overall macroeconomic environment is in reasonable balance (no runaway inflation, no overvalued exchange rates), special purpose initiatives capable of alleviating key sectoral constraints can be sufficient to set the growth process in motion, even while broader dysfunctions in the business environment continue.

A second reason for the success of the strategy is more directly governance-centric. As chapter 8 explores conceptually, in personalized-competitive settings the emergence of a new arena for profit becomes also an invitation for predation, as outsiders to the activity look to shake down a share of these new rents for themselves. For islands to thrive, this threat of predation must be forestalled. How? The remedies of open access won't work. In personalized-competitive settings, there is no impartial and impersonal justice system on which to rely; on the contrary, rent capture and allocation is integral to the political process.

One source of protection from predation is the business process itself: Insofar as production, financing, and marketing call for specialized skills, the effort to predate would almost immediately kill the goose laying the golden eggs. A second source of protection is more political. Bangladesh's garments' entrepreneurs organized collectively into sectoral associations and leveraged their collective power to ensure that rules of the game supportive of the sector remained in place.[8] What made this especially effective was that the number of firms rapidly became large, with the major entrepreneurs varying in their affiliations across the two dominant political parties. Because the firms were overwhelmingly export-oriented, all had an incentive to assure that the country sustained a good reputation as a manufactures platform for the global market. Entrepreneurs connected to the government of the day had no incentive to use these connections to undercut other producers. So who was in power didn't really matter; either way, the channels to protect the interests of the sector were strong.

Yet for all of Bangladesh's striking successes, the country's experience also signals the limits of growth under a personalized-competitive umbrella. Bangladesh's institutional arrangements have been strong enough to support a thriving garments export industry, but the capital investments required for garments production are modest, and positive returns can be realized in very few years. The institutional arrangements have *not* been strong enough to support larger investments involving much longer time horizons.

Electricity shortfalls comprise one of the most binding constraints in the Bangladeshi business environment. For well over a decade, the Bangladeshi authorities have worked to attract private investment in electricity generation. Yet these efforts have consistently failed, undermined by the interaction of political rivalry, the large rent opportunities associated with these investments, and the resulting uncertainty confronted by putative investors.

A further limitation of personalized, competitive, and clientelistic growth is the fragility of the platform itself. Bangladesh's political arrangements are volatile and continually threaten to derail. They may be good enough to lift the country from low- to low-middle income, but they are unlikely to be good enough to take the next steps. Indeed, volatility risks reversal of the gains that have been achieved. Bangladeshi development is thus in something of a race between on the one hand the risk of reversal and, on the other, the emergence of a middle class with sufficient critical mass to help push Bangladeshi politics and institutions to a next level. The crisis of 2006/2007 (more on that at the end of this chapter) serves as a stark reminder of this fragility.

Zambia—Eking Out Gains from the Jaws of Disillusion

Zambia is the second example of personalized competition that we examine in depth.[9] For a country of only 12 million people, it has enjoyed a strikingly high profile in the development community, partly because as of independence in 1964, its strong copper mining sector made it one of the wealthiest and most urbanized countries in Africa, partly because it has consistently been an island of peace and stability in a Southern African sub-region beset by conflict, and partly because it was a pioneer in Africa's embrace of democratization and economic liberalization in the early 1990s.

My first engagement with the country came in the mid-1990s, when I was co-leader of a World Bank team tasked with exploring what might be the opportunities for diversification of the country's overwhelmingly copper-dependent economy. At that time, it already was becoming apparent that a seemingly comprehensive embrace of the "Washington Consensus" formulae was not yielding the hoped-for economic turnaround; we were asked to suggest new ways forward. My second engagement was a decade later: Though growth had finally picked up, the Zambian experience remained a disquieting one: I was asked to explore, from a governance and political economy perspective, the puzzle that I introduced in chapter 2, namely the continuing gap between the ambitious programs that were negotiated and agreed between government and donors, and weak implementation. Wrestling with Zambia's combination of accelerating growth and disappointing governance was, for me, a key step in coming to grips with the logic of personalized competition.

Zambia's track record over the past two decades lays bare a difficult truth that Bangladesh's successes obscure: Though an elite bargain forged under an umbrella of personalized competition may work as a system of political order, it lacks a positive, inspirational vision. As a result, countries growing along a personalized-competitive trajectory often are viewed, not as perhaps having managed to assemble "just enough" of a platform for economic development to proceed, but rather, as with Zambia, as disappointments. The experience thus brings into sharp relief the questions raised at the outset of this chapter: Is the combination of growth plus personalized competition (often underpinned also by vertical links between patrons and clients) to be welcomed as a viable way forward or, given its governance limitations, is it an avoidable failure? And, insofar as it is viable, what might be the possibilities for doing better, even if only incrementally?

The search for a viable institutional platform.   The first three decades of Zambian independence witnessed a sequence of three far-reaching institutional experiments. Each was welcomed at its outset with huge optimism, only for inflated expectations to be dashed against the rocks of seeming failure.

The first failed experiment—"failure," that is, when viewed through the eyes of the former colonial power—came within the first decade of independence. When the British left in 1964, and the flag of an independent Zambia was first unfurled, the erstwhile colonial power likely looked on its handiwork with some satisfaction. There had been a successful first democratic election, which resulted in a legitimate elected parliament and president; there was a strong independent judiciary; property rights were protected. As a country with a per capita income in 1964 of $2,700 (in calendar year 2000 dollars), among the highest on the African continent, and a thriving copper mining sector, development prospects seemed good.

But this optimistic perspective did not reckon with some fundamental disconnects that underlay the institutional façade. Though political power had transferred to the African majority, ownership, control, and access to income opportunities continued to reflect the now-ended colonial order. The best paid and most senior jobs in both the public and private sectors were almost all held by Europeans; 60 to 70 percent of all marketed agricultural goods were produced by white settler farmers on large commercial farms; the copper mines, which dominated the nonagricultural part of the economy, were wholly owned by South African, British, and American interests.[10] Inequality pervaded Zambian society, with startling poverty at the bottom: only one-third of adults were literate; average life expectancy at birth was 40 years; and 230 of every 1,000 children died by the age of five.

Along with these economic inequities, there was also an underlying tendency toward fragmentation in a "new" country that had no natural national identity of its own. Zambia (then Northern Rhodesia) had been cobbled together as part of the European scramble for Africa in the late nineteenth century.[11] Its land area was vast, inhabited by multiple scattered indigenous populations that had little in common other than their colonial overlord. Notwithstanding the collective euphoria over the end of colonial rule, any sense of collective national interest was fragile, and once independence was won, entropy began to set in. Between 1964 and 1966, the number of person hours lost due to labor disruptions led by the powerful copper mineworkers union rose five-fold. Regional, and sometimes ethnically based opposition emerged from among the many factions that had come together under the umbrella of the nationalist struggle for independence.

The result of these disconnects was a progressive unraveling of the institutional arrangements inherited at independence. On the economic front, President Kaunda declared his intent in the 1968 Mulungushi Declaration to "Zambianize" the economy; the government subsequently took a majority equity share in both mining and industry. On the political front, in 1970 a breakaway faction threatened to pose a serious electoral threat to United National Independence Party's (UNIP) hegemony; 100 members of the faction were detained. In 1972, all political parties except UNIP were banned. The following year, a new constitution was passed initiating a "one party participatory democracy," under the aegis of UNIP.

Early-stage dominance thus became the second of Zambia's far-reaching institutional experiments. Kenneth Kaunda, leader of UNIP, sought to govern in an inclusive way, coopting aspirant elites and potential rivals into the governing coalition via the distribution of rents to powerful urban and ethnic constituencies, represented by key elites who were awarded positions in the cabinet, carefully balanced ethnically. This dominant model proved economically unsustainable; in part because political considerations repeatedly trumped the economic dimensions of development policymaking, but also because of a sustained collapse of the price of copper from 1973 onwards (copper mining was the dominant industry and accounted for over 90 percent of export revenues). As economic conditions worsened, political discontent rose.

Then came the third institutional experiment: the embrace of political competition. In response to political discontent President Kaunda decided to mount multiparty elections in 1990. To his surprise, they were won by the opposition party. To his credit he left office peacefully (an early pioneer of Africa's sweeping democratic transition of the 1990s). Zambia's democratic transition in 1991 was greeted with euphoria, as a leading edge of an African (and global) wave of democratization in the wake of the fall of the Berlin wall and the collapse of the Soviet Union. Almost immediately after the new Movement for Multi-Party Democracy (MMD) government, led by the former trade union leader, Frederick Chiluba, took power, it won further kudos from the development mainstream by aggressively embracing the Washington Consensus package of macroeconomic stabilization, exchange rate and market liberalization, and privatization. Hitherto far-reaching price controls were eliminated entirely; radically overvalued exchange rates became market determined; privatization, especially of commercial enterprises, proceeded rapidly and, for the most part, transparently, accelerated by the establishment of the Zambia stock exchange. In support of these far-reaching reforms, aid flows increased rapidly, reaching a peak of 27 percent of total government spending in 2002.[12]

But, again, the euphoria turned to disillusion, this time among protagonists of democratization and economic liberalization.[13] The MMD split less than two years after it came to power, with some of the most committed reformers leaving office. Consistent with the logic of personalized competition (though not the hopes and dreams of democracy's champions), top-down presidentialism and political management via the allocation of rents became the order of the day, both during President Chiluba's period in office, and during the presidencies of his successors, Levy Mwanawasa and Rupiah Banda. Indeed, in 1999 President Chiluba sought to reverse some of the democratic gains by pushing for a constitutional amendment that would allow him to run for a third term in office. But disillusion had not descended that far; he was forced to back down in the face of sustained civic opposition.

Patronage remained the order of the day, however. For ambitious individuals, the path to individual gain and opportunities for patronage was via success in the never-ending game of winning access to the president's (revolving door) inner circle through the continual forming, unforming, and reforming of political coalitions under the MMD umbrella. With the ending of a leadership code during the Kaunda era that had (not always successfully) prohibited senior public officials from owning businesses, the opportunities for extracting rents were many.[14] Over time, insiders found ways of circumventing the rules governing privatizing and acquired former parastatals, including tourist lodges, manufacturing firms, and trade enterprises for little or no compensation. Procurement contracts were directed to businesses owned by public officials (with many documented cases of overinvoicing and of payment for work not done). President Chiluba had direct control of a Presidential Discretionary Fund and the resources of a Presidential Housing Initiative.

Poor economic performance contributed further to the general disillusion. Notwithstanding the ambitious reform agenda, for the first decade following the democratic elections the economy failed to recover; with no growth between 1991 and 1996 and a paltry annual average of only 1.7 percent between 1996 and 2000. But perhaps the low point of governance by personalized competition and patronage was the process of privatization of Zambia's copper mines and its aftermath.

Following pressure from donors, the government began the process of privatizing the Konkola Deep mine in 1996 and initiated a transparent, competitive bidding process. By the end of 1997 bidding had been completed, and negotiations with the winning bidder (a consortium comprising South Africa's Anglovaal Mining, the Canadian company Noranda, Phelps Dodge, and the Commonwealth Development Corporation) were completed, with finalization of the agreement scheduled for March 1998. Initially, independent observers considered the process and its (seeming) outcome a success, but in a surprising move the government turned it down at the last minute. Two years later, the company was sold to the Anglo American Corporation (its original owner and longstanding participant via management contract) for a significantly lower price: $60 million up-front (versus $150 million earlier) and a commitment to $300 million in follow-up investment (versus $1 billion earlier).

The turnaround.   If the story of Zambia's experience under personalized competition were to end in 2002, the conclusion would be clear: that, at least in the Zambia case, the vision of growth via democratization was a chimera; that the combination of competition, personalized elite bargaining and difficult economic circumstances proved too noxious to yield any positive development result. But the story does not end in 2002.

Over the course of the subsequent decade, growth accelerated from less than 2 percent per annum between 1996 and 2000, to upward of 6 percent between 2006 and 2009, barely slowing in the wake of the global financial crisis. Urban poverty fell, from 45 percent of city residents in the early 2000s, to 28 percent by 2010. Zambia also had successfully further consolidated its democracy in 2011, with a peaceful transfer of power following an electoral victory by the opposition Patriotic Front.

It would be a mistake to interpret these gains too glibly as delayed evidence that liberalization and democratization were, after all, the right remedies. Copper remained king, and rising copper prices comprised a key driver of Zambia's growth acceleration; prices were up from $2,000 per ton in 2002, to $4,000 per ton in 2005, reaching $8,000 per ton by 2007. But Zambia's growth was not by copper alone.

One of my most pleasant surprises when I returned to the country in 2007, a decade after my initial foray, was that the economy was in the process of diversifying. The mining sector was diversifying, with products other than copper accounting for 15 percent of metals and minerals exports. But what was especially gratifying was to learn that nonminerals exports had also accelerated, reaching 20 percent of total export value by 2009.

Our mid-1990s study of the economy had highlighted smallholder cash crop agriculture as a promising area, with cotton growing especially attractive. The country's cotton ginneries had recently been privatized. We highlighted what seemed to be a promising new-style partnership, with the ginneries providing support services to small farmers, and the World Bank and other donors participating as financiers of roads, irrigation, and other infrastructure. Though the process was messier than the initial vision, the headline story seemed to be that what we had hoped for: Exports of seed cotton had become Zambia's leading nonminerals export, with the total volume of Zambian production up four-fold, from 50,000 tons per annum in the early 1990s to close to 200,000 tons by 2005.[15]

That, in classic personalized-competitive fashion, is the good news. The more difficult news concerns the way in which this growth was achieved. For cotton, the headline numbers gloss over what has been a roller coaster of booms and busts, including a bust in 2007 when production fell back to close to 100,000 tons. As chapter 10 details, underlying these cycles are institutional weaknesses of a kind that are endemic to personalized competition.

When one looks behind the headline of rapid recovery, at least as troubling a story emerges for copper mining. Investors drawn to personalized-competitive environments walk clear-eyed into settings replete with political uncertainties and do so in search of returns that are commensurate with the risks involved. Managing these risks often takes the form of a willingness to deal, to share the rents with key local political elites. This presumably helps explain what happened between 1997 and 1999, when Zambia ended up with terms for the privatization of Konkola Deep that were only one-third as favorable as what was on the table just two years earlier. But 1997–1999 turns out to be just the beginning of the saga.

In 2002, for reasons that remain obscure (or, taken at face value, reflect what in retrospect must have been one of the world's worst business decisions), the Anglo American Corporation decided to walk away from a mine that, just three years previously it had purchased at a fire-sale price. Suddenly, there was a risk that the mine could close, at enormous risk to the industry more broadly. But this is not what happened. Instead, rapid-fire negotiations produced a new agreement with the Indian-owned (and London Stock Exchange quoted) Vedanta Corporation.

Vedanta purchased the mine for $25 million cash, plus an additional $23 million over the subsequent three years. Even though Vedanta inherited none of the earlier obligations of the mine, it was granted the right to carry forward all past losses against future tax obligations. Then copper prices boomed. Vedanta's sweetheart deal meant that it was able to clear over $1 billion in profit before having to pay a penny in income tax to the Zambian fiscus.[16] In 2006 alone, Vedanta earned $300 million of profits, tax free, from its Zambia venture.

Unsurprisingly, these arrangements provoked an outcry, both within Zambia and internationally. So in April 2008 (too late for the now waning copper boom), the Zambian parliament passed a new mining taxation regime, which introduced a new windfall tax and tightened up on write-off allowances.

I allowed myself a sigh of relief when I learned of this arrangement; perhaps Martin Luther King's adage that "the arc of the moral universe is long, but it bends toward justice" applied after all, even in personalized-competitive settings. But I did not reckon with what came next. In early 2009, parliament repealed the windfall tax that it had promulgated just a year earlier and also restored the right to write-off the full amount of capital invested against future profits. Barring another unexpected turnaround, Zambians thus look set to miss out again when the next commodity cycle comes around; the details about how local actors benefited personally from the various copper deals remain obscure but are surely relevant to the outcomes described above.

Personalized Competition and its Discontents

The Bangladesh and Zambia examples show that personalized competition can indeed be compatible with growth but that the combination can be a discomfiting one. Moreover, as chapter 7 shows, this mixed pattern seems to be quite widespread. Between 2000 and 2010, many countries combined pluralistic politics, rapid growth, weak (and often worsening) formal institutions, and high corruption. Some of the emerging lessons from the Bangladesh and Zambia case studies may thus be of quite general interest.

In both countries, politics is organized around factions; the factions can be more individualized (as in Zambia), or more group-oriented (as in Bangladesh). Political parties compete for the loyalty of these factions, with the terms of this competition having more to do with the benefits that may be available than with specific ideas. As Mushtaq Khan puts it for Bangladesh:

> *Leaders want to incorporate the largest number of the most important organizers into the party at the lowest price in terms of the rents they demand.*[17]

Political competition thus takes the form of a bidding war, as leaders work to assemble a winning coalition in advance of upcoming elections. The importance of bidding wars implies that loyalty to a specific party or individual leaders within that party is fluid.

The systems are stable, not because of the de jure institutions, which are weak, but because the de facto institutional arrangements are aligned with the incentives of the participants. This could be because (as with Bangladesh's garment sector) the institutions are set up in ways that make the costs of reneging higher than the potential benefits, or it could be because (as with Zambia's fluid membership of political parties) reneging now might set a "bad" precedent for the future, when current losers could become winners, and vice versa.[18]

This stability can (and did for both Bangladesh and Zambia) provide a sufficient platform for economic growth to accelerate. But it does not provide a sufficient platform for public service provision via standard, top-down approaches. The reason is that in personalized-competitive settings, control over public resources is at least as much about access to spoils as it is the provision of services to citizens. At the limit, the result could be complete impunity with respect to how political actors use their authority, although in both Bangladesh and Zambia there are restraints on that impunity: In Bangladesh, a vibrant nongovernmental sector offered an alternative channel for service provision; in Zambia, though there was little incentive for effective service provision (except to elite constituencies), formal checks and balances arrangements created enough space for citizens that impunity was not unbounded—but this bounded impunity created an extreme tilt to the status quo, which repeatedly short-circuited efforts at reform.

Is there no alternative other than to settle for this type of discomfiting reality? Surely democracies, even early stage democracies, can do better?

Transformational alternatives?   Pressure to change a status quo of personalized competition could come from the bottom up, spurred by the inequities of a system where the game is stacked in favor of the powerful. It could also be catalyzed from the top down, with incumbents seeking to use their authority to stack the deck in favor of their holding on to power and provoking, in turn, a powerful reaction from the opposition. Where might such disruption lead? Zambia and, especially, Bangladesh, offer some potentially sobering insights.

Consider, first, pressure that comes from the bottom up. In a personalized-competitive setting, creating an organization that will act on behalf of the poor is no easy challenge. It's much easier to imagine elite actors using populist tactics, built around promises that subsequently prove empty, to advance their narrow interests. Zambian citizens currently are in the process of finding out how much room for transformation electoral remedies offer in practice. The opposition Patriotic Front led by veteran politician (and one-time MMD cabinet minister) Michael Sata won the 2011 on the basis of promises that the Front would, finally, act on behalf of the broad majority of the population, rather than a narrow group of elites. Time will tell whether the Front's election represented a new departure for Zambia or another in a long round of empty promises.

Now consider disruption coming from the top down. Here Bangladesh offers a potent cautionary tale. The country repeatedly has had to reckon with incumbents seeking to use their authority to stack the deck in favor of their retaining power, and provoking, in turn, a powerful reaction from the opposition. It was precisely to address this vulnerability that the institutional innovation of a caretaker government was introduced. Though the arrangement worked for a while, it came unglued in 2006 when the party in power (the BNP) found new ways to stack the deck, and the military stepped in. What happened next sheds powerful, and sobering, light on the extent to which countries with open, but weak, institutions can lift themselves out of the seeming institutional mire of personalized, clientelistic competition.

When Bangladesh's military took power in early 2007, it had to decide how to move forward. Should it simply clear the decks so that a fair election could take place within months? Or should it try to "drain the swamp," and clean up the corrupt environment? It chose the latter, setting up a new caretaker government and appointing Fakhruddin Ahmed, a former World Bank official, as its leader.

The next few months witnessed an extraordinary effort to transform the country's political game. The caretaker leadership took on virtually the entire political elite of the country. The leaders of the two political parties, Khaleda Zia and Sheikh Hasina, were arrested and charged with corruption. Up to 100,000 people from across the political spectrum were jailed, many on corruption charges.

Meanwhile, the government geared up a radical program of institutional reform. A blueprint for change had been written a few years earlier by World Bank staff and issued publicly in 2002. The document, titled *Taming Leviathan: Reforming Governance in Bangladesh, an Institutional Review*,[19] is extraordinary both for its forthrightness and the sweep of its proposals. Its dozens of recommendations included:

- Strengthen accountability by reinforcing the role of parliament, tightening public
- financial accountability, and protecting the independence of the media.
- Energize administrative reform by fostering merit based recruitment and promotion, increasing pay for senior staff, delegating more authority to lower levels, and exploiting the potential of e-government; and
- Decentralize to local levels by delegating control over finances and personnel to local governments and strengthening the voice of poor, local communities.

Caretaker leader Ahmed was well aware of the document; he had been thanked in its acknowledgements for his valuable comments. Enjoying the backing of the military, and with seemingly unrestrained authority, he set about the task of building institutions of good governance. He invited new actors to step forward and encouraged Mohammed Yunus, Bangladesh's Nobel Prize winning pioneer of microfinance, to set up a new political party.

Almost none of the efforts worked. After some reflection, Mohammed Yunus prudently declined the offer to establish a new political party. The task of prosecuting those arrested for corruption bogged down. And the task of building new governance institutions from scratch turned out to require more time and more commitment at all levels than was available. Meanwhile, street protests began to build against any entrenchment of military rule. And in the face of rising uncertainty, economic growth itself started to slow, threatening the continuing viability of the Bangladeshi model of poverty reduction.

With options narrowing, and with their reputations and earnings as valued United Nations peacekeepers under threat (the Bangladeshi army provides more troops to UN peacekeeping operations than any other country on Earth), the military concluded that the only viable course of action was to try and unscramble the egg: They backed off efforts at far-reaching institutional reform, dropped corruption charges against the political leaders, and invited the Awami League and BNP to compete in a new election. This they duly did, with the Awami League emerging as the victor and proceeding to govern in a familiar personalized and clientelistic fashion.

If that had been the end of the story, one might have been able to conclude that the events of 2006–2008 had, at least, a silver lining: that they served both as a brake on the worst extremes of impunity, and as a reminder of the crucial importance for Bangladeshi stability of the constitutional commitment to put in place an impartial caretaker government in advance of national elections. But there was more to come.

In 2011, Sheikh Hasina and her Awami League, notwithstanding its long history as champions and beneficiaries of the arrangements, used its large parliamentary majority to revoke the provision in the Bangladeshi constitution that mandated the establishment of caretaker governments.[20] As of the time of writing, what this portended for the run-up to upcoming elections remained to be seen, although another "edge of chaos" moment seemed distressingly likely to unfold.

Incremental ways forward.   At the outset of this chapter, I cautioned that democratic triumphalism can all too easily give birth to its opposite—that when we finally are confronted with the practical limits of our vision of what is good, noble, just and true, we recoil and succumb to cynical disappointment. But cynicism and disappointment are just as false as triumphalism. They change nothing and especially not the reality that the caravan, personalized-competitive or otherwise, keeps moving on.

With easy transformational options seemingly unavailable, the challenge is to find creative ways of moving forward. Given the way things are, what is to be done? Here, to conclude this chapter, are some guideposts for engaging creatively within personalized-competitive settings.

First, do no harm. A close look at countries in the early stages along the competitive trajectory rarely reveals an edifying spectacle. What looms large are personalized power, greed, careless impunity in the face of endemic, grinding poverty, and the ever-present risk of things falling apart. The temptation to reshuffle the institutional deck will naturally be strong. But a close look can also reveal that, from a dismal starting point, and in a very messy way, things are getting better, that a growing number of people are being lifted out of poverty, that a middle class with the desire and interest for society to function differently is beginning to emerge. In such an environment, pressing for far-reaching change, if it has any effect at all, might do as much harm as good.

Second, focus on concrete results, not on processes. Why? Because, as chapters 8 through 10 explore, a focus on results provides a potentially potent entry point for engaging stakeholders with high-powered incentives to see the outcomes achieved, and these stakeholders may, in turn, help lock-in commitments from political leaders. Inclusive coalitions can be built around results, and results are potentially readily monitorable and so can provide a basis for holding leaders to account for follow through. By contrast, Manichean campaigns to root out corruption polarize; instead of bringing people together, they demonize potential allies who may have had little alternative other than to operate within a personalized and clientelistic system's rule of the game and, as influential stakeholders, may turn out to be key parts of any effective change effort. Obviously, the achievement of results is going to require some changes in processes too, but there are limits as to how much can be achieved. Contra much of the governance discourse it is important not to put the process cart ahead of the results horse.

Third, focus more on microlevel interventions than on systemic changes. As chapters 9 and 10 show, islands of effectiveness can be organized around self-standing, narrowly focused institutions. And the cumulative consequences of an islands approach can be powerful: Individual islands can grow exponentially, pulling a wide variety of related activities in their wake; many localized island-based interventions can over time add up into far-reaching social change, as a vibrant middle class takes hold. Dynamism from many, seemingly haphazard islands is what has propelled Bangladesh forward. Getting a few islands to work can be difficult enough; pressing for more broad-ranging change in an unpropitious environment will almost surely be a misdirection of energy.

Fourth, learn more as to which are the crucial pillars of stability, which all parties can agree are untouchable. Bangladesh's strong track record of macroeconomic stability, and the common observation that, in many countries, central banks work better than other institutions, may offer one set of clues. Mushtaq Khan offers a different kind of pointer when he highlights the rules surrounding the caretaker government as the critical choke point for Bangladesh. In practice, we currently know all too little to distinguish clearly between what is urgent, and what is merely desirable; the overheated rhetoric of good governance has short-circuited a process of learning. Less triumphalism and more humility could perhaps yield some more robust, practical lessons.

Finally, even as we recognize that personalized competition may indeed sometimes provide "just enough" of a platform for development to proceed, we need to remind ourselves that not all binding constraints to development can necessarily be eased through incremental measures. There are many countries where the economic environment is too dysfunctional, and institutions are too weak, for incremental reforms to be enough to kick-start growth. Moreover, even in those countries (such as Bangladesh and Zambia) where a "just enough" approach can be sufficient to provide a spark, as growth proceeds society changes profoundly, with new pressures, and new opportunities building up. At some point, as chapter 6 explores in depth, countries that have managed to sustain a "just enough" high-wire act will need either to more systematically strengthen institutions and foster inclusion, or risk losing their hard-won, but still fragile, development gains.

Annex Table A5.1 **Countries in Competitive Trajectory, by Rule of Law, Income, and 2000–2010 Real Growth Rates**

	Per Capita Income, 2000			Total Number of Countries
	Low (under $500)	Medium ($500–$1,500)	Higher ($1,501–$10,000)	
Quality of the rule of law, 2000	High (ROL > 0.45)			
			Estonia 50%	8
			Poland 48%	
			Uruguay 37%	
			Mauritius 36%	
			Czech 34%	
			Chile 28%	
			Costa Rica 24%	
			Hungary 23%	
Medium High (−0.25 < ROL < 0.45)	India 76%		Lithuania 63%	9
	Mongolia 73%		Slovakia 59%	
	Senegal 17%		Panama 53%	
			Thailand 48%	
			Argentina 39%	
			South Africa 26%	

continued

Annex Table A5.1 (continued)

	Per Capita Income, 2000			Total Number of Countries
	Low (under $500)	Medium ($500–$1,500)	Higher ($1,501–$10,000)	
Medium Low (−0.75 < ROL < −0.25)	Madagascar −1%	Philippines 30% Bolivia 18%	Dominican Republic 40% Brazil 26% Mexico 6% Jamaica 2%	7
Low (ROL < −0.75)		Honduras 18%	Romania 56% El Salvador 13% Venezuela 13% Guatemala 9%	5
Number of countries	4	3	22	29

Sources: Table A2.1 and chapter 7.

Annex Table A5.2 **Countries in Intermediate Trajectory, by Rule of Law, Income, and 2000–2010 Real Growth Rates**

	Per Capita Income, 2000			Total Number of Countries
Quality of the rule of law, 2000	Low (under $500)	Medium ($500–$1,500)	Higher ($1,501–$10,000)	
High (ROL > 0.45)			Botswana 34%	1
Medium Higher (−0.25 < ROL < 0.45)	Ghana 37%	Sri Lanka 50%	Bulgaria 62%	10
	Lesotho 16%		Latvia 52%	
			Lebanon 49%	
			Turkey 35%	
			Namibia 34%	
			Croatia 29%	
			Guyana 22%	
Medium Low (−0.75 < ROL < −0.25)	Moldova 68%	Armenia 110%	Peru 48%	11
	Zambia 36%	Indonesia 44%	Macedonia 25%	
	Mali 36%	Ecuador 33%		
	Nepal 28%			
	Malawi 20%			
	Benin 9%			

continued

Annex Table A5.2   (continued)

	Per Capita Income, 2000			Total Number of Countries
	Low (under $500)	Medium ($500–$1,500)	Higher ($1,501–$10,000)	
Low (ROL < −0.75)	Nigeria 80%	Georgia 83%	Russia 63%	17
	Sierra Leone 79%	Ukraine 63%	Colombia 32%	
	Mozambique 77%	Albania 63%		
	Bangladesh 52%	Paraguay 23%		
	Niger 23%	Papua New Guinea 16%		
	Kenya 16%	Cote d'Ivoire 15%		
	Guinea Bissau 1%			
	Nicaragua 0%			
	Central African Republic −11%			
Number of countries	17	10	12	39

Sources: Table A2.1 and chapter 7.

97

CHAPTER 6

Virtuous Circles in Action

Virtuous circles, we saw in chapter 3, unfold in three distinct phases: Momentum begins; it builds; and (if a circle takes hold) it is sustained. Chapters 4 and 5 used the country examples of Korea, Ethiopia, Bangladesh, and Zambia to explore how the momentum of virtuous circles might be initiated along each of the dominant and the competitive trajectories and what might be useful ways of supporting this process. This chapter shifts the angle of vision and takes a longer-run perspective. The focus is less on distinctive patterns of incentive and constraint along each trajectory and more on what might sustain the momentum of virtuous circles that link governance and growth.

A useful point of departure for the discussion is Daron Acemoglu and James Robinson's widely acclaimed 2012 book, *Why Nations Fail*. Taking a very long-run view of history, Acemoglu and Robinson delineate how virtuous circles of political and economic inclusion, and of institutional change, can propel development forward:

> *The virtuous circle of inclusive institutions . . . works through several mechanisms. First, the logic of pluralistic political institutions makes usurpation of power much more difficult. . . . Pluralism enshrines the principle that laws should be applied equally to everybody. . . . The principle of the rule of law . . . powerfully introduces the idea that people should be equal not only before the law but also in the political system. Second, inclusive political institutions support and are supported by inclusive economic institutions [which] remove the most egregious extractive economic relations. . . . Finally, inclusive political institutions allow a free media to flourish, and a free media often provides information about, and mobilizes opposition to threats against inclusive institutions.*[1]

Why Nations Fail derives from this analysis a bracingly clear policy implication:

> *It is the societies with inclusive institutions that have grown over the past 300 years and have become relatively rich today . . . Nations can take steps toward prosperity by transforming their institutions from extractive to inclusive. . . . Authoritarian growth is neither desirable nor viable in the long run, and thus should not receive the endorsement of the international community as a template for nations in LAC, Asia and Africa. . . . Attempting to engineer prosperity without confronting the root cause of the problems—extractive institutions and the politics that keeps them in place—is unlikely to bear fruit.*[2]

By contrast to the above, a central message of this book is that development pathways are varied and circuitous, that no one size fits all and that, for all the evident imperfections, the way forward in many settings is to work with the grain. In the final section of this chapter we explore further the reasons for these different policy implications. But the differences notwithstanding, Acemoglu and Robinson's analysis usefully directs attention toward two central aspects of the evolution of virtuous circles that thus far have received limited attention in this book and this chapter explores in depth.

First, *Why Nations Fail* brings to the forefront the challenge of inclusion. Earlier chapters focused on the elite bargains that underpin political settlements, with little attention to broader popular interests and influence. However, without broad acceptance institutional arrangements are unlikely to be stable over the long run. Some countries may indeed be able to make a leap from rule-by-law dominance (cell #4 in Figure 6.1) to sustainable democracy (cell #6); Korea, as we shall see in the next section of this chapter, offers a

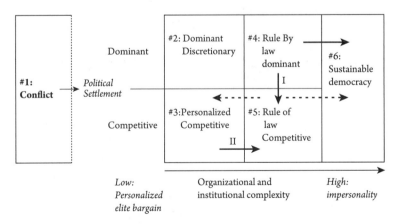

Figure 6.1 **Democratic Transitions**

powerful illustration. But where inclusion has not yet been adequately consolidated, a move to democracy takes a country from cell #4 to cell #5, rather than cell #6. As the dotted arrows along path I in Figure 6.1 imply, and as the example of South Africa in the next section underscores, whether a country moves forward from cell #5 toward sustainable democracy, or backward toward more personalized institutions, is likely to depend importantly on how effectively the challenge of inclusion is addressed.

Second, Acemoglu and Robinson's long view of history surfaces the question of how institutions evolve. They suggest that over the very long run there are just two stable equilibria: one characterized by extractive political and economic institutions, with low incomes, and the other by inclusive political and economic institutions, with high incomes. This is a bold and compelling proposition, with which the analysis laid out in this book is entirely consistent. But countries do not begin their development journey with well-functioning, inclusive institutions already in place. A key analytic task is to understand better how institutions get from here to there; how, for example, the Path II trajectory in Figure 6.1 is traversed. We began our exploration of this issue in chapters 2 and 3. This chapter takes the analysis further, focusing first on the evolution of bureaucracies, and then on the evolution of checks and balances institutions. It turns out to be surprisingly difficult to find twentieth-century examples of countries that have successfully traversed the Path II trajectory, open throughout. So the second section of this chapter draws in its discussion on an intriguing earlier example, the 1880s–1920s Progressive Era in the United States.

The Challenge of Inclusion

In the spring of 1987, living in Korea, I was witness to a democratic transition of a kind that I never expected to see in my home country of South Africa. Astonishingly, and unexpectedly, less than three years later, I found myself watching on television in my Washington, DC, home as Nelson Mandela walked out of Pollsmoor Prison, a free man. Over the next four years, erstwhile enemies negotiated what has universally come to be viewed as a model constitution. In 1993, F.W. De Klerk (the last apartheid state president) and Nelson Mandela were jointly awarded the Nobel Peace Prize for their work in ending apartheid. The world watched transfixed as, in April 1994, the country's population, black and white, held a peaceful, nonracial election; as, a few weeks later, Nelson Mandela (who had been imprisoned for twenty-seven years) was sworn in as the country's president; and as, over the next few years, he governed in a spirit of reconciliation, an inspiring demonstration of the possibility of transcending deep wounds.

Table 6.1 **South African and Korean Governance Trends, 2000–2010**

	South Africa			Korea		
	2000	*Change: 2000–2010*	*2010*	*2000*	*Change: 2000–2010*	*2010*
Rule of law	+0.10	No change	+0.10	+0.83	+0.16	+0.99
Government effectiveness	+0.69	−0.31	+0.38	+0.70	+0.49	+1.19
Voice and accountability	+0.72	−0.14	+0.58	+0.55	+0.17	+0.72
Control of corruption	+0.61	−0.52	+0.09	+0.25	+0.17	+0.42

Source: Worldwide Governance Indicators. For details, see chapter 7.

But two decades on, the trajectories of the Korean and South African transitions look very different. Korea's is an unqualified success. As Table 6.1 shows, between 2000 and 2010 the quality of its governance institutions (already relatively high at the outset of the decade) continued to improve. Along with the scores in the table, the Worldwide Governance Indicators (WGI) also report a country's percentile rank globally. Korea's scores in Table 6.1 locate it in the 84th and 81st percentile of performers globally for government effectiveness and the quality of the rule of law, and in the 70th percentile for the remaining two indicators. But the future of South Africa's democracy is less certain. As of 2010, South Africa's gross domestic product was (measured in purchasing power parity) $10,290 per person—middle-income status but only one-third of Korea's per capita equivalent of 29,460. Over the 2000–2010 decade, the country witnessed a reversal in three of the four governance indicators in Table 6.1, with especially stark declines in government effectiveness (for which South Africa's global relative ranking fell from 76th percentile in 2000 to 66th percentile in 2010) and the quality of control over corruption (for which the ranking fell from 73rd to 61st percentile).[3] Why?

This section explores some links between these divergent trajectories of governance and parallel differences in patterns of economic inclusion. Acemoglu and Robinson define economic inclusion in a relatively narrow way that focuses on the pattern of growth: the presence of competitive markets and the extent to which growth is employment-creating and is accompanied by opportunities for accumulation of capital (including, importantly, human capital) across a broad swathe of society. Their focus directs attention to the trajectory of change in access to assets, and thus to the growth of the middle class. The focus here is broader: Along with inclusive growth, it incorporates also inequality, and broader perceptions of the "legitimacy" of the social order. Equity is defined in terms of the distribution of asset ownership. Both inclusive growth and equity, operating through a variety of channels, are drivers of broader perceptions of legitimacy.

Inclusive growth and the middle class.   Identification of the middle class as a key driver and buttress of democracy dates back at least to Karl Marx. The idea was elaborated by modernization theorists, including Lipset, and Huntington, explored in comparative historical perspective by Barrington Moore, and formally modeled by Acemoglu and Robinson in their 2005 book, *The Economic Origins of Dictatorship and Democracy.*[4] Both the Korean and South African cases illustrate vividly the influence of an emerging middle class on democratization, though with some surprising twists and turns.

The Korean story is the classic one. As described in chapter 4, a rapidly growing middle class was pivotal in fostering that country's democratic transition. In the mid-1950s, only about 30 percent of the relevant age cohort was in high school; by the early 1990s, the country had achieved near-universal high school education: The share of the relevant age cohort enrolled in tertiary education rose from 7 percent in the mid-1970s to over 50 percent by 2002.[5] For most of the period of military rule under Generals Park and Chun, the middle class was politically acquiescent, but in 1987 it came out in support of students. Government responded by agreeing to competitive elections, setting in motion the fifteen-year process of democratic consolidation described above.

The role of South Africa's middle class as a driver of that country's transition to democracy is less straightforward but equally compelling. Paradoxically, the principal actor here is the "white" middle class. A classic history of the 1930s and 1940s, *Volkskapitalisme,*[6] argues that when the apartheid-championing National Party came to power in 1948, it had very specific, targeted economic goals in mind. One goal was to broadly raise the levels of living of the Afrikaans-speaking white population, in part by entrenching pre-existing prohibitions which prevented black workers from building their skills and competing in the workplace. A second goal was to leverage state resources to build an Afrikaner counterweight to the economic power of the British-linked local elites. In both, apartheid succeeded spectacularly. By the 1980s, the Afrikaner population had been transformed from poor and state dependent to an increasingly self-assured middle and upper class. Control over the state no longer seemed necessary to sustain these economic gains.[7] An end of apartheid could be considered as a realistic option.

What of South Africa's black middle class? It was one of multiple players in the struggle to overthrow apartheid, but not the major one. To be sure the African National Congress (ANC), which was founded in 1912 and had led black resistance to white rule was (at least initially) an aspirant middle-class movement. Both repression and resistance intensified with the coming to power of the National Party in 1948, culminating in the banning of the ANC in 1960. Its political leaders all either went into exile, or (as with Nelson Mandela, the world's most famous political prisoner) were expected to languish for the rest of their lives in jail.

In the latter 1970s, rebellious schoolchildren, not their parents or elder siblings, set in motion the events that resulted in apartheid's end. A resurgent black labor movement also was a major force propelling the struggle forward, as part of a broader United Democratic Front. The exiled and jailed leadership of the ANC added to pressure for change by combining largely symbolic military operations within South Africa with a hugely successful campaign to build international opposition to apartheid. While debate continues as to the relative importance of domestic and exile drivers of democratization, none of these players can plausibly be described as "middle class."

Indeed apartheid, by design, retarded enormously the emergence of a black middle class. A rising black middle class would both have given the lie to the country's racist ideology, and would have transformed South Africa's cities racially, which was precisely what apartheid sought to avoid. But by the early 1980s, these policies had both become untenable politically. Accompanying the country's political transformation, white elites increasingly had come to recognize that a thriving black middle class could be an important buttress in favor of an open, rule-bound democratic society, and against more radical/ populist policy reforms. This, as described further below, is how things have played out post-apartheid, at least so far, but only in part.

Inequality.   A voluminous literature suggests that, working through multiple direct and indirect channels, very high levels of inequality can both slow the rate of economic growth, and can inhibit the emergence of inclusive political and economic institutions.[8] Again, the contrasting cases of Korea and South Africa illustrate.

At the outset of its growth spurt, Korea enjoyed the benefits of high initial levels of equality. The country's equitable distribution of assets and income had its roots in far-reaching land reform undertaken in the aftermath of Japanese colonial rule. In 1940, the richest 3 percent of landowners controlled two-thirds of agricultural land; by the mid-1950s, the richest 6 percent controlled only 18 percent of the land. At the outset of its growth miracle, Korea's Gini coefficient measure of inequality was an unusually low 0.37. Even as Korea's economy grew, inequality did not rise very much. As of 1998, the top 10 percent of income earners received only 22.5 percent of national income. As one analysis underscores, Korea's relatively equitable distribution was an important contributor to its high-performing government. It resulted in government being free from capture by powerful vested interests. And it

provided (via land reform) the broad income base that enabled the rapid accumulation of human capital needed to staff a performance-oriented public
bureaucracy.[9]

South Africa, by contrast, continues to be bedeviled by deep-seated
structural imbalances. It was ruled for centuries by and on behalf of its white
minority elites (who accounted for less than 20 percent of the country's population). They dominated control of assets, opportunities, and access to public
services. In 1993, the last year of white minority rule, the top 10 percent of that
country's income earners received 53.9 percent of national income. (The top
20 percent, overwhelmingly white, received 71.6 percent.) The country's Gini
coefficient was measured at 0.66.

The first decade of democracy witnessed some important moves in the
direction of greater economic inclusion, with major gains for citizens at the
bottom of the income distribution. Access to electricity, to piped water, and to
educational and health services expanded rapidly; universal public pensions
and child support grants were introduced. The percentage of the population
living on less than $1.25 per day fell from 24.3 percent in 1993 to 13.7 percent
in 2008.[10] By one measure, the size of the country's black "affluent middle"
class rose from less than 2.2 million in 1993 to 5.4 million (out of a total population of about 50 million) by 2008.[11] All of this engendered a rising tide of
optimism. When South Africa hosted the soccer World Cup in 2010, to the
world as a whole the country's inspiring miracle seemed intact.

Yet for all of the gains, genuine inclusiveness turned out to be hard to achieve.
The underlying structure of the economy remained unchanged. After the first
flush of transformation, the growth of the middle class began to slow. An upper
tier of employed workers (supported by strong labor unions) enjoyed some
income gains, but unemployment remained stubbornly above 25 percent.[12]
Meanwhile, the upper end of the income distribution did disproportionately
well. With political risk reduced, and new opportunities opening up, asset prices
rose rapidly, and the asset owners were, overwhelmingly, the preexisting elite.

By 2008, the Gini coefficient of income inequality had risen to 0.70. The
share of income going to the top 10 percent of the population (a somewhat
higher proportion of whom were now black) had risen to 58 percent. Taxes
and transfers had some progressive impact. Even so, as of 2010 average per
capita expenditure (measured in purchasing power parity dollars) for the
poorest decile of the population was approximately $1,400 per annum;
for the 8th decile approximately $2,400 per annum; and for the 4th decile
$6,000—but $49,000 per person for the top decile.[13]

Even more ominously for the future, though public spending on education
was both high as a share of national income and equitably distributed, as of
2007, South Africa's average performance in international standardized tests
rated below Kenya (which has a per capita national income one eighth that of

South Africa), and only marginally better than that of Malawi (one-twentieth the per capita national income).[14] Two decades after the end of apartheid, inequality, and elite privilege (though no longer organized exclusively along racial lines) appeared to again be rising, rather than declining.

Expectations and legitimacy.   In a textbook definition, legitimacy "involves the capacity of a political system to engender and maintain the belief that existing political institutions are the most appropriate and proper ones for the society".[15] Francis Fukuyama expands on this: Political power, he suggests,

> *is ultimately based on social cohesion. Cohesion may arise out of calcu-*
> *lations of self-interest, but simple self-interest is frequently not enough.*
> *Political power is the product not just of the resources and numbers of*
> *citizens that a society can command but also the degree to which the*
> *legitimacy of leaders and institutions is recognized. . . . Legitimacy means*
> *that the people who make up the society recognize the fundamental justice*
> *of the system as a whole and are willing to abide by its rules. . . . It has to*
> *be understood in terms of the ideas people hold about god, justice, man,*
> *society, wealth, virtue and the like.*[16]

At the heart of South Africa's democratic miracle was hope, the expectations of the large majority of the population that a better future lay ahead. The stability of the country's new democracy was underpinned by a seemingly contradic-tory combination of, on the one hand, a robust constitution anchored in the rule of law with strong checks and balances against the abuse of state power and, on the other, de facto dominance by the ANC, which in the first decades of majority rule enjoyed an unchallengeable electoral majority by virtue of its ability to position itself as the party that liberated the black majority from the yoke of apartheid.

Close to two decades later, the realities increasingly were hitting home of an economy that lacked dynamism, of limited job opportunities in the formal sector, and of some continuing shortfalls in the provision of public services. As evidenced by the contentious politics within the ANC in the run-up to its 2012 reelection of Jacob Zuma as its leader, and by an ongoing drumbeat of allegations of corruption and impunity among the country's leadership, the optimism that accompanied the South African miracle has been fading. What if citizens cease viewing the rules of the game as "legitimate" but begin to see them as another stacked deck? What if hope disappears?

One possible option is that constitutional democracy continues on a sus-tainable basis, with a combination of economic and political competition both making space for personal ambition and providing a continuing spur for better public-sector performance. A second possibility is ethnic populism, a Zimbabwe-style reversal in the direction of discretionary dominance. A third possibility is an acceleration of patronage, with newly empowered elites using their clientelistic networks to keep a lid on nonelite discontent.

The ANC brings together many disparate interests under one organizational umbrella. The combination of top-down, within-party organizational control and a (so far) strong electoral majority gives further momentum to a patronage-oriented outcome. In an unequal, middle-income country such as South Africa, patronage is doubly seductive: It puts an implicit cap on the need to respond to the dissatisfaction of the bottom half of the population, and it offers huge rewards to emergent elites who gain access to spoils. As per Figure 6.1, in the parlance of this book's framework, an acceleration of patronage would constitute a backward movement from "rule of law competitiveness" to "personalized competition" (or perhaps even, insofar as the ANC further consolidates its de facto control, to "discretionary dominance").

In sum, South Africa's continuing shortfall of economic inclusion, and its corrosive political consequences, comprise a vivid example of a struggle for the soul of democracy that, notwithstanding easy talk of democratic triumphalism, is underway across the developing world- and whose outcome remains profoundly uncertain.

The Evolution of Institutions

Now let us build on the discussion of institutions earlier in the book, with the aim of looking beneath Acemoglu and Robinson's divergent very long-term equilibria, and getting some more granular insights into how institutions evolve. For all the criticism in this book of "good governance," there is a sense in which its protagonists are obviously correct. Both well-functioning bureaucracies and well-functioning checks and balances institutions are necessary for the sustainability of democracy. The former provides a platform that enables politicians to deliver on their promises. The latter provide equality for all before the law; rules that assure open political and economic competition; plus credible commitment that the rules of the game will indeed remain stable. But how do these well-functioning institutions evolve out of earlier, more personalized arrangements? This section considers this question in turn for bureaucracies and for checks and balances institution.

The evolution of bureaucracy.   What induces a public bureaucracy to make the Path II journey from being principally a patronage machine for conferring rents on political allies and clients to a rule-based organization committed to public services provision? Efforts to improve the capacity and performance of the public bureaucracy have become a standard part of the toolkit of development practice, one that we explore in depth in chapter 8. This section highlights some of the longer-run dynamics within which specific reform efforts are situated.

Bureaucracies play very different roles in the early stages of the dominant and the competitive trajectories. Along the dominant trajectory, as the examples of Korea and Ethiopia illustrated, political leaders committed to development, with a strong hold over the levers of power, and with a long-time horizon have both the incentive and the ability to support the emergence of a strong bureaucracy. By contrast, as a recent book by Harvard's Merilee Grindle, *Jobs for the Boys*, underscores, in personalized, competitive settings, the incentives to build bureaucratic capacity are weaker.

Grindle explores for nine countries the drivers of successful reforms to move from patronage to more Weberian approaches to governing the civil service; five cases (Prussia, Great Britain, Japan, the United States, and France) focused on the historical experience of contemporary high-income countries. Four cases are from Latin America; in three (Argentina, Chile, and Mexico), the reforms were undertaken within the past two decades; in the fourth (Brazil), the reforms date back to the *Estado Novo* of the 1930s and early 1940s. Grindle finds that comprehensive public-sector reform generally depends on top-down decision making:

> *Initiatives to introduce and consolidate civil service systems can be described as elite projects. They were led by small groups of individuals who designed the reforms, did most of the work in negotiating them, and made most of the decisions about getting reforms approved.*[17]

For the many developing countries that were part of what Samuel Huntington termed the third wave of democratization[18] but where (as per chapter 7) top-down decision making is weak, the conclusion that comprehensive public-sector reform requires consolidated top-down authority would seem to be bad news. Grindle does, though, identify one clear exception to the overall pattern: the late-nineteenth-century United States.

Between the 1870s and the 1920s, fuelled by Progressive Era activism, the United States went from a middle-income country[19] rife with patronage to become, a half-century later, a high-income country with a solidly performing public sector. Here is how patronage worked in the USA for much of the nineteenth century:

- All federal positions were patronage appointments, either made directly by the president, or allocated by him among members of congress to distribute as "spoils";

- Federal employees had no job tenure; they were removed upon the defeat of their political benefactors;
- Employees were required to be politically active on behalf of their sponsors, and to contribute 2 to 10 percent of their salaries to party coffers—else risk losing their job.

The turnover of post office employees (at the time the post office was the largest employer in the federal government) provides an egregious example of the system's functioning. In 1885, when Democrat Grover Cleveland won the presidency, he fired all 40,000 (Republican appointee) postmasters, and appointed his own loyalists. In turn, when Republican Benjamin Harrison won the presidency in 1890, he replaced all (now) 50,000 democratic appointees with Republican supporters.[20]

As another example, consider this depiction of how supporters used patronage to try and help incumbent president, Benjamin Harrison win a Republican primary in Baltimore in March, 1891. The story begins on March 24, 1891, in the office of Theodore Roosevelt (between 1889 and 1895, Roosevelt, who subsequently served as America's president from 1901 to 1908, worked as a commissioner on the federal Civil Service Commission):

A Mr. John C. Rose, counsel to the Maryland Civil Service Reform League was shown into Roosevelt's office. He had serious irregularities to report: The local postmaster and US marshal were using their offices as emergency campaign chests. Senior officials were going around "assessing" subordinates for contributions in open defiance of the Civil Service Code ... to be used to bribe election judges.

  Roosevelt chose to arrive in Baltimore, unannounced, on the morning of election day. ... As he wandered through the noisy wards he saw enough evidence of wanton illegality by federal employees to fill a fleet of police wagons. ... On every sidewalk fists flew and money—taxpayers' money— changed hands, while election judges sat in impassive groups of three, like monkeys who saw, heard, and spoke no evil. ... Carts rumbled in bringing hundreds of rural voters with no apparent connections to the local Republican party. Ward workers entertained these transients in saloons where the beer flowed freely, compliments of Postmaster Johnson and Marshal Airey. ... None of the federal employees saw anything wrong in influencing the course of a presidential election. "As far as I could find out," Roosevelt recalled, "there seemed to be no question of principle at stake at all, but one of offices merely ... [in the event, the anti-administration forces won the primary]."

Party reaction to Roosevelt's visit was immediate and violent. The president, apparently was "very mad" with Roosevelt. Frank Hatton (editor of the Washington Post) delightedly fanned the flames with a front-page story headlined "TEDDY AT THE POLL—Helping to Hurt Mr Harrison". The article alleged that Roosevelt's tour through the wards had caused many government employees to "desert the field", resulting in a humiliating defeat for the administration.[21]

Change to America's patronage system came from both top-down legislative reforms and from individual acts of public entrepreneurship. The top-down reforms came in the form of the 1882 Pendleton Act, which introduced a Civil Service Commission to administer competitive examinations for entry into "classified" positions, and provided a variety of other protections against arbitrary discharge. The catalyst for its passage was the assassination of President James Garfield by a disgruntled patronage seeker. But a crucial underlying driver of civil service reform was economic dynamism—the emergence of a national market, the growth of a middle class and the business sector, and corresponding pressures for better public services. Indeed, the first targets for applying the Pendleton Act were government offices that had a direct impact on commerce: urban post offices and customs houses and executive branch offices in Washington, DC. But as of 1884, the Act covered only 11 percent of all federal jobs; it took another quarter century for its coverage to reach two-thirds of federal employees.[22]

Alongside the top-down reforms, a series of entrepreneurial initiatives by career civil servants also were important contributors to the emergence of high-performing agencies within the federal civil service. These acts of public entrepreneurship combined internal initiatives to strengthen individual agencies with external initiatives to build supportive constituencies. In a landmark book, *The Forging of Bureaucratic Autonomy*, Daniel Carpenter describes, agency by agency, how this works. He summarizes his conclusions as follows:

Bureaucratic autonomy occurs when bureaucrats take actions consistent with their own wishes, actions to which politicians and organized interests defer. . . . In these episodes, it was less the case that social movements built the bureaucratic state than that the bureaucracy built social movements.

Carpenter documents agency by agency, a series of prodigious acts of leadership. Consider the example of Harvey Wiley, who was recruited in 1883 into the Department of Agriculture as chief chemist of the United States; he subsequently hired well-qualified young graduates into his agency, using the protections of the Pendleton Act. He also built alliances with a wide variety of civil society organizations (including college officials, women's organizations, and the American Medical Association). By the early 1890s, he was "taking neither orders nor agendas from anyone but himself." In 1906, he leveraged his organizational reputation and external constituencies to drive, against political opposition, passage of new "truth in advertising" legislation to combat food adulteration. These efforts have withstood the passage of time; the contemporary US Food and Drug Administration is built on the platform established by Wiley a century ago.

Viewed through the lens of hierarchical approaches to the functioning of bureaucracies, there is something unusual, perhaps even wildly inappropriate, about public entrepreneurs like Harvey Wiley taking onto themselves advocacy for specific goals- a function that, some would argue, lies more properly in the domain of the interactions between citizens and politicians. But in settings where politics is clientelistic, and bureaucratic decision making is personalized and geared toward patronage, is bottom-up public entrepreneurship necessarily a bad thing? Parts III and IV of the book return to this dilemma.

The evolution of checks and balances institutions.   There has been no shortage of "how-to" advice for strengthening checks and balances from advocates of democracy. Much has been written about political tactics for fostering democratization, and about how to facilitate free and fair democratic elections; both of these themes fall beyond the scope of this book. An equally abundant literature extols the virtues of the rule of law in underpinning democracy and good governance. However, as contributions by Tom Carothers, Stephan Haggard, and others underscore, empirically anchored knowledge as to how to foster the rule of law remains frustratingly thin.[23]

What makes the emergence of checks and balances so difficult is that, as was explored in Part I, they require actors with power to agree on rules that restrain that power. But in the earlier, personalized stages of democracy, elites have little incentive to surrender discretionary authority or to bring in outsiders who could challenge their dominance. How do checks and balances institutions that restrain arbitrary state power emerge? With what implications for the prioritization of initiatives aimed at strengthening their operation? This subsection explores these questions.

In *Violence and Social Orders*, North, Wallis, and Weingast offer a hopeful perspective on the prospects for improvements over time in the quality of checks and balances institutions. They draw on the theoretical framework of new institutional economics and the economic history of Europe and North America to sketch out an ambitious framework for understanding how rule of law institutions might[24] emerge endogenously out of personalized "limited access orders". Their argument builds on North's earlier exploration of "lock-in" between organizations and the rules of the game (that is, the institutions) that govern them, and can be traced back further to Martin Lipset, Samuel Huntington and other modernization theorists cited earlier.[25] North, Wallis, and Weingast argue, as we saw in earlier chapters, that stable "limited access orders" can offer a platform for economic growth and the emergence of increasingly complex organizations. But they go beyond this: They suggest a sequence through which impersonal institutions can emerge out of limited access orders and can then provide a platform for a transition to sustainable democracy.

In their suggested sequence, it is interactions between institutions and organizations that drive the process forward: Stronger organizations push for ongoing improvements in the rules of the game that underpin their capabilities; the resulting strengthened institutions lead to further gains in both growth and organizational capabilities, providing a further spur for institutional improvements. This cumulative process potentially culminates in the achievement of a series of "doorstep conditions" that underpin impersonality. One of these is rule of law among elites; the others are consolidated political control over the military, and the emergence of "perpetually lived" organizations. And these doorstep conditions, North, Wallis, and Weingast argue, can provide a platform for the inclusion of progressively broader groups under the umbrella of impersonality until, at the limit, universality—an "open access order" or, in the parlance of Figure 6.1, sustainable democracy—is achieved.

Note an implicit corollary of the above for policy: It suggests that, if indeed a country's economy is developing rapidly, patient restraint vis-à-vis a push for democratization will provide time for the rule of law to strengthen so that, as and when democratization comes, the platform of a vibrant middle class will be a more solid one.[26] But, as another look at the Korean and South African country examples underscores, it is important not to overstate this claim. Both examples contradict any simple-minded nostrum that there is a seamless sequence from strengthened rule of law to sustainable democracy.

In Korea,[27] substantial presidential discretion remained the order of the day as late as 1985, just two years before the country's embrace of democracy. This discretion was exemplified by the dismemberment in that year of the Korean chaebol, the Kukje Group, for its unwillingness to agree to payments solicited by senior government officials. The decisive breakthrough for the rule of law came, not prior to the democratic transition, but subsequently – more than a decade after the 1987 election—when, in the aftermath of the 1997 Asian financial crisis, the government (under reformist president Kim Dae Jung) embraced far-reaching financial sector reforms, and new rules for transparent corporate governance. The 1999 prosecution and subsequent imprisonment of a former chief executive of the Daewoo chaebol (which had been especially close to the military government) signaled that Korea's business-government relations had shifted decisively from the pattern described back in chapter 4.

By contrast, in South Africa the rule of law was consolidated very early, at least for (white) elites, and was part of the country's political discourse for very many decades prior to any impetus to democratization. How early? As early, perhaps, as the eighteenth and nineteenth century, which was when the country's Roman-Dutch system of jurisprudence took shape. Perhaps 1910 might be a more prudent date: 1899–1902 had witnessed the brutal Anglo-Boer war, a war in which the British pioneered the incarceration in concentration camps of civilian families, plus scorched earth military tactics designed to starve out their Boer opponents. By 1902, the boer republics had been defeated. Eight years later, the Union of South Africa took legal form. From that time on, if you were part of the European-descended minority, you were protected by law. Yet it took another eighty years before South Africa broke with apartheid, and embraced a multiracial democracy.

For all of the above complexities in the sequences of leads and lags through which checks and balances institutions evolve, there is a common underlying theme: the potential for forward movement to be sustained via virtuous circles that link economic transformation and institutional change. But what if momentum slows? Difficult times are inevitable, so, for all the power of cumulative causation, it cannot be the whole of the story of how a country traverses the institutional path toward sustainable democracy. While some countries can go through difficult times without getting trapped in a downward spiral, in others what it has taken many decades to build, can be destroyed much more rapidly. Why?

Part of the explanation may be that some key determinants of the quality of checks and balances institutions lie outside the process of economic development. In a magisterial analysis, Francis Fukuyama[28] explores how religious legal systems provided an antecedent for the rule of law. These religious systems established a precedent that the rule of law could be sovereign over leaders, including secular leaders. They provided a codification of the law into an authoritative text, with the content determined by specialists in the law, not political authorities. And they provided institutional autonomy, a set of structures separate from the political hierarchy, with their own resources, and powers of appointment. In England and continental Western Europe, over time periods measured in centuries, the rule of law gradually lost its explicit anchoring in religious roots, driven forward by secular political conflict, political ideas of the enlightenment, and the emergence of economically and socially vibrant cities. But, suggests Fukuyama, the prior development in a religious context provided both the precedent and the institutional platform upon which secular rule of law was built.

Acemoglu, Johnson, and Robinson suggest a different (but also exogenous) causal link. They trace variations across developing countries in the quality of property rights to divergent patterns of colonial rule.[29] In some colonies, the focus of the imperial power was on extraction; in these, the rule of law remained underdeveloped and growth was stunted. But in others, the emphasis was more on settlement, the development of a productive base, and consequently the establishment of a set of institutions that supported property rights.

In sum, a long-run historical perspective suggests that virtuous circles between governance and growth comprise only part of the story. For reasons that are deeply rooted in their histories, some countries will be better endowed with checks and balances than others, and be more likely to sustain them in the face of threats to their reversal.

Viewed from the perspective of governance reform the above view is pessimistic: It suggests that many important forces that shape the quality of checks and balances may lie outside of the purview of reformers. But even accepting that endogenous processes are not the whole of the story, perhaps something more hopeful can be said. Recognizing that the challenge is an uphill one, perhaps reformers might focus on some minimum set of checks and balances that, in personalized democracies in particular, is both capable of protecting against institutional reversals even in difficult times, and is compatible with the incentives of elites, and so can provide a good enough platform for sustaining forward momentum. What might be the components of such a minimum set? The historical experience of the United States is (again) instructive.

The Progressive Era of the 1880s to the 1920s is an example of a virtuous circle in action. Rapid social and economic transformation in the aftermath of the country's 1861–1865 civil war had created a new urban middle class, anxious about its place in society, and aggressive in its efforts to forge a social reality that was consistent with their values.[30] The result was a mushrooming of social movements, ranging from advocacy for women's suffrage, to a quest for clean government, to trust-busting and other efforts to control big business, to campaigns to prohibit alcohol, plus sundry other initiatives aimed at the "moral improvement" of the population. Public entrepreneurs were shaped by this climate of reformist zeal. And they, in turn, leveraged it to build alliances in pursuit of the objectives they took on for themselves.

But why did it all play out that way? Why did social conflict result, not in an unraveling, but in a cumulative strengthening, of American institutions?[31] To address these questions, we need to go back another century, to a distinctively American "civil religion" variant of the exogenous roots of the role of law. An explicit goal of the participants at the 1787 Philadelphia Convention was to write a constitution that could simultaneously underpin an effective federal government, and constrain executive authority via a robust separation of powers, vertically between the federal and state governments, and horizontally between the legislature, executive, and judiciary.[32] Indeed, a vision of restraining absolutism was one of the motivations for the American war of independence against the British.

What was created by America's founding fathers hardly constituted institutions of good governance. For most of the nineteenth century, American checks and balances were entirely consistent with a government that was rife with patronage and corruption. But these institutions also provided a framework within which a century later, as the economy and society changed and pressures for better government grew, a progressive movement of reform could emerge.

The American experience suggests what might be a minimum set of four checks and balances institutions capable of underpinning stability even in otherwise contentious personalized-competitive settings. Here are the first three:

- Credible electoral rules and their monitoring and enforcement. Credibility that electoral competition offers the potential for powerful groupings outside the circle of power to become insiders is fundamental to the stability of the personalized-competitive system.
- Openness to critical discourse as to how those currently in power are exercising it.
- Constraints on the use of coercive executive power to settle scores with opponents in other parts of the domestic elite.

Note the synergy between the elements of the list. Only if outsiders can feel confident that their life, liberty, and property are not vulnerable to the arbitrary exercise of state power would they be willing to channel any disaffection they feel into "voice" and refrain from the threat of destabilizing violence. Conversely, only if elections are credibly competitive do insiders, knowing that their turn will come to be on the outside, have an incentive to exercise restraint.

The fourth component of the minimum set is even more fundamental than the first three. No institution can be sustained in a societal vacuum. In Zambia, as described in chapter 4, it was a popular outcry that prevented the incumbent president Frederick Chiluba from amending the constitution, a decade after the country's transition to democracy, so that he could run for a third term. In Bangladesh, it took popular pressure to have a free and fair election in 1996, and to get the military to return to its barracks in 2007, and (though as of this writing it is too soon to say) it may take popular pressure for subsequent rounds of elections to be conducted fairly. When bad times come, a minimum set of painstakingly negotiated checks and balances may, perhaps, provide something of an institutional buttress, but ultimately, as rule of law reformers increasingly are coming to recognize, a country's democracy is only as strong as the commitment of its people to a democratic order.[33]

Sustaining Forward Momentum

Chapter 3 introduced the idea that interactions between governance and growth can set in motion a cascading chain of economic, social, institutional and political changes. This chapter has explored a variety of further mechanisms through which inclusion, institutional change and economic growth can support a virtuous circle of development. One way to summarize the overall discussion is in terms of three mutually reinforcing virtuous subcircles.

The first subcircle, based on the discussion in chapter 3, links institutional improvements and inclusive growth. In this subcircle improvements in the provision of public services, plus gains in investor confidence that property rights will be protected, strengthen the business environment, and support continuing economic growth. Sustained growth, in turn, leads to a stronger private sector and a growing middle class, which generates new pressures and incentives to strengthen institutions.

The second and third subcircles build on this chapter's analysis of inclusion and the evolution of institutions. The second subcircle links growth and expectations. The promise implicit in inclusive growth is one of hope, of continually expanding access to economic opportunity, of a growing middle class, and a better future for all. Growth can thus provide a powerful platform of legitimacy. And the resulting sense of confidence that things are on the move can in turn, further spur growth.

The third subcircle links expectations and institutions. In this sub-circle, public institutions provide a "container" for politics, a set of stability-enhancing rules for channeling collective action and citizen engagement. Citizens pressure to enhance the quality of the rules. Insofar as their pressure is successful, they gain increasing confidence that the rules of the game have the potential to work for them, "unstacking" a deck that had hitherto been skewed to serve a privileged few. By nurturing compliance rather than confrontation, growing legitimacy lowers the transactions costs of cooperation, further strengthening institutions.

The top panel in Figure 6.2 uses the example of the United States' sixty-year-long "Progressive Era" to illustrate how the three subcircles can reinforce one another. Transformed expectations in the aftermath of civil war helped kick-start an era of rapid economic growth via the growth-expectations virtuous circle. Rapid growth generated new demands for better government from both the private sector and civil society, resulting, via both the expectations-institutions and growth-institutions virtuous circles, in a cumulative transformation from a patronage-oriented to a relatively high-performing public sector and, by the mid-1920s, a high-income, high-performing democracy. The Progressive Era comprises a powerful illustration of inclusive economic and political institutions in action.

In the case of South Africa (illustrated in the second panel of Figure 6.2), initial momentum came from gains in legitimacy and social stability in the wake of the new, post-1994 political institutions. But this has not been supported by the other subcircles. Though public services for the majority improved rapidly in the first decade post-apartheid, growth accelerated only moderately, and the pattern of growth remained highly dualistic. There was no mutually reinforcing growth-expectations virtuous circle. Instead, expectations gradually soured, with pressures from disaffected groups in society threatening to corrode the institutional gains. South Africa's elites would, indeed, do well to take heed of the dictum to "choose (economic, not only political) inclusion."

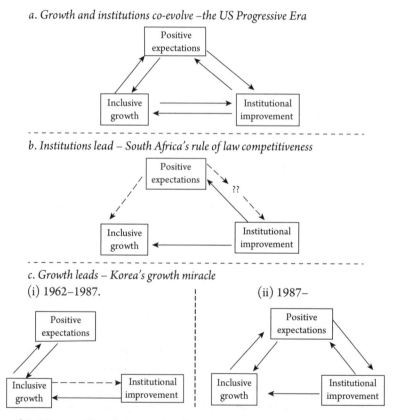

Figure 6.2 **Virtuous Development Circles**

Both the Progressive Era United States and South Africa illustrate the practical relevance in at least some settings of Acemoglu and Robinson's policy prescription to "choose inclusion". But, as I noted at the outset of this chapter, in contrast to their prescription a central message of this book is that development pathways are varied and circuitous, that no one size fits all, and that, where there is evidence of positive momentum, the way forward is to work with the grain.

To be sure, not all instances of rapid growth qualify as "positive momentum". In low-income countries, major new investments in extractive industries can lead to an extraordinary acceleration of economic growth over the medium-term; they offer momentum and an injection of resources. But all too often, the benefits accrue very narrowly, and so end up entrenching an Acemoglu and Robinson-style extractive equilibrium. Unless the difficulties are successfully addressed, the consequence will be the classic resource curse,[34] where initially weak institutions and unequal, extractive growth fuel one another to drive the country (following an initial surge of optimism) into a downward spiral of deepening political and institutional dysfunction. Chapter 10 explores some efforts to forestall this dismal logic.

But even where economic growth accelerates along inclusive lines, there can be leads and lags in the transformation of institutions. Of particular interest is the transformation of political institutions: Sometimes inclusive political institutions might strengthen rapidly, at other times the pace might be slower (and at times there might seemingly be no movement at all). Efforts to force the pace of political reforms can, however, have unintended consequences. In chapter 5, we saw one example of these unintended consequences in the way in which the Bangladeshi military's abortive efforts to engineer "good governance" played out. The bottom panel of Figure 6.2 further addresses the question of whether to force the pace of political reform, using the example of the complex pattern of leads and lags through which Korea traversed the path to sustainable democracy.

In Korea, it was the institutions-growth nexus that set the virtuous circles in motion, as an authoritarian government signaled its commitment to use state intervention to foster rapid growth, with a strong role for the (tightly controlled) private sector. Sustained development momentum followed, via the growth-expectations virtuous subcircle, as General Park successfully delivered on his promise to deliver economic growth, thereby winning acquiescence for his top-down development strategy. Civil society demands for greater political openness were repeatedly suppressed, so institutional change was much slower in coming.

A collision between a dominant political leadership and a growing and restive middle class carries with it the risk that the cumulative process as a whole could derail. But that is not what happened in Korea. Instead, in 1987 (as per the bottom-right panel), the third virtuous subcircle finally came into play, setting in motion a transformation of institutions. Over the subsequent decade, this institutional transformation locked in political legitimacy, the positive expectations needed for continued growth—and, in time, sustainable democracy. In sum, what the Korean and American examples share, and the South African one may not, is the potential for interactions among the subcircles to sustain momentum over time.

This brings us to a central policy implication. As we have seen throughout this book, many countries enjoying rapid, inclusive growth also are characterized by institutions that seem both dysfunctional and resistant to change. In these countries, the temptation can be strong to try and override opposition and press forward with far-reaching institutional reforms. But discontinuous change is, almost by definition, unpredictable, and carries with it a risk of losing momentum. As an alternative, this book explores the potential of incremental, momentum-sustaining, with the grain institutional reforms.

The case for giving priority to momentum-supporting, incremental reforms does not, of course, apply equally across all countries. In countries that have long been mired in stasis and dysfunction, discontinuous policy and institutional reforms, perhaps even discontinuous political change, may be necessary, indeed desirable. Further, countries with a religious, cultural, or political inheritance that makes their institutions resilient may be able to take in stride a temporary loss of momentum. But many countries do not have this kind of inheritance. For them, resilience to shocks builds through cumulative interactions between governance and growth. In such settings, if momentum stops too soon, virtuous circles can all too easily go into reverse, wiping out hard-won gains.

Note, finally, that the practical implications of a call to give top priority to sustaining momentum are more ambiguous than they might first appear. The call might be interpreted as saying "do no harm": Avoid reform overreach that risks disrupting the continuing momentum of an ongoing virtuous circle. But it could also be interpreted in a very different way, as pointing to the need to give priority to addressing those areas where continuing lags most threaten reversals of the momentum of virtuous circles.

The process of development is a knife edge. Too much pressure for change risks derailing the positive momentum of virtuous circles; but with insufficient attention to what needs to be changed, the process risks grinding to a halt. Much can be learned about incremental with-the-grain options to improve public service provision and sustain economic dynamism even in the absence of a full set of good governance institutions; these are the focus of Part III of this book. But in the final analysis, in navigating the knife edge and crafting a way forward, no simple reform dictum can substitute for in-depth country-specific knowledge and informed judgment.

CHAPTER 7

Patterns of Governance and Growth

Argument by anecdote has an obvious limitation: Anecdotes can, by accident or design, be wholly unrepresentative outliers. To address the question of representativeness, this chapter presents a set of descriptive statistics that provide a bird's-eye view of patterns of governance and growth for forty-one countries, the thirty-eight countries identified in Annex Table A3.1 as having achieved decadal growth between 2000 and 2010 in excess of 50 percent, plus an additional three countries, identified as explained below. The chapter comprises a brief detour from the overall approach of the book; readers who so prefer, can proceed directly to Part III without loss of continuity.

Propositions and Measurement

Before turning to the forty-one countries, it may be helpful to say more about the relevant empirical propositions, and the data that will be used to assess them.

Some empirical propositions. A large and impressive literature has explored econometrically the relationships between governance and growth, from a variety of different perspectives. For the most part, that literature and the perspective of this book are complementary—but they address different questions and have different time horizons.

The book's analytic framework centers around the differences between the dominant and competitive trajectories (and, within each, between personal and impersonal institutions). No prediction is implied as to what fraction of countries with a particular trajectory will grow, let alone whether one trajectory is more likely to be supportive of growth than another; within each trajectory, some countries will grow and others will not. Rather, the central idea is that rapid growth is possible within each of the trajectories, but that the way governance and growth can interact to kick-start development varies along the dominant and competitive trajectories:

- Along the dominant trajectory, the platform for growth is hypothesized to come from gains in bureaucratic capability, plus consistent, longer-term oriented leadership.
- Along the competitive trajectory, the platform is hypothesized to come from elite bargains that provide sufficient basis for the emergence of islands of effectiveness, organized around strategic interactions among government, private sector and civil society actors.[1]

Along both trajectories, as per chapter 6, an initial surge in development momentum is proposed to have the potential to set in motion a virtuous circle of cumulative gains in positive expectations, inclusive growth, and improvements in institutional quality.

Table 7.1 suggests some specific propositions as to how early-stage performance might vary along each trajectory vis-à-vis three sets of variables and contrasts them with the "good governance," "Washington Consensus" assertion that effective institutions are necessary for sustained economic development. One of the three variables is control over corruption, which is considered further in the final section of this chapter. The other two are government effectiveness and the quality of the rule of law (the latter as a leading example of checks and balances institutions more broadly).

How do the propositions in Table 7.1 align with the findings of the econometric literature? There is relatively little to say about the relation between economic growth and the effectiveness of the public bureaucracy; it has been under-researched statistically, in part because of difficulties in coming up with a robust measure of bureaucratic quality. One well-known study reported a

Table 7.1 **Governance Patterns Among Rapidly Growing Countries—Some Hypotheses**

	Analytic Category		
	Washington Consensus	*Early-Stage Dominant*	*Early-Stage Competitive*
Government effectiveness	Strong	Strong and/or rising	Low
Rule of law quality	Strong	Weak but with potential for incremental improvement as growth proceeds	
Extent of corruption	Low	Low/unaddressed	High

statistically strong relationship between the extent of bureaucratic "Weberianism" (on which more in chapter 8) and rates of economic growth, but the analysis did not fully distinguish among competing hypotheses as to what might be the underlying causal influences.[2] Note that the hypothesis in Table 7.1 does not predict a straightforward linear relationship; rather, it suggests that one key underlying determinant of bureaucratic effectiveness for many early-stage countries is whether the political settlement is dominant or competitive—and that, controlling for other influences, one important subgroup of rapidly growing dominant countries is likely to have stronger than "expected" bureaucratic capability. The next section of this chapter explores in a preliminary way to what extent these patterns are evident for eighteen countries that grew rapidly along the dominant trajectory between 2000 and 2010.[3]

Now let us look at the alignment between the econometric literature and Table 7.1's propositions as to the relationship between growth and the rule of law. Again, a key issue concerns the direction of causality, and here the analysis of causality has been robust. Some of the econometric studies explore causality only in one direction; they test the hypothesis that better (exogenous) rule of law institutions will, on average, lead to higher per capita incomes (and, often, more rapid growth en route). Others explore the extent to which causality between the rule of law and economic growth operates in both directions. Two-way causality is fundamental to the approach adopted in this book: It underpins the idea that development momentum might be sustained by a virtuous circle of interaction between the quality of institutions, inclusive growth and associated gains in the influence of the middle class, the private sector, and civil society. The econometric evidence supports both the proposition that better institutions lead to higher incomes, and that causality can be two-way.

To begin with causality from institutions to income, the econometric results demonstrate a positive and significant exogenous impact of the rule of law on economic performance, using a variety of measures of the rule of law, a variety of different data sets, and diverse econometric methodologies.[4] Similar results have been obtained for tests of exogenous impact vis-à-vis other institutional measures.[5] Considered as a whole, the evidence is convincing that, on average, countries initially endowed with better institutions will have better economic performance than those where the initial institutional conditions are weaker: Their per capita incomes will be higher, as will (by definition) be their long-term average growth rates that brought them from low to higher incomes.

The causal relationship from income to institutions also has been probed by a variety of studies. Some of these have focused narrowly on the relationship between income and democracy, including the classic modernization hypothesis that economic modernization can provide a platform for subsequent democratization; they do not find systematic support for the hypothesis that causally relates modernization and democracy.[6] Other studies have explored two-way causality between per capita income[7] and a variety of different types of institutions. These latter studies indeed find that two-way causality between growth and at least some subset of institutions is an important part of the development story.[8]

One final empirical proposition needs to be considered. Implicit in Table 7.1 is the idea that, as long as a baseline of peace and stability has been achieved, there is no minimum threshold of institutional quality below which growth cannot move forward. Superficially, the evidence that the quality of institutions has a positive exogenous impact on income might seem to support the notion of some minimum threshold. But this would be a misreading; the results that demonstrate causality in one direction, though significant, leave much variation unexplained. Moreover, a positive exogenous relationship does not rule out the possibility of two-way causality, and thus a virtuous circle of development gains in countries where the initial institutional conditions are weak—though the probability of gains might be lower, and their magnitude smaller than in institutionally better endowed countries. Indeed, as we shall see in later sections of this chapter, consistent with the notion that there is no minimum necessary threshold of institutional quality, in the first decade of the twenty-first century the combination of rapid growth and weak rule of law turned out to be exceedingly common.

Measurement. The discussion in the sections that follow is organized around four sets of variables. The first variable, constructed from the widely used Polity IV data set, locates countries along the dominant-intermediate-competitive spectrum.[9] The remaining three variables are from the Worldwide Governance Indicators (WGIs)[10]. They are:

- *Government effectiveness*—constructed by the WGI authors "to capture perceptions of the quality of public services, the quality of the civil service and the degree of its independence from political pressures, the quality of policy formulation and implementation, and the credibility of the government's commitment to such policies"
- *Rule of law*—constructed by the WGI authors "to capture perceptions of the extent to which agents have confidence in and abide by the rules of society, and in particular the quality of contract enforcement, property rights, the police, and the courts, as well as the likelihood of crime and violence." And,
- *Control of corruption*—constructed by the WGI authors "to capture perceptions of the extent to which public power is exercised for private gain, including both petty and grand forms of corruption, as well as "capture" of the state by elites and private interests."

Measurement of governance is notoriously imprecise; all indicators have strengths and weaknesses.[11] A key strength of the WGI indicators is their broad multicountry coverage, which is a principal reason why they are used here. A well-known limitation, one that is a direct consequence of the fact that they are calculated by aggregating across multiple distinct sets of governance data, is that the concepts that they measure are imprecisely defined (note, though, that the aggregation methodology also yields confidence intervals for the WGI estimates).[12]

The WGI variables are calibrated to range between –2.5 and +2.5, with a mean score of zero for each variable; the calibration is based on the WGI's full universe of over 200 countries. Using this universe as a starting point, we exclude countries with year 2000 per capita incomes above $10,000, and with populations of less than one million. This leaves 119 countries, including the forty-one countries that are the focus of this annex. Since high income countries (not included in the 119) generally score better on governance measures, the mean score for each variable for the group of 119 will be considerably less than zero.

Patterns of Governance Among Rapidly Growing Dominant Countries

This section explores the empirical relevance of the Table 7.1 propositions for dominant countries, using data for all eighteen countries in the group with decadal growth of 50 percent or more. The countries can be categorized into three subgroups. A first subgroup (Table 7.2) comprises eight rapidly growing, non-oil-exporting, non-former Soviet Union countries.

Five of the eight countries in the first subgroup (Bhutan, China, Rwanda, Vietnam, and Ethiopia) mirror fairly closely the Table 7.1 "developmental state" expectation of above-average and/or improving government effectiveness along the dominant trajectory. In China, government effectiveness was relatively high at the outset of the period, and continued to improve modestly over the course of the decade. In Ethiopia and Rwanda (and, more modestly, Vietnam) government effectiveness rose over the course of the decade (Rwanda also had strikingly large gains in the quality of rule-of-law). As for the remaining three countries, the low scores for government effectiveness in Cambodia and Laos (and, though somewhat more borderline, for Tanzania) are not consistent with the logic of growth via the dominant trajectory.

The second subgroup (Table 7.3) comprises six rapidly growing dominant countries that, prior to 1991, had been part of the Soviet Union. The pattern of institutional change for Kazakhstan fits well with the expectations for

Table 7.2 **High-Growth, Non-Oil, Non-Former Soviet Union Countries on the Early-Stage Dominant Trajectory**

Country	Growth 2000–2010	Government Effectiveness			Rule of Law		
		2000	Change 2000–2010	2010	2000	Change 2000–2010	2010
Countries with "good enough" and/or improving government effectiveness							
Bhutan	78%	+0.78	−0.21	*+0.57*	+0.18	−0.07	+0.11
China	156%	−0.09	+0.21	*+0.12*	−0.48	+0.13	−0.35
Rwanda	70%	−0.65	+0.60	*−0.05*	−1.35	+1.04	−0.31
Vietnam	77%	−0.44	+0.13	*−0.31*	−0.34	−0.16	−0.50
Ethiopia	71%	−0.91	+0.56	*−0.35*	−0.87	+0.12	−0.75
Countries with weak, nonimproving government effectiveness							
Tanzania	59%	−0.42	−0.08	*−0.50*	−0.39	−0.13	−0.52
Cambodia	88%	−0.96	+0.14	*−0.82*	−0.99	−0.10	−1.09
Laos	67%	−0.81	−0.17	*−0.98*	−0.95	+0.05	−0.90

Source: Worldwide Governance Indicators.

Table 7.3 **High-Growth Former Soviet Union Countries on the Dominant Trajectory**

Country	Growth 2000–2010	Government Effectiveness			Rule of Law		
		2000	Change 2000–2010	2010	2000	Change 2000–2010	2010
Kazakhstan	100%	−0.71	+0.43	*−0.28*	−1.08	+0.46	−0.62
Azerbaijan	241%	−0.98	+0.15	*−0.83*	−1.11	+0.26	−0.85
Uzbekistan	72%	−0.95	+0.15	*−0.80*	−1.10	−0.27	−0.83
Tajikistan	75%	−1.21	+0.31	*−0.90*	−1.43	+0.24	−1.19
Belarus	115%	−0.65	−0.48	*−1.13*	−1.02	−0.02	−1.04
Turkmenistan	196%	−1.34	−0.24	*−1.58*	−1.21	−0.24	−1.45

Source: Worldwide Governance Indicators.

the dominant trajectory. But for the other countries in the group, government effectiveness remained low throughout the decade. For these countries, "bounce-back" from the disruption associated with the disintegration of the Soviet Union-plus, for some, (Azerbaijan, Turkmenistan, and Kazakhstan) growing value of oil exports—provide more plausible explanations for the observed growth accelerations.

Table 7.4 **High-Growth Oil-Exporting Countries on the Dominant Trajectory**

Country	Growth 2000–2010	Government Effectiveness			Rule of Law		
		2000	Change 2000–2010	2010	2000	Change 2000–2010	2010
Angola	120%	−1.46	+0.34	*−1.12*	−1.63	+0.39	−1.24
Chad	67%	−0.76	−0.74	*−1.50*	−1.03	−0.47	−1.50
Myanmar	118%	−1.21	−0.46	*−1.67*	−1.33	−0.18	−1.51
Equatorial Guinea	245%	−1.51	−0.17	*−1.68*	−1.30	+0.04	−1.26

Source: Worldwide Governance Indicators.

The third subgroup comprises four high-growth oil exporting countries classified as dominant using the Polity IV assessments. As Table 7.4 shows, all score very low on government effectiveness, with major declines over the decade for two of the four. As these data suggest, for countries with weak institutions that are enjoying rapid, resource-led growth, the likely governance trajectory is less that of a development state than it is the dismal logic of the resource curse. Chapter 10 explores some options for improving the odds that the curse can be overcome.

Patterns of Governance Among Rapidly Growing Competitive Countries

This section explores the empirical relevance of the Table 7.1 propositions for early-stage competitive countries, using data from twenty-three countries. The group includes twenty countries with decadal growth in excess of 50 percent, and that were in the competitive or intermediate trajectories for all (or most)[13] of the decade from 2000 to 2010, plus three countries (Ghana, Mali, and Zambia) that are included as additional examples of relatively rapidly growing low-income countries, even though their decadal growth was in the 30 to 50 percent range.

There is an inherent limitation in using a multicountry data set to assess the extent to which these countries' patterns of growth and institutional change fit with the hypothesized patterns for early stage personalized competition. By contrast to the hypothesis for early-stage dominant countries, the hypothesis here is a "negative" one, namely that growth in early stage personalized competition will not be accompanied by strong and/or improving government effectiveness and the rule of law. Rather, growth is hypothesized to be driven principally by rent-sharing agreements that provide a platform of stability on the basis of which "islands of effectiveness" can emerge. Assessing this proposition requires detailed country-specific analysis; governance indicators can offer only an initial indication of whether the "negative" indeed holds empirically.

The twenty-three countries can usefully be categorized into four subgroups. The first subgroup comprises nine early-stage competitive countries, listed in Table 7.5, for which the "negative" is indeed evident. For all nine, government effectiveness was low in 2000, and showed no significant improvement over the decade. Three countries (Sierra Leone, Ukraine, and Mozambique) show some improvement in the quality of the rule of law, from a very low base. It is worth noting that seven of the nine—Bangladesh, Mali, Moldova, Mongolia, Sierra Leone, Ukraine, and Zambia—have seen strongly contested elections, plus some electoral alternation, notwithstanding their classification as "intermediate" using Polity IV measures. As the example in chapter 5 of Bangladesh illustrated, in many of these countries the electoral processes have been turbulent, including, at the limit, ethnic violence in Kenya and state collapse in Mali (until a turnaround in 2013,

Table 7.5 **Rapidly Growing Competitive and Intermediate Countries with Consistently Weak Formal Institutions**

Country	Growth 2000–2010	Government Effectiveness			Rule of Law		
		2000	Change 2000–2010	2010	2000	Change 2000–2010	2010
Mozambique	77%	−0.43	−0.11	**−0.52**	−0.77	+0.29	−0.48
Mongolia	73%	−0.31	−0.30	**−0.61**	−0.12	−0.30	−0.42
Mali	36%	−0.87	+0.0	**−0.87**	−0.46	0.00	−0.46
Bangladesh	52%	−0.56	−0.19	**−0.75**	−0.95	+0.18	−0.77
Zambia	36%	−0.86	+0.06	**−0.80**	−0.54	+0.07	−0.47
Moldova	68%	−0.58	−0.06	**−0.64**	−0.56	+0.16	−0.40
Ukraine	63%	−0.75	−0.03	**−0.78**	−1.14	+0.30	−0.84
Nigeria	80%	−0.96	−0.22	**−1.18**	−1.11	−0.10	−1.21
Sierra Leone	79%	−1.46	+0.25	**−1.21**	−1.47	+0.52	−0.95

Source: Worldwide Governance Indicators.

Table 7.6 **Six European Union Accession Countries**

Country	Growth 2000–2010	Government Effectiveness			Rule of Law		
		2000	Change 2000–2010	2010	2000	Change 2000–2010	2010
Slovakia	59%	+0.57	+0.29	**+0.86**	+0.29	+0.29	+0.58
Estonia	50%	+0.72	+0.50	**+1.22**	+0.58	+0.57	+1.15
Lithuania	63%	+0.06	+0.66	**+0.72**	+0.24	+0.52	+0.76
Latvia	52%	+0.26	+0.44	**+0.70**	+0.14	+0.65	+0.79
Bulgaria	62%	−0.04	+0.05	**+0.01**	−0.23	+0.15	+0.08
Romania	56%	−0.43	+0.28	**−0.15**	−0.19	+0.34	+0.15

Source: Worldwide Governance Indicators.

with the support of foreign troops). These difficult experiences comprise sobering reminders of the risks confronted by countries that combine openness and weak formal institutions even if, for the moment, they might be enjoying rapid growth.

The second subgroup comprises six countries, listed in Table 7.6, which acceded to the European Union during the 2000–2010 period. As chapter 3 discusses, in the later-stage-competitive group politics is hypothesized to be programmatic; political leadership seeks to deliver on its electoral promises, and does by building on (and perhaps further strengthening) both public sector capability and the rule of law. Indeed, four of the six countries in the table had strong institutions at the outset of the decade, and achieved far-reaching further gains over the course of the subsequent ten years in both government effectiveness and the quality of the rule of law; their patterns of growth and institutional change align well with the hypothesized pattern for later stage competitive countries (Bulgaria and Romania were the institutional laggards).

Tables 7.7 and 7.8 list the eight remaining rapid growers along the competitive and intermediate trajectories. The four countries in Table 7.7 fall somewhere between the early-stage (Table 7.5) and later-stage (Table 7.6) countries. For all four countries, the 2000 WGI scores for both government effectiveness and the quality of the rule of law clustered around zero. By mid-decade, three of the four were rated by Polity IV as robust democracies (Sri Lanka is the exception). But none of the countries saw significant gains in institutional quality; indeed, in both India and Sri Lanka scores for

Table 7.7 **Rapid Growers with Mixed Institutional Quality**

Country	Growth 2000–2010	Government Effectiveness			Rule of Law		
		2000	Change 2000–2010	2010	2000	Change 2000–2010	2010
Panama	53%	+0.24	−0.10	**+0.14**	−0.20	+0.07	−0.13
Ghana	37%	+0.02	−0.06	**−0.04**	+0.09	−0.16	−0.07
India	76%	−0.14	+0.13	**−0.01**	+0.28	−0.34	−0.06
Sri Lanka	50%	−0.35	+0.18	**−0.17**	+0.17	−0.25	−0.08

Source: Worldwide Governance Indicators.

Table 7.8 **Four Formerly Communist Intermediate Countries**

Country	Growth 2000–2010	Government Effectiveness			Rule of Law		
		2000	Change 2000–2010	2010	2000	Change 2000–2010	2010
Georgia	83%	−0.73	+1.02	**+0.29**	−1.12	+0.91	−0.21
Armenia	110%	−0.57	+0.42	**−0.15**	−0.46	−0.01	−0.47
Albania	63%	−0.83	+0.56	**−0.27**	−1.24	+0.80	−0.44
Russia	63%	−0.77	+0.37	**−0.40**	−1.13	+0.36	−0.77

Source: Worldwide Governance Indicators.

the quality of the rule of law worsened. Careful comparative case studies of countries in this group (and also Bulgaria and Romania, which display similar patterns) could offer important insights as to the challenges associated with moving from personalized to more impersonal institutions along the competitive trajectory.

The final subgroup comprises the four countries in Table 7.8. All four were in the communist block prior to 1990, but their Polity IV scores for 2000 (and, indeed, throughout the decade) locate them in the intermediate, not the dominant, category. All four show major gains in government effectiveness; three of the four also show major gains in the quality of the rule-of-law. Indeed, the patterns of institutional change of all four are more consistent with the logic of later-stage programmatic competition (or, perhaps, of the dominant trajectory) than of personalized competition.

Patterns of Corruption—Shades of Gray

The data presented in the previous two sections have, hopefully, shown that the typology that underpins this book has quite broad empirical relevance. But the data also underscore that things are more complex than a few "ideal types"

Table 7.9 **Control of Corruption in Forty-One Countries, 2000–2010**

Dominant	2000	Change 2000–2010	2010	Competitive and Intermediate	2000	Change 2000–2010	2010
Bhutan	+038	+0.45	+0.83	Estonia	+0.65	+0.23	+0.88
Rwanda	−0.65	+1.13	+0.48	Lithuania	+0.19	+0.12	+0.31
				Slovakia	+0.15	+0.12	+0.27
				Latvia	−0.29	+0.43	+0.14
				Ghana	−0.07	+0.15	+0.08
Tanzania	−0.95	+0.43	−0.52	Georgia	−0.88	+0.76	−0.12
Vietnam	−0.59	−0.01	−0.60	Bulgaria	−0.21	+0.02	−0.19
China	−0.24	−0.37	−0.61	Panama	−0.39	+0.04	−0.35
Ethiopia	−0.49	−0.24	−0.73	Romania	−0.48	+0.27	−0.21
Belarus	−0.50	−0.24	−0.74	Mozambique	−0.40	+0.01	−0.39
				Sri Lanka	−0.26	−0.19	−0.45
				Albania	−0.82	+0.33	−0.49
Kazakhstan	−1.06	+0.06	−1.00	India	−0.37	−0.15	−0.52
Laos	−0.78	−0.30	−1.08	Zambia	−0.85	+0.27	−0.58
Azerbaijan	−1.09	−0.11	−1.20	Armenia	−0.65	−0.01	−0.66
Tajikistan	−1.05	−0.15	−1.20	Mali	−0.66	−0.02	−0.68
Cambodia	−0.85	−0.37	−1.22	Moldova	−0.54	−0.15	−0.69
Uzbekistan	−0.91	−0.36	−1.27	Mongolia	−0.40	−0.33	−0.73
Chad	−0.82	−0.51	−1.33	Sierra Leone	−0.91	+0.15	−0.76
Angola	−1.52	+0.18	−1.34	Ukraine	−1.07	+0.08	−0.99
Turkmenistan	−0.95	−0.50	−1.45	Bangladesh	−0.94	−0.06	−1.00
Eq. Guinea	−1.53	+0.03	−1.50	Nigeria	−1.13	+0.13	−1.00
Myanmar	−1.31	−0.38	−1.69	Russia	−0.92	−0.17	−1.09

Source: Worldwide Governance Indicators

can capture, that there are shades of gray. What governance patterns might lie in-between the neat boxes of the typology?

Table 7.9 offers one way to explore these shades of gray. It uses WGI data to distinguish among the forty-one rapidly growing countries on which this chapter focuses according to the success with which they control corruption. A corruption measure offers a useful birds-eye view of the quality of governance; It shifts the focus of attention away from the quality of specific institutions per se towards the extent to which the political and institutional order as a whole delivers one key outcome—constraining opportunism in service of private ends, and thereby enhancing the focus on public purposes. Looked at through this lens, the disparity is stark between countries on the dominant and the competitive/intermediate trajectories.

Along the twenty-three rapidly growing countries on the competitive trajectory, the track record on control of corruption, while hardly stellar, is fairly positive, with strong performance in some countries, signs of improvement in others, and very few reversals:

- Five countries (Estonia, Latvia, Lithuania, Slovakia, and, intriguingly, low-income Ghana) had control of corruption scores for 2010 which were greater than zero; Ghana's score of 0.08 positioned it in the 60th percentile globally;
- A further four (Georgia, Albania, Romania, and Zambia) achieved gains of at least 0.25 points over the 2000–2010 period, improving their global percentile ranking by at least ten points (Georgia, it is worth noting, leapfrogged from the 20th to the 55th percentile).

Among the remaining countries, only four had scores at or below –1.0 (at that score a country would be in the weakest 15 percent globally), and only one (Mongolia) had a decline over the decade in excess of 0.2 points.

By contrast, among the eighteen rapidly growing countries on the dominant trajectory the pattern is much more negative:

- Eleven of the eighteen had 2010 scores at or below –1.0, which placed them in the weakest 15 percent globally; over the course of the decade six of these (Laos, Cambodia, Uzbekistan, Chad, Turkmenistan, and Myanmar) witnessed declines in their WGI scores of at least 0.3 points;
- A further three (China, Ethiopia, and Belarus) experienced declines of over 0.2 points; their global control of corruption rankings fell over the course of the decade by over 10 points, to the 32nd, 27th, and 25th percentiles, respectively.

Only one dominant country (Bhutan) had a control of corruption score above zero throughout the 2000–2010 period, and only two (Tanzania and, again, Rwanda) made major gains over the decade, with Rwanda showing truly extraordinary improvement, moving from the 31st to 71st percentile globally.

The evidence in Table 7.9 on the extent of corruption among the rapidly growing dominant countries suggests that, for many countries along the trajectory, David Booth and Tim Kelsall's notion of "development patrimonialism," introduced in chapter 4 as a hybrid combination of clientelism and a developmental state, may indeed have some empirical traction. But for many of the countries even that is perhaps an optimistic gloss. Trends in corruption can usefully be interpreted as a leading indicator of the changing extent of commitment of a country's political and bureaucratic leadership to development; as leaders become entrenched in power they risk losing what might initially have been a strong commitment. Indeed, once a willingness to act opportunistically in pursuit of private gain takes hold, the risks rise of development going into reverse. The evidence on corruption suggests that while for some countries the dominant trajectory may indeed offer a path of progress, for many others what it seemingly contributes to development, it may subsequently all too readily take away.

ADDRESSING GOVERNANCE CONSTRAINTS

Part III shifts the focus from the broad macrodynamics of how governance and growth interact to the specifics of microlevel governance initiatives, less as ends in themselves than as means to address binding constraints on development. It examines a variety of different approaches to reform, each better adapted to some country circumstances than to others.

Table III.1 unbundles potential governance interventions across two dimensions: whether the approach is comprehensive or incremental, and whether the focus is on hierarchical ("principal–agent") or horizontal ("principal–principal") improvements. As the top row of the table shows, this gives us two types of comprehensive reforms: hierarchical reforms that focus on system-wide strengthening of the public bureaucracy, and horizontal reforms that focus on strengthening checks and balances institutions (targeting improvements in electoral systems, and in the capabilities of the judiciary, parliament, and other nonexecutive institutions of accountability). Taken together, these comprise the agenda of "good governance" reform.

If they were implemented effectively, comprehensive "good governance" reforms would, of course, remove binding governance constraints to development. However, as we have seen, comprehensive reform only will gain traction if it is compatible with prevailing political and institutional arrangements, and windows of opportunity for far-reaching change are rare. In most places, most of the time, the incentives, authority and long-term horizon needed for comprehensive reform to take hold will be lacking. In these latter settings, finding a "good fit" calls for a different set of reform options.

A principal goal of Part III is to explore options for easing governance constraints to continuing forward momentum on growth and development in settings where there is little prospect of a great leap forward to good governance. This search is especially relevant for countries where politics is open and competitive, but power is

Table III.1 **Addressing Governance Constraints—Four Approaches to Reform**

	Hierarchical *("principal–agent")*	Horizontal *("principal–principal")*
Comprehensive	System-wide public management reform	Strengthen checks and balances institutions
Incremental	Targeted improvements in public management (specific functions, sectors, agencies- or locales)	Strengthen multi-stakeholder governance

fragmented and contested, time horizons are short, and the rules of the game are personalized. As the chapters that follow explore, the incremental governance initiatives highlighted in the bottom row of Table III.1 offer the best prospects for getting development in this latter group of countries.

Chapter 8 explores conceptually how to achieve a "good fit"—which conditions are more propitious for top-down public-sector reform to succeed and which are such that incremental and multistakeholder approaches are more likely to add value. Chapters 9 and 10 explore multistakeholder approaches empirically. Chapter 9 uses the examples of basic education and community-driven development to assess the potential of transparency and participation initiatives to address weaknesses in top-down public service provision. Chapter 10 explores some ways in which multistakeholder engagement can support private-sector development.

To be sure, an incremental approach lacks the bold allure of comprehensive governance reform. But, as per Parts I and II of this book, the case for incrementalism is based on a different theory of change, one where microlevel initiatives provide a platform for the emergence of "islands of effectiveness" within a broader sea of dysfunction, securing some gains in the short term, and serving as a platform for cumulative gains over the longer-run in both governance and poverty reduction.* Paradoxically, it is in these more microlevel incremental initiatives that the human factor, the scope for public entrepreneurship, becomes especially relevant. Public entrepreneurs with the commitment, skill, and staying power to build both internal capabilities and external alliances play a central role in enabling islands of effectiveness to take root within a broadly dysfunctional public sector.

---

* For other contributions which build on idea that the governance agenda could usefully be re-imagined, building up from the microlevel, see Sue Unsworth, *An Upside Down View of Governance,* Synthesis Report of a Centre for the Future State Research Programme, Institute of Development Studies (Sussex, 2010). Also David Booth, *Development as a Collective Action Problem: Addressing the Real Challenges of African Governance,* Synthesis Report of the Africa Power and Politics Programme, Overseas Development Institute (London: 2012).

CHAPTER 8

Function Versus Form in Public-Sector Reform

While I was part of the core team that wrote the 1997 World Development Report (WDR) on *The State in a Changing World,* I no longer am comfortable with its core message that an effective state is key for development. Gains in state effectiveness are, to be sure, a central part of the development process. I decidedly am *not* indulging in the vacuous "states-versus-markets" debate (and most certainly am not aiming to make the case for the "markets" side of the debate). The trouble with the message of the 1997 WDR was that it blurred the outcome of a cumulative process of development and the multiple paths for getting from here to there. One cannot begin at the end point.

But this hardly makes the institutions of governance irrelevant. Development is quintessentially about interdependence, and this interdependence is governed by institutions, introduced in chapter 2 and formally defined by Douglass North as "the humanly devised constraints that govern human interaction."[1] Development needs workable institutions to govern market transactions. It needs institutions to provide credible commitment that the rules of the game will remain stable, so that skillful investors will be able to realize the promised returns to their entrepreneurial efforts. It needs institutions to provide those public goods and services that have large social benefits but that are not adequately provided by the market.[2] And it needs institutions to assure that resources intended for social objectives indeed are used for the purposes intended.

In countries where formal state institutions work well, meeting these challenges is (relatively) straightforward: Public bureaucracies can be relied upon to deliver services, and the justice system and other checks and balances institutions can be relied upon to assure compliance with the rules of the game. As we have seen, though, these more benign institutional arrangements can be relied on only in a subset of countries. In many, indeed perhaps the majority of developing countries, the "rules of the game" are more personalized, with little prospect of this changing into the medium term.

The next three chapters will explore microlevel initiatives that aim to support the emergence of institutions capable of fulfilling the public role outlined above, with a focus on how this challenge can be addressed in difficult governance settings. This chapter introduces conceptually a varieties of approaches to achieving public goals, and provides an overview of the potential and limits of each; the next two explore some applications of the less familiar approaches laid out here. Conventional approaches to building public-sector capacity comprise an important part of this chapter's discussion, but they are not the only part.

Dani Rodrik's distinction between form and function, also introduced in chapter 2, is especially relevant to analysis of the role of institutions in developing countries. Rodrik makes the distinction as follows:

> First-order economic principles do not map into unique policy packages. Good institutions are those that deliver these first-order principles effectively. There is no unique correspondence between the functions that good institutions perform and the form that such institutions take. Reformers have substantial room for creatively packaging these principles into institutional designs that are sensitive to local constraints and take advantage of local opportunities.[3]

In some settings, efforts to strengthen public-sector capacity may straightforwardly fill the institutional gap. But in other settings, if progress is to be achieved, other institutional arrangements will be needed.

Public-Sector Maximalism

The scope of the stated ambition of the World Bank is extraordinary. Though from the outside, it still often is perceived to be staffed principally by economists and engineers pre-occupied only with economic growth, it has in fact become something very different: education, health, governance, the environment—all of these and more have become part of its professed global expertise. The immodest mission statement in the entrance to the building pronounces that "our dream is a world free of poverty." It also is an organization with an exceptional range of skills: "from one hundred countries, and ten (prestige) universities" is the way the organization's diverse staff sometimes is wryly described.

Given the Bank's combination of noble purpose and range of skills, it might be expected to be a hotbed of creativity, of continuing search for new ways of getting results. Indeed, one of its strengths is that it provides space for innovators. But the dominant organizational culture generally has not welcomed innovation. Throughout the almost quarter century in which I was a staff member, there was ongoing tension between boundary-breakers and "keepers" of the dominant way of doing things. Part of this tension could be traced to the usual kinds of bureaucratic tension; inevitable in any organization, but perhaps more endemic in one filled with a highly educated and highly ambitious staff, and with a complicated, ambiguous, and difficult to measure "bottom line." But there also turned out to be an even more fundamental source of tension than fights over turf or personal ambition, namely the conflict between competing "first principles" as to what could provide a viable platform for moving forward with development.

I confronted one of these fights to the (professional) finish while I was leading the Bank's Africa public-sector reform group. As discussed in chapter 2, I was becoming increasingly aware of the very uneven results from efforts at public-sector reform. Meanwhile, some remarkable gains were beginning to be reported from "bottom-up," community-based approaches to development work. Surely, I reasoned, there were opportunities for synergy: Participatory approaches potentially offered the gains in accountability that were missing from many public management reforms. Conversely, public management reforms offered the potential for longer-run institutionalization, the Achilles' heel of the community-driven approaches. But what I had not reckoned with was the degree of mutual (professional) detestation among champions of each of these two approaches.

All too often, protagonists of working with communities derided government as the enemy to be avoided at all costs. And, in a mirror image of virulence, all too often public management types derided their community-oriented counterparts as short-sighted romantics. So, all too often, bringing these warring tribes into the same room felt like facilitating a dialogue of the deaf. (Actually, in classic bureaucratic fashion, the meetings themselves generally had a tone of formal, distant politeness; it was in the corridors, or behind closed doors, that the true virulence of mutual professional dislike was voiced.)

"You're both right!!" This message was one that I often repeated in an effort to find a way through these wars of principle, ideology, and turf between champions of top-down and bottom-up approaches to development work. But it often fell on deaf ears. Certainly, mealy mouthed, empty platitudes hardly are likely to cut through wars unto the death. I continue to believe, though, that it's the right message. Why? Because the right balance between top-down and bottom-up strategies depends (as always) on context.

Public-sector reform as a managerial challenge.   What does it takes to improve the performance of a public bureaucracy? At first glance, the recipe seems fairly straightforward. In his classic, early twentieth-century work, the German sociologist Max Weber outlined the core elements of a "rational" ("Weberian") bureaucracy. These included an explicit division of labor among different parts of the bureaucracy; a hierarchical structure; rule-governed decision making; meritocratic recruitment; and a predictable, long-term career ladder for staff within the bureaucracy.[4]

Weber's characterization seemingly suggests that the challenge of improving bureaucratic performance is principally a managerial one, namely to strengthen the skills of public employees, to reengineer public systems to make them more efficient, and to stamp out fraud, waste, and abuse. These are "capacity-building" tasks, which seemingly can be addressed straightforwardly within the parameters of the ongoing discourse between donors and developing country governments. Indeed, donors have supported very extensive programs of public-sector capacity building; some focus on strengthening "core of government" public financial and administrative management systems and others more on building sector-level capacity.[5]

The public-sector capacity-building approach was made somewhat more complicated by the fact that what in the early twentieth century had seemed to be the epitome of high-performing organization had become in the later twentieth century a term of opprobrium. "Bureaucratic" increasingly came to mean slow, inflexible, and unresponsive. But again, a solution seemed to be at hand. The last two decades of the twentieth century saw a worldwide mushrooming of new public management (NPM) reform efforts aimed at strengthening the results orientation of the public sector.

Worldwide, the intent of reforms was to shift the focus of control from inputs to outputs.[6] Policy makers were to define clearly *what* should be done, and to set performance targets as a basis for monitoring the performance of frontline providers. Against the backdrop of clarity with respect to goals and accountability for results, frontline providers were to be given the flexibility to decide *how* things are to be done. Reforms that aimed to shift toward a more results-oriented approach to public management generally incorporated four sets of interdependent changes:

- *Reorienting input controls.* Traditional bureaucracies have long been governed via tight controls over inputs. The NPM approach to input control aimed to reduce rigidities on frontline providers, but in a framework that ensured effectiveness and probity in how the resources are used.
- *Clarifying the performance framework within which frontline providers are to operate.* The providers could be either public or private firms working on contract. For public providers, this framework could take the form of agreed up-front targets of performance. For private providers, the framework could comprise the regulatory rules of the game that set the constraints within which profit-seeking activity might proceed.

- *Strengthening the rewards for achieving agreed-upon results—and the penalties for falling short.* Measures here included performance contracts between organizational leaders and their controllers, and initiatives to link budgets or staff promotion to performance.
- *Strengthening systems for monitoring and evaluation* and thereby providing an empirical basis for assessing results (outputs—whether resources achieved their intended proximate objectives; and outcomes—whether the social purpose for which the resources were deployed was achieved), and thereby providing a basis (other than compliance with input controls) for assessing performance.

The pioneers in the design and implementation of the above agenda were the United Kingdom, New Zealand, and other higher-income countries. Preaching the gospel of NPM rapidly became a growth industry in developing countries as well. The agenda was hugely attractive to independent consultants, and also to donors and governments for whom there was much to gain from embracing the rhetoric of public-sector reform.

There are, however, two difficulties with this NPM-modified agenda of public-sector capacity building. The first difficulty is that even in high-income countries the track record of NPM reforms was (to put it gently) uneven. Here is the conclusion of a landmark review of public administrative reform in ten OECD countries, including such noted public management reformers as Australia, New Zealand, Sweden, the United States, and the United Kingdom[7]:

> *Reform-watching in public management can be a sobering pastime. The gaps between rhetoric and actions . . . are frequently so wide as to provoke skepticism. The pace of underlying, embedded achievement tends to be much slower than the helter-skelter cascade of new announcements and initiatives. Incremental analysis and partisan mutual adjustment seem to have been very frequent features of public management reform, even if more-than-incremental changes were frequently hoped for.*

The second difficulty is even more fundamental. The agenda presupposed that NPM reforms build on a pre-existing platform of a reasonably well-functioning Weberian public bureaucracy.[8] However, as the 2004 WDR, *Making Services Work for Poor People* underscored, in many developing countries the reality on the ground was very far from Weberian.

Public-sector reform as a challenge of accountability.   The point of departure of the 2004 WDR was a growing disconnect between a rapid expansion in the provision of resources for service provision and corresponding expansion in access to services, but continuing shortfalls in service quality and results. Substantial evidence was emerging that money often was not used for its intended purposes[9]:

- In Zambia, an expenditure tracking study conducted in the early 2000s found that only 24 percent of a fund for schools actually reached the schools themselves.[10] A landmark study a decade earlier showed a similar result in Uganda.
- In Bangladesh, unannounced visits to a sample of the country's primary health centers found that 35 percent of staff were absent.
- Similarly, in India, only 45 percent of teachers were actually teaching at the time of unannounced school visits, and 25 percent of the teacher cadre was absent;
- Across a sample of six countries (the above two plus Ecuador, Indonesia, Peru, and Uganda), the average absenteeism rate was 19 percent for teachers, and 35 percent for health workers.
- Studies in Ghana and Nigeria in the early 1990s found that about 30 percent of public clinics lacked drugs.

The WDR showed that only (at best) a modest part of the performance gap could be attributed to shortfalls of financial resources. In so doing, it also blew the lid off the comfortable presumption that the problem was one of capacity. The report argued that though there are many proximate causes of failure in the provision of public services, the core failure was in relationships of accountability:

> *Too frequently those seeking improvement have focused only on internal organizational reforms—focusing on management of the frontline workers. If organizational failures are the result of deeper weaknesses in institutional arrangements (weak political commitment, unclear objectives, no enforceability), direct attacks on the proximate determinants (more money, better training, more internal information) will fail.*[11]

What is the accountability challenge? At its heart, the task is to assure credible commitment. When one party gets what he or she wants immediately upon making a promise, but is required to deliver his side of the bargain only subsequently, the incentive to renege can be irresistible. As Nobel Prize-winning economist Oliver Williamson and other new institutional economists have underscored in their work on the governance of private firms, locking-in commitment in a way that assures follow through, and thereby getting the deal made, is a ubiquitous challenge.[12] The all-too-human dilemma that promises can be easy to make, but difficult to keep, is the stuff of romance, of finance, of private investment, of the employment relationship (in both the public and private sectors), and of the arena of public action.

To address accountability, the 2004 report borrowed from the literature on the governance of private firms and embraced a hierarchical ("principal–agent" in academic parlance) framework for improving service provision. Superficially, this seemed a natural move to make: The frontline units responsible for the provision of public services overwhelmingly were staffed by public employees,[13] and the shortfalls (absenteeism, skill gaps, fraud and the like) seemed to be those of a dysfunctional employer-employee relationship, public or private. As per the literature on the private sector, the challenges of managing employees seemingly had a straightforward solution: strengthen the mechanisms for monitoring and enforcement.

But this seemingly straightforward analogy between public and private organizations is profoundly misleading. Here is the public governance variant of the accountability challenge: Political leaders win power on the basis of their promises; public officials get paid to carry out public functions that deliver on these promises. But with power won and with an employee's salary paid, there is a potential disconnect between the particular public purpose being pursued, and the private ends of those who have been delegated the authority to pursue it. How is this disconnect addressed?

The chain of principal–agent accountabilities that needs to be in place if public bureaucracies are to work along the lines posited by reformers from Weber to the WDR is long:

- Political leaders need to take hold of the reins of executive authority, and translate their general vision for the country into a strategy for action.
- Within the framework provided by that strategic direction, public-sector bureaucracies need to design and assess the benefits and costs to society of specific policy options, and assign budgetary resources to the highest return priorities.
- Frontline service providers need to take responsibility for delivering on these priorities;
- Bureaucracies need to have internal management structures and control systems that align staff efforts with organizational goals and monitor internally how resources in fact are used (including whether frontline employees show up and put in an honest day's work).
- Underpinning all of this are elections and other mechanisms that hold political leaders accountable for following through on their promises, including checks and balances institutions capable of reining in powerful political and bureaucratic leaders in the event that they begin to abuse power for private purposes.

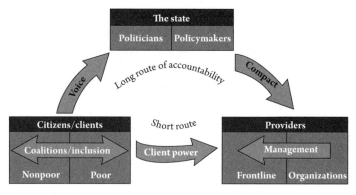

Figure 8.1 **The WDR Accountability Triangle**

The 2004 report famously described this impersonal, institutionally robust chain of authority and delegation as "the long route of accountability." As Figure 8.1 illustrates, it organized the chain into two broad sets of links: "voice," which links citizens to politicians, and thence to policymakers, and a "compact" that links policymakers and service providers.

As some of the most successful examples of the past six decades signal—the reconstruction of Europe in the aftermath of World War Two, and the "East Asia Miracle" countries (from Japan, to Korea, to contemporary China, with many others in between)—when bureaucracy works, and can be harnessed in service of development, extraordinarily rapid economic and social gains can be achieved. It is this vision of what is possible that underpins the ardent commitment of the champions of public management reforms.

But for all of these advantages, the long route of accountability is dauntingly complex; each of the many distinct links of the chain has to work for the system to be robust. The anchor for this cascading chain is politics, and only very distinctive political conditions provide a platform that is robust enough for the system as a whole to work. What of the other countries?

Incremental Options for Public-Sector Reform

An overarching principle of a "with-the-grain" approach to development policy is that successful reforms need to be aligned with a country's political and institutional realities. For any specific reform, an incentive compatible approach begins by asking, who might be the critical mass of actors who both have standing and have a stake in the proposed arrangements—and so are in a position to support and protect them in the face of opposition? Without these actors, there will be no one to defend reforms in the face of the ever-present incentives to renege in search of private advantage. This principle has especially stark implications for the maximalist reforms to strengthen public administrative management described in the previous section.

The politics of public-sector reform.   As noted above, the maximalist agenda of public management reforms generally includes better budgetary and financial controls, clearer, more differentiated functions across agencies, more merit-based ways of recruitment and promotion within the civil service, and better management across the range of public organizations. Such reforms generally are painstaking to implement, and take a long time to yield results. As we saw back in chapter 2, comprehensive public-sector reforms generally are successful only in a subset of countries, those where (as Merilee Grindle emphasizes in *Jobs for the Boys*) top-down reforms have the potential to gain traction.

As Grindle details, the search for "windows of opportunity" that can enable reformers to "move decisively towards the formal acceptance of their initiative" has long been something of a holy grail among development practitioners.[14] They have a long (and mostly unsuccessful) track record of putting a far-reaching reform agenda on the table, and then exhorting local leaders to show "political will." Occasionally, as the examples of Georgia and Rwanda in chapter 7 suggest, they may indeed stumble upon the right combination. So, given the potential, it always is wise to remain open to the possibility that a window of opportunity for far-reaching change indeed has opened up. However, along both the dominant and the competitive trajectories there are reasons for caution.

Along the dominant trajectory, the effectiveness of reform efforts depends on the extent to which political leaders are developmentally oriented (this, of course, varies widely from one leader to another) and the extent to which the leadership has an unequivocal hold on power. Where these are present, the opportunities for ambitious public management reforms gaining traction are good. But where these are weaker, efforts at comprehensive public management reform are unlikely to get much traction.

Along the competitive trajectory, leadership supportive of ambitious public management reforms can emerge where political competition is between programmatically oriented political parties, which differ in the details of their platforms, but have a shared incentive to have a capable public sector in place.[15] But this basis for political competition generally comes only when institutional arrangements are impersonal: quite prevalent among more later-stage countries but less likely among early-stage, personalized-competitive countries.

For early-stage, personalized-competitive countries, comprehensive public management reforms and the logic of politics are seemingly diametrically opposed to one another. A principal purpose of comprehensive public management reforms is to limit the personalized discretion that lies at the heart of governance in early-stage, competitive settings. But as the examples in chapter 5 of Bangladesh and Zambia highlight, in many early-stage, competitive countries, politics is organized around personalized interactions (and distribution of rents) among elites, and between elites and nonelites. Reform affects rents and their distribution, so control over both the process and the content of the reform agenda is likely to be contested. Even if reform can somehow be promulgated (in order, for example, to satisfy conditionalities imposed by the World Bank or other donors), there are unlikely to be credible arrangements for monitoring, and for enforcing noncompliance at lower levels. As should by now be evident, personalized rules of the game cannot be superseded simply by wishing it so.

In sum, public-sector maximalism has been built on a brittle foundation of technocratic exhortation, the search for reform "champions", and the willingness to see as windows of opportunity a few carefully chosen turns of phrase by senior officials eager to seem to accommodate the aspirations of donors. On occasion it works, but in all too many settings these maximalist preoccupations have been a distraction from the pursuit of more incremental, but real results—and a corresponding focus on more modest, but achievable, reforms.

Public management "lite."   Refocusing the reform agenda on more incremental approaches to public-sector reform yields a rich trove of potential options. Some of these can usefully be described as "public management lite." Others differ from the standard, top-down approach in more fundamental ways.

"Public management lite" reforms comprise piecemeal—incremental, but perhaps cumulative—variants of the more comprehensive agenda. They potentially have relevance along both the competitive and the dominant trajectories, especially for the many countries that inhabit "shades of gray" between the pure forms of the ideal types of the conceptual model.

Along the competitive trajectory, "public management lite" approaches are most likely to be useful in countries where "rule-of-law competitiveness" is not yet locked in, and elite contestation remains predominantly personalized, but where the momentum of development is continually strengthening the position of private-sector, middle-class, and civil-society stakeholders looking for better performance from government. The almost forty year, step-by-step process of transformation of the United States bureaucracy, described in chapter 6, illustrates how an incremental approach to public strengthening might work. Grindle suggests that public sector strengthening in the United Kingdom followed a similarly incremental path, though one that was less dependent on participatory mobilization than the American example. And in Mexico, efforts to reduce discretion and strengthen rule-boundedness came only in the early 2000s, in the wake of democratization, when the country was already firmly in the middle-income range, and when all political parties judged that their longer-run interests might be best served by a less politicized civil service; even then, the Mexican reform agenda remained quite limited.[16]

Along the dominant trajectory, "public management lite" approaches are likely to be especially relevant in countries where leaders combine at least some commitment to achieving development results with the continuing use of discretionary conferral and withdrawal of favors as a principal tool of governance. As we saw in chapter 7, this combination of political dominance, rapid growth, and weak nonimproving institutions was ubiquitous over the period from 2000 to 2010. Grindle offers some added insight into how dominant patrimonial governance and growth might be compatible. She argues strongly that discretion and patronage need not be antithetical to results-oriented government. As she puts it:

> *Patronage systems are not synonymous with bad governance. . . . Ministers and other high level officials have the capacity to use their appointment power to attract highly qualified staffs to carry out specific policy initiatives. . . . Managers with discretion over hiring have significant opportunities to create islands of excellence. . . . Discretion in hiring can provide means for escaping the rigidity of personnel laws and regulations.*[17]

But she also notes:

> *Inherent in the flexibility that makes patronage systems available for a variety of goals is the problem of their instability and politicization. . . . with considerable potential for unwise use and the undermining of the public purposes of government. . . . The fatal weakness of patronage systems is that they are capricious, not that they are inevitably incompetent.*[18]

How, as development unfolds, might countries move incrementally to reduce discretion and enhance formal rule-boundedness in public management? A variety of entry points potentially are compatible (or at least not starkly incompatible) with the incentives of political leaders in settings where patronage remains the principal mode of governance. Each focuses narrowly on a carefully delineated subset of the broader public-sector reform agenda.

First, narrowly targeted efforts to strengthen merit-based recruitment and promotion, introduce market-related pay among a selected subset of officials, and strengthen civil service protections against arbitrary political action appear to have greater prospects for success than efforts that seek change for all public employees.[19] The key is to target the efforts to introduce meritocratic systems to positions where the developmental returns potentially are high and the political resistance relatively low. In Mexico, civil service reform efforts in the early 2000s explicitly bypassed both the very top tier of political appointees and politically protected less-skilled employees (with the latter comprising well over half of the public service); Mexico's 2003 reform law targeted only 43,000 of a total of over 330,000 public employees, and as of 2007 fewer than 9,000 public employees had been incorporated into the new professional career system.[20] In Albania, a determined effort focused on the top 1,000 or so employees was able to provide protections against arbitrary political interference for close to a decade; in Sierra Leone, reforms targeted a narrow swathe of a few hundred technical professionals, staying away from both the very top jobs (where political connections and control dominated decision making), and the many low paid patronage jobs at the bottom of the system.

Second, efforts to improve public financial management systems seem to get quite good traction: A comprehensive assessment identified improvements in fifty-four of eighty-seven countries where the World Bank provided support for these reforms, and major improvements in twenty-four of these[21] (by contrast, the same study identified improvement in only thirty of seventy-one countries where the World Bank had provided support for public administrative reform—and major improvements in only seven of these).

Drilling down further, initiatives aimed at ensuring that finances are delivered predictably to frontline units appear to get better traction than ambitious efforts to set multiyear expenditure priorities, or to put in place robust "value for money" control systems.[22] One plausible explanation for these patterns is that public financial management reforms that enhance the ability to get finance to where it has been targeted are less politically threatening than those that limit discretion in either hiring or procurement. To make the point differently, strengthened financial management controls need not be inconsistent with either patronage employment practices or corruption in procurement; what they do is provide a management tool for targeting resources to priority activities, and assuring that they indeed get there. What happens next is up to the local managers, and their political masters.

A third possible entry point is to focus public management reform efforts on specific sectors, agencies and locales. By contrast to reforms of core systems, this downstream focus can more straightforwardly be linked to the achievement of concrete development results, making the reforms both more readily monitorable, and more readily linked to specific constituencies.

This last entry point brings us to a fundamental divide in the agenda of public-sector reform: the distinction between supply-side and demand-side approaches. The 2004 WDR brought this distinction to center stage in its contrast of the "long route" of accountability and an alternative "short route." The "short route" comprises the interactions between providers and their clients: between teachers and students or parents, between municipal garbage workers and slum-dwellers, and so on. As per the other name used for the "short route" in the WDR, "client power," it offered the potential to introduce countervailing power in settings where frontline officials had high levels of discretion (note that sometimes this discretion could flow from the characteristics of a specific task, how teachers teach, for example; at other times it could be a consequence of broader shortfalls in political oversight).

Introduction of the demand side of client power was an important corrective to the narrowly technocratic preoccupation of many public-sector reformers. But the WDR's approach had two limitations. One limitation is that it presupposed that the recipients of services indeed have leverage over frontline behavior, a power relationship that sometimes may be true, but oftentimes is not.

The second limitation was that a preoccupation with the "demand side," as defined in the WDR, offered a very constricted view of the range of alternatives to top-down technocratic reforms: By focusing primarily on two polar patterns, a hierarchical long-route, and a frontline short route, the WDR deflected attention from the vast spaces in the middle: the many layers within a specific sector in-between the top-levels of policymaking and the service provision frontline and the many countries where governance falls well short of "good" but is better than disastrous. As we shall see, viewed through the lens of multistakeholder governance these in-between spaces are where many opportunities for achieving gains in performance are to be found.[23]

The Logic—and Politics—of Multistakeholder Governance

Nurturing commitments among equals offers an alternative option to the hierarchical, principal–agent approach to accountability laid out in the 2004 WDR. Elinor Ostrom, in her 2009 Nobel Prize acceptance speech, observed that collective action was "the path not followed," and devoted her professional life to exploring where it might lead. As she put it:

The market was seen as the optimal institution for the production and exchange of private goods. For nonprivate goods, without a hierarchical government to induce compliance, self-seeking citizens and officials would fail to generate efficient levels of public goods. . . . The most important lesson for public policy analysis derived from the intellectual journey I have outlined . . . is that humans have a more complex motivational structure and more capability to solve social dilemmas than posited in earlier rational-choice theory. . . . We need to ask how diverse institutions help or hinder innovativeness, learning, adapting, trustworthiness, and levels of cooperation.[24]

Far more than is commonly recognized, collective action has huge potential as an approach to addressing challenges of public-sector performance. This is for three reasons:

- First, collective action potentially can be unbundled. It can comprise an institutional platform for "islands of effectiveness" to thrive, even where the broader governance environment is difficult. It has the potential to go (institutionally) where the long route cannot.
- Second, though collective action generally has been associated with situations where the principals are nongovernmental, this need not be the case. In principle, the relevant principals can comprise both governmental and nongovernmental actors—although including governmental actors as a co-equal among the principals presumes that, in the context of the specific collaborative endeavor being considered, they have similar standing as co-principals as do nongovernmental actors. (It is to signal this broader framing that the terms "multistakeholder governance" and "collective action" are used interchangeably here.)
- Third, as the next sub-section details, the range of activities in which a collective action approach potentially is relevant is ubiquitous.

The ubiquity of collective action.[25]   Though Elinor Ostrom focused her work principally on the role of collective action in the governance of "common pool" resources, including irrigation systems, inshore fisheries, communally owned land, groundwater resources, and forests[26], the range of applications is far, far wider. It can be a way of addressing shortfalls in the provision of public service via, for example:

- Participation in the governance of schools, health clinics, and other frontline service provision facilities by multistakeholder groups that include service recipients and others with a stake in the efficiency and effectiveness of service provision;

- Community engagement in processes for prioritizing, constructing, and maintaining small-scale local infrastructure;
- Multistakeholder oversight of public-sector procurement: for example, through joint commitments by private bidders and public agencies to govern specific large-scale, procurement-intensive public projects through "integrity pacts."
- Public–private partnerships and/or other collaborative, multistakeholder arrangements to govern the operation of formally state-owned entities, and of other arms-length public agencies.

Chapter 9 explores the first two of these in depth.

Collective action involving private firms potentially has an important direct role to play in economic growth, as chapter 10 explores in depth. Examples to be considered there include cluster initiatives among private (manufacturing and other) firms within a given sector or value chain to facilitate mutually linked investments, or to jointly invest in learning or market facilitation; and outgrowing arrangements in which processers and small-holder farmers collaborate around common rules governing the provision of inputs and the sale of crops; these can combine vertical (i.e., between farmers and processers) and horizontal (i.e., between groups of farmers and groups of processers) institutional arrangements.

More broadly, collective action arguably lies at the heart of government policymaking. It can usefully characterize the process through which coalition governments (or, for that matter, powerful factions in cabinet government) reach agreement as to which development initiatives to prioritize. And it may also be a useful depiction of how governments at an early stage along the competitive trajectory reach agreements at the macrolevel to achieve political stability—and, at more microlevels, as to which are the domains in which they will refrain from destructive conflict, and thereby allow development initiatives to proceed.

Of more immediate relevance for the present chapter, a focus on the strategic interplay among stakeholders—that is, on the logic of collective action—potentially offers a rich new set of insights into how public bureaucracies function in personalized-competitive settings, and how their performance might be improved. As noted earlier, personalized-competitive settings are likely to be characterized by much more competition and ambiguity than is implied by either the "long-route" or the "short route" depictions in the 2004 WDR. Rule-setting processes are likely to be contested, and trade-offs between objectives less likely to be clarified. Agreements that are reached are likely to be subject to weaknesses in both monitoring, and in sanctions for noncompliance.

These ambiguities and weaknesses undercut the potential for principal–agent governance to work. But they also create new spaces where there is expanded scope for external stakeholders to engage and for managers to exercise discretion. The outcomes could serve narrow interests—but, as the example in chapter 6 of the American Progressive Era illustrates, they need not. It all depends on the quality of multistakeholder engagement: Who are the stakeholders and the managers, what are their incentives, and how do they interact with one another and with the broader supply-side public-sector processes?

Two sets of challenges in particular shape the quality of these multistakeholder engagements. There is the ubiquitous challenge of facilitating cooperation among participants to achieve joint benefits, in a way that limits the classic free rider and other moral hazard problems. This is the classic challenge on which most work on collective action (including Ostrom's) has focused. But there is also a second challenge. When cooperation works, it creates a valuable asset (a quasi-rent, in formal economic parlance). Especially in the absence of formal institutions of restraint, this asset potentially can attract the attention of powerful actors seeking to capture the returns from multistakeholder governance for themselves, even though over the longer term this predation would kill the goose that laid the golden egg. To be successful, collective action must fend off predation. Let us consider each challenge in turn.

The theory of collective action.   In the long-route, the key institutional task is to align the behavior of agents with the goals of their principals. But collective action does not fit into a principal–agent world. Rather, it is the process whereby:

> *a group of principals can organize and govern themselves to adopt coordinated strategies to obtain (and maintain) higher joint benefits when all face temptations to free-ride, shirk, or otherwise act opportunistically.*[27]

What does it take for a group of principals to co-operate successfully? Over an almost forty year career, Ostrom analyzed the governance of hundreds of common pool resources in dozens of countries. She also was among the pioneers of structured laboratory-style experiments to assess the incentives for co-operation, part of the burgeoning field of behavioral economics.[28] Based on this work, she went beyond the standard depiction (introduced in chapter 2) of institutions as a set of rules, monitoring and enforcement arrangements, and laid out a disaggregated framework of "working rules" that, she argued, could be used to describe any and all institutional arrangements. With these rules as backdrop, she identified a set of eight "good practice" principles for the successful governance of collective action. Table 8.1 summarizes the principles, grouping them into four broad categories, and linking them (loosely) to their associated working rules.

Table 8.1　**Institutional Analysis: Working Rules, and their "Good Practice" Design Principles**

The Working Rules	Principles for "Good Practice" Design
I: Rules governing eligibility	
Boundary rules—define who is eligible to enter a position	*Clearly defined participant boundaries:* Clear and locally understood boundaries between legitimate participants and nonparticipants are present.
Position rules—create positions for participants to enter	
II: Operating rules	
Payoff rules—assign rewards or sanctions	*Proportional equivalence between benefits and costs.* Rules specifying the amounts that a participant benefits are proportional to the distribution of labor, materials, and other costs.
Aggregation rules—determine how collective decisions are to be arrived at	*Collective-choice arrangements:* Most individuals affected by the collaborative initiative are authorized to participate in making and modifying its rules.
Choice rules—specify what a participant occupying a position must/must not/may do at a particular point in a decision process	*Conflict-resolution mechanisms:* Rapid, low-cost, local arenas exist for resolving conflicts among participants, or with officials. *Graduated sanctions:* Sanctions for rule violations start very low but become stronger if a user repeatedly violates a rule.
III: Rules governing monitoring	
Information rules—assign the obligation/permission or prohibition to communicate to participants in positions . . . and the language/form in which the communication will take place	*Monitoring:* Monitors who actively audit participant behavior are at least partially accountable to the participants and/or are the participants themselves.
IV: Rules governing delegation of decision authority	
• Operational rules • Collective choice rules • Constitutional rules	*Minimal recognition of rights:* The rights of participants to set rules (or participate in rulemaking) are recognized by the government. *Nested initiatives:* Governance activities are organized in multiple nested layers, with a clearly defined, autonomous domain of decision making for local-level collective action

Source: Adapted from Ostrom (2005).

Taken together, the rules and principles in Table 8.1 address the core challenges of facilitating co-operation. For collective action to be effective:

- Goals need to be jointly agreed, so it needs to be clear who are the principals with "standing," hence the rules governing eligibility;
- Once goals are agreed upon, institutional arrangements are needed to assure that everyone lives up to their commitments to cooperate, that some of the (co-equal) principals do not free-ride on the efforts of others, hence the operating rules;
- Insofar as this cooperation is voluntary, the operating rules need to be perceived by participants as fair, thereby helping to nurture trust and build social capital, hence the emphasis in the good practice principles on inclusion, proportionality and incrementalism;
- In the spirit of "trust, but verify," there need to be mechanisms to assure that all participants live up to their obligations—hence the rules governing monitoring.

Ostrom concluded that "robust systems for governing common pool resources had met most of the good practice principles, and that those systems that had collapsed or were performing ineffectively were not so structured."[29] We put these principles to work in chapters 9 and 10.

Bringing in politics.   The good practice principles focus principally on the challenge of facilitating cooperation among participants to achieve joint benefits, in a way that limits the classic free rider and other moral hazard challenges. But what of the second challenge: fending off predators seeking to capture for themselves the returns from multistakeholder governance?

As we have seen, in a large fraction of low-income democracies politics is likely to be hotly contested, competitive electorally, and personalized. In these settings, development gains do not come easily; they are the result of struggles, at all levels, involving political leaders, public officials, private-sector players, and civic activists. Using the analytic lens provided by collective action, these struggles can usefully be conceived as conflicts among principals: some developmentally oriented, others more predatory.

Predation, as used here, refers specifically to actions that use channels of political support external to the specific arena of cooperation to override with impunity the formal and informal rules of the game associated with the collective effort.[30] The threat from predators can manifest at either or both of two levels:

- At the level of the multistakeholder initiative itself, predators might choose to ignore with impunity mechanisms agreed among participants for monitoring and enforcement, as not applying to them. Additionally,

- Predators might leverage their influence networks to put themselves out of reach of any formal legal frameworks to which participants might otherwise have had recourse for resolving disputes and sanctioning illegal acts.

Ostrom implicitly addresses predation in the group of good practice principles in Table 8.1 which govern the delegation of decision authority. These principles address the importance for collective action of a clearly defined autonomous zone of decision making. As she put it, "what can be done at one level will depend on the capabilities and limits of the rules at that level and at a deeper level."[31] The dilemma, though, is that in personalized-competitive settings, these higher-level arrangements are ad hoc, personalized, and discretionary. Except as an unhelpful counsel of despair, the assertion of the need for an autonomous zone does not address the complexities that follow from these political realities.

How might autonomous zones of decision making—islands of effectiveness—come about in difficult governance environments?[32] A useful point of departure is to recognize that all collective action initiatives are populated with multiple interested stakeholders. Some are directly associated with the collective endeavor; others are on the periphery. Some are protagonists of the development purpose, others are predators who seek to capture for their own private purposes what the protagonists are seeking to build.

Predators and protagonists each have their own channels of influence. "Threat" resources comprise the influence networks on which predators might draw to override with impunity rules intended to facilitate achievement of the development purposes. "Trumping" resources comprise the countervailing influence networks on which protagonists might draw to facilitate compliance with rules. These influence networks—the structure of the alliances that bind them together, and their relative weight—are, in turn, shaped by the broader political and institutional dynamics within which the collective endeavor is embedded.

Under what conditions might trumping influence networks prevail over the threat from predators? Three broad conditions seem to be key for multistakeholder engagement to be effective, namely that[33]:

- There are stakeholders with strong incentives to have the collective effort succeed. The stakeholders could be direct participants in the collective effort, or they could be "outsiders." Their incentives could be based on their own self-interest, insofar as they directly benefit from the fruit of the collective effort. They could also derive from the self-defined mission of an active civil society organization; *and*

- These stakeholders are well-connected politically, with influential ruling factions; and/or the external stakeholders are able to draw on widely held social norms of justice and fairness; *and*
- Leaders are skillful in mobilizing and coordinating the stakeholders in support of the collective purpose; these leaders could come from within the collective endeavor, or could be external stakeholders who are skillful in mobilizing to bring to bear pressure for good performance.

Where all three conditions are met, protagonists of a development initiative potentially can triumph over predators; but in the absence of any of the three, efforts at collective action are hypothesized to fail.

Especially in personalized-competitive settings, these threat-trumping dynamics potentially are ubiquitous. They potentially can play out at the service provision frontline—the "short route" of accountability in the approach laid out in the 2004 WDR. Additionally, as noted earlier, they also potentially can play out in the vast spaces in the middle; the many layers between top-levels of policymaking and the service provision frontline where rule-setting processes are likely to be contested, trade-offs between competing goals likely to be left unresolved, and agreements reached likely to be subject to weaknesses in both monitoring and sanctions.

Figure 8.2 expands the 2004 "accountability triangle" in Figure 8.1 in four ways to illustrate how this might work:

- First (in "A"), it highlights that the institutional arrangements which prevail for public service provision can vary from one country setting to another, depending on the prevailing "political settlement";
- Second (in B1–B3), it unbundles the accountability triangle's "compact" in a way which highlights the hierarchical arrangements within public bureaucracies—and thus the possibility that contestation over goals and performance can play out at multiple levels (not only at the senior-most interface between politicians and policymakers);
- Third (in C1–C4), it signals that external stakeholders potentially can work to influence policy at multiple levels—as voters (in "C1"); by engaging directly with senior or mid-level government officials to try and influence decisions (in C2 and C3); or as clients (in C4), using public services and seeking better performance.
- Fourth (in D1–D3), it underscores the possibility that public officials themselves might have some discretion which they potentially could use to further either their private interests, or in pursuit of public ends—and, indeed, might manage interactions among diverse stakeholders in ways that enhance that discretion.

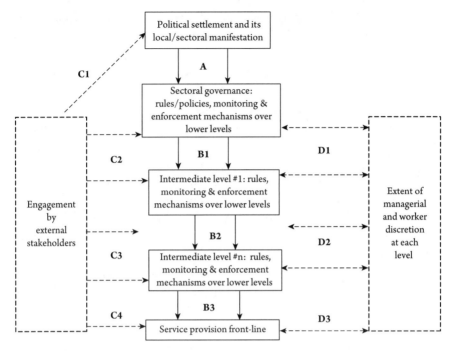

Figure 8.2 **Multiple Levels of Contestation.** Source: Levy and Walton (2013).

Whether each of the "middle spaces" toward which Figure 8.2 points result in capture or achievement of a specific development intent is not fore-ordained. Chapters 9 and 10 draw on a variety of disparate examples to explore the ways in which the outcome might depend on how the three conditions play out in practice, on the quality of leadership, and the balance between threat and trumping influence networks.

Expanding the Toolkit of Public-Sector Reform

There is a story one often hears about global development policy experts. It is apocryphal, but it contains an uncomfortable element of truth. It explains how they manage to fly from country to country, and always have ready, as they land at the country's international airport, a draft of the report that they are expected to spend the next two weeks writing. The secret, it is said, lies in their facility with the "find-and-replace" tool on computer word process-ing programs. Nothing much changes in their advice other than the name of the country.

In my experience, most development practitioners are much more committed, both personally and professionally, to their mission than this story implies. But the story is an example of where "best practice" approaches to policymaking, taken to the limit, might lead—and many technically specialized development practitioners are indeed purveyors of best practice thinking. This tendency to focus on, and endlessly refine, the "best practices" package has been exacerbated by the incentives and corporate cultures of the World Bank and other development agencies and experts: each has a large stake in building a mystique around the special value added of globally useful technical expertise.

By contrast, a central goal of this book is to provide a conceptual platform for a "good fit" approach to development policymaking that stakes out the middle ground between "one-size-fits-all" best practices on the one hand, and "every country is unique" on the other. The country typology laid out in Parts I and II of the book addresses part of that challenge. It highlighted some key characteristics that are shared in common among some sub-groups of countries but not others—and used the contrasts to facilitate more effective comparison of "like with like," and thereby be more targeted and effective in identifying feasible options for moving forward.

But if the advice itself remains the same, regardless of circumstances, distinguishing systematically among different groups of countries does not contribute much to a "good fit" approach to development policymaking. Thus a principal goal of this chapter has been to broaden the menu of options for public-sector reform. The intent is not to prescribe some mechanical formula, but rather an initial orienting framework to clarify which among an array of alternative options is potentially most relevant in a specific country settings, as a platform for further learning (what Matt Andrews calls problem-driven iterative adaptation, on which more in Part IV[34]).

Table 8.2 brings together public-sector reform options and country characteristics. As per the table, one set of options is to focus on comprehensive reforms that seek to build a high-performing core of government along Weberian (or NPM) principles, and cascade reform downward throughout the operating units of the public hierarchy. Other approaches proceed more incrementally, via

- Targeted efforts to improve public management, focused on specific functions, sectors, public agencies and locales where there exist credible champions and an appetite for reform;
- Multistakeholder initiatives that bring to center stage the participatory engagement of nongovernmental as well as governmental stakeholders in the (microlevel) processes of formulating the relevant rules and policies, and assuring their implementation.

Table 8.2 **A "Good Fit" Approach to Public-Sector Reform**

Country Types	Approach to Public-Sector Reform		
	Comprehensive public management reform	Incremental public management improvements	Multistakeholder governance
Sustainable democracy	Good performance if consensus on agenda across political parties	Good performance if political mandate for targeted reform	Could add value if it helps resolve principal–agent problems
Personalized competitive	Poor performance • multiple principals with lack of clarity on goals • high risk of capture by managers/staff	Some potential, if combined with multistakeholder engagement	Good potential if developmental influence networks stronger than predators
Dominant, developmental	Good performance if sustained leadership commitment to agenda	Good performance if political mandate for targeted reform	Could add value if it helps resolve principal–agent problems
Dominant patrimonial	Poor performance insofar as it reduces opportunities for public employment patronage		
Dominant, predatory	Capture by predatory principal		Unlikely to be effective as countervailing power to predator

Source: Adapted from Levy and Walton (2013).

The "public management lite" and multistakeholder approaches share one key feature that so far in the discussion has only been implicit: each depends for its efficacy on public (or civic) entrepreneurship. The presence of leadership capable of skillfully mobilizing and coordinating stakeholders was identified above as a necessary condition for multistakeholder engagement to be effective. And the example in chapter 6 of the Progressive Era in the

United States highlighted the central role of public entrepreneurs with the commitment, skill, and staying power to build both the internal capabilities and external alliances needed for islands of effectiveness to take root within a broadly dysfunctional public sector. In the final chapter of the book, I will have more to say about the entrepreneurial dimensions of governance reform.

As Table 8.2 signals, comprehensive approaches can work in settings where formal institutions (or leadership) and a commitment to achieving development results are strong. In these settings, multistakeholder engagement can be a useful tool to help principals monitor their agents more effectively (the Ethiopian authorities' embrace of bottom-up monitoring mechanisms, described in chapter 4, is a good example).

In more patronage-oriented settings, there is little prospect of comprehensive reforms gaining traction, both because the reforms reduce opportunities for discretion in hiring decisions, and (in the more competitive settings) because of a lack of consistent leadership with a longer-term orientation. In these settings, multistakeholder engagement takes on heightened relevance, as a complement to targeted initiatives to improve public-sector capacity incrementally and, in more politically fragmented settings, as the basis for building and sustaining islands of effectiveness even in the absence of a supportive public sector.

The contours of the "supply-side" agenda of public-sector reform and capacity building (in both their comprehensive and incremental variants) are well-known, and will not be elaborated further in this book.[35] Debate continues, but largely on the margin. However, there is less consensus as to the opportunities and limits of multistakeholder approaches. So it is to these that we turn in the next two chapters.

CHAPTER 9

Transparency and Participation— Getting the Fit Right

In 2003, in an audacious effort to combat corruption, the government of Brazilian president Luiz (Lula) da Silva invited the media and civil society organizations to witness a lottery.[1] The "lucky" winners were selected randomly from the full set of Brazil's 4,500 municipalities with fewer than 450,000 inhabitants. The "prize" was an intensive review of public spending practices by a team of ten to fifteen public auditors—with the results of the audit posted on the Internet and made available to the media. The process was repeated monthly; by mid-2005, 669 municipalities had been audited.

Were the audits, as some critics doubtless claimed, simply a form of political theater, telling voters nothing they did not already know? By happenstance, in June 2004—at which point about half of the 669 audits had been conducted—Brazil held municipal elections. This created an almost ideal natural experiment.

For each municipality, the auditors reported on the irregularities they uncovered—frauds in procurement, the use of fake receipts or "phantom" firms, overinvoicing the value of services provided. The impact of these reports on election results was large. On average, incumbent mayors had a 41 percent chance of being reelected—and among those municipalities audited after the election, there was no systematic relationship between the number of violations (subsequently) found and the probability of reelection. By contrast, the probability of reelection rose to 53 percent among mayors who had been audited in advance of the election and received a clean audit— and fell to 31 percent for the mayors of municipalities where audits uncovered two irregularities and only 20 percent where three or more violations were detected. Evidently, the completed audits provided voters with new information that affected their behavior.

The Brazilian municipal audits are just one example of what has become a tidal wave of informational and participatory initiatives aimed at improving governance. It would be nice to be able to report that these "bottom-up" initiatives have achieved universally positive results and have been universally applauded by protagonists of development. But neither is true. The array of initiatives has been bewilderingly broad and the advocacy and criticism correspondingly cacophonous. A vast new "he said," "no, she said" literature has arisen. Advocates and critics selectively report on the initiatives that support their conclusions, pay less attention to less favorable empirical results, and repeatedly restate their prior convictions. A dialogue of the deaf seemingly continues, barely affected by research findings.

Transmission Mechanisms for Transparency and Participation

One useful way to surface the controversies is to distinguish among different types of transparency and participation initiatives—or, more precisely, among different transmission mechanisms through which these initiatives might support service provision. Three distinct mechanisms are evident.

In the first mechanism, transparency and participation work "upstream" to enable citizens to better hold politicians accountable for delivery on their promises. This is the mechanism characterized in the 2004 World Development Report as the "voice" channel of the long route of accountability—and the Brazilian municipal audits offer a vivid example of the mechanism in action. For this mechanism to improve service provision, all of the long-route requisites highlighted in chapter 8 need to be in place: For example, in order for the publication of audit results to affect the quality of service provision in Brazil's municipalities, mayors need to be directly elected; their ability to garner votes (and their nomination as candidates) needs to be influenced by their performance in office; once in office they need to have the incentive and the tools to affect how the municipal bureaucracy performs.

The second mechanism, by contrast, does not presuppose relatively strong-background state institutions. In this mechanism, the goal is for transparency and participation to support public provision more directly, working from the bottom up. The aim is not to strengthen the chain of accountability as a whole but rather to achieve specific localized gains, perhaps within specific sectors, perhaps in specific departments or locales within a sector, perhaps in specific agencies, perhaps even (as per the logic of the "short route") in specific frontline units. As per the discussion of multistakeholder governance in chapter 8, this transmission channel works not via the influence of "voice" on politicians but more directly—by strengthening the influence networks of developmentally oriented actors, thereby enhancing their ability to prevail in local-level "threat-trumping" conflicts. It can be thought of as a complement to pure public-service provision.

The third mechanism goes even further than the second in its distance from long-route approaches to strengthening "voice"—and, potentially, in the opportunities it offers for bottom-up approaches to support development even in difficult circumstances. This mechanism bypasses the public sector entirely and embraces parallel, participatory arrangements for service provision (and potentially for financing as well). Advocates of this approach suggest that such initiatives potentially offer two sets of benefits: They can achieve important short- and medium-term gains in service provision in otherwise unpropitious settings; additionally, from a longer-term perspective, they can help build institutions from the bottom up by strengthening a culture of citizenship.

With these three mechanisms as a backdrop, consider the following conclusions from recent reviews of transparency and participatory initiatives. The first is taken from a flagship World Bank-sponsored 2013 research review of experience with participatory initiatives:

> *Local oversight is most effective when higher-level institutions of account-ability function well and communities have the capacity to effectively monitor service providers and others in charge of public resources. Thus, induced participatory development appears to increase, rather than di-minish, the need for functional and strong institutions at the center. . . . Reforms that enhance judicial oversight, allow for independent audit agencies, and protect and promote the right to information and a free media appear to be necessary for effective local participation.*[2]

Then there is this conclusion, from a 2011 review by eminent scholar-practitioners:

> *Civil society action can help to the degree that it can fix failures in political incentives for development policies; or in cases when the political leader-ship has incentives to use civil society input to address failures.*[3]

Finally, there is this carefully qualified conclusion from an eminent scholar and advocate of democratic decentralization. While published a few years earlier than the others, it reflects a continuing view among champions of democratic local government:

> The proliferation of user committees, most of which are single-purpose bodies, has (it appears) often had a damaging impact on elected multi-purpose bodies. . . . User committees often produce confusion and dislocation. . . . there is confusion about overlapping jurisdictions . . . much more damage is done when user committees usurp roles and function that had previously been assigned to elected multi-purpose councils. On occasion (it is not clear how often) they also deprive them of revenues.[4]

While each conclusion focuses on different aspects of transparency and participation, they share a common feature. They suggest that for bottom-up initiatives to add value, they need to support (or be supported by) the broader framework of formal institutions. Put differently, they embrace the first transmission mechanism highlighted above and are more skeptical as to the value added of the second and third mechanisms.

In contrast to these conclusions, a central theme of this book is that there is no one right way to address institutional weaknesses; depending on the context, a variety of very different options each potentially can add value to development. Building on that theme, this chapter explores the possibility that in some settings where formal institutions are weak, transparency and participation can offer an alternative way of addressing governance weaknesses at the micro level via the second and third transmission mechanisms. At least on the surface, transparency and participatory approaches might seem to have particular promise in personalized-competitive democracies, which often offer an environment of openness but without formal institutional buttresses—and, for reasons discussed in chapter 8, with little prospect of strengthening formal institutions even over the medium term. In these settings, the second and third transmission mechanisms offer the hope that progress need not only be dependent on what happens at the apex of power but can be made through many small victories, one island of effectiveness at a time.

The remainder of this chapter explores whether this hopeful perspective is supported by the empirical evidence. The next section uses examples of bottom-up efforts to strengthen the public provision of basic education to explore empirically the potential and limits of the second mechanism. The subsequent section uses the example of community-driven development (CDD) to explore whether, even in difficult institutional environments, the third mechanism might nonetheless sometimes be able to achieve some short-term gains in service provision and, over the longer term, help nurture a culture of citizenship. As we shall see, the evidence is incomplete, but—at least for some settings—encouraging.

Bottom-Up Supports for Public Provision—The Case of Education

The idea that transparency and participatory bottom-up initiatives can add value even in the absence of more broadly effective arrangements for accountability has been part of the development discourse for almost two decades. A celebrated early initiative reported remarkable improvements in the provision of urban services in Bangalore, India, in response to a series of service delivery scorecard surveys conducted between 1994 and 2003.[5] In the health sector, a rigorous, peer-reviewed study found that an informational initiative yielded, within eighteen months, a 33-percent decline in the under-five mortality rate in a subset of Ugandan villages; numerous other studies also report strong improvements in health as a result of bottom-up initiatives.[6] Service delivery scorecards and right to information legislation, participatory budgeting and expenditure tracking, participatory implementation and third-party oversight—these, and many others, have become staples of the design of development implementation.

As noted above, the notion that involving recipients of public services could lead straightforwardly to improvements in public service is a hopeful one. It suggests that there is a way forward even in settings where bureaucracies and politics don't work well. Even better, it suggests that the mechanism works by activating citizenship, by involving ordinary people in shaping their futures, giving them a sense of control over their lives and communities, nurturing a sense of both efficacy and of mutual obligation. But is this hopeful vision credible—at least in some places and at least some of the time?

Consider the following (quite typical) circumstance of a basic education system in a country with weak governance. After years of pressure, effort, and donor support, near-universal primary-school enrollment has been achieved. But quality is abysmal; teachers often are underqualified, and teacher absenteeism is rife. Teaching jobs are prized politically as building blocks for networks of patronage and political support. The combination of weak, clientelistic governance and politically connected teachers also often makes teachers unions unusually powerful.

Getting systemic reforms in such settings requires political engagement at multiple levels; the opportunities and constraints to education reform have been analyzed comprehensively in influential studies by Merilee Grindle, Robert Kaufman, and Joan Nelson.[7] For reasons that should by now be clear, only in a subset of countries is there likely to be the political space, authority, and motivation to proceed with far-reaching reforms of a country's educational policies. In other settings, might focusing more narrowly on using tools of transparency and participation to open up space for engagement by parents and communities, working on behalf of their children, offer a way forward? This could be done by creating new participatory structures (or leveraging existing ones) for involving parents and communities in school affairs—or simply by putting into the public domain information on key aspects of school performance. If microlevel institutional innovations along these lines were put in place, could they indeed transform school performance—even in the more difficult governance settings where there is limited scope for systemic reforms?

The central idea is that, as explored in chapter 8, in ambiguous governance environments there may be space between the "long route" and the "short route" where educational outcomes potentially can be shaped by contestation at the local level. Hierarchical governance may fall well short of good, but it may be better than disastrous. Throughout the system, there could be public actors—school principals, district officials—eager to improve performance but hemmed in by political obstacles. In such settings, bottom-up transparency and participatory initiatives could provide entry points for improving school performance at multiple levels by helping to buttress the developmentally oriented actors in threat-trumping struggles. Schools could succeed insofar as they are supported by developmentally oriented influence networks capable of fending off predatory pressures to abuse school resources for private and political purposes; district officials could similarly leverage influence networks to win support for improving the schools they oversee. The volume of careful, empirical research on transparency and participatory initiatives to improve education has been growing rapidly. What can one learn from that research as to the viability of bottom-up approaches to education sector reform?

Some empirical findings.   At first sight, the evidence is encouraging that initiatives that work via the second transmission mechanism indeed can enhance school performance. Table 9.1 reports the results of some careful impact evaluations of three distinct types of bottom-up initiatives:

- Public expenditure tracking studies (PETS), which monitor and report on whether public monies indeed find their way to their intended purpose. The Uganda education PETS is the pioneering example.
- School performance scorecards. (School performance can straightforwardly be measured using robust, comparable tests of literacy and numeracy.) In addition to the Pakistan example in Table 9.1, other settings in which public dissemination of school performance scorecards have been used as a governance tool include the state of Parana in Brazil; multiple countries in Central America; and Uganda, Nigeria, and Namibia in Africa.[8]

- Participatory governance of schools by committees that include parents and other community members. Along with the El Salvador, Kenya, and Indian examples in Table 9.1, there are many additional examples world-wide of such initiatives.

Table 9.1 **Five Bottom-Up Basic Education Initiatives**

	Context and Intervention	*Impact*
Uganda public expenditure tracking	An expenditure tracking survey found that only 20% of funds allocated for nonwage school spending actually reached schools. In response, the Ministry of Finance made direct transfers to schools—with information on transferred amounts posted at public facilities and in local media	Share of grants actually reaching schools rose from 20% to 90%; largest impact was in locales with strongest local media coverage
Pakistan rural	A randomized control trial in which parents in "treatment" schools receive report cards with information on their child's performance, performance of their child's school relative to others, and of all schools in their village relative to others	Two years after intervention, schools in treatment communities were more likely to have textbooks; test scores were higher; time spent in classroom rose
El Salvador EDUCO	Creation of community-elected school-level committees to take responsibility for school governance, including monitoring of funds transferred directly to schools, and for hiring, firing, and monitoring of teachers	Student enrollments in EDUCO schools went from 8,500 students in 1991 to more than 320,000 a decade later. The probability of a student continuing school was 64% higher in EDUCO schools; teacher effort was higher and absenteeism lower

continued

Table 9.1 **(continued)**

	Context and Intervention	*Impact*
Kenya extra teacher program	A randomized control trial in which two treatment groups each received funding to hire an extra contract teacher from the local area as a supplement to the cadre of government-employed, "civil service" teachers. In one of the two treatments, a school committee was mandated to monitor the performance of the contract teacher and to decide whether to renew the contract—and was provided with training as to how to do these tasks	The extra teacher improved student performance. In schools without the additional school committee mandate, attendance of civil service teachers fell by 21 percent. In schools with empowered school committees, incumbent teachers were 8 percent more likely to be found teaching in class during random spot checks than before the intervention
India village education committees	Four randomized control trials that provided information and training on the roles of village education committees. Prior to the initiative, the committees had formal mandates but were nonfunctional; learning achievement was poor	Mixed results. No meaningful gains in literacy and numeracy in one treatment group; more positive results in the others—but the benefits of the intervention were distributed unevenly

Sources: Many individual research studies, synthesized in Barbara Bruns, Deon Filmer, and Harry Patrinos, *Making Schools Work: New Evidence on Accountability Reforms* (Washington, DC: World Bank, 2011).[9]

The results reported in Table 9.1 affirm that transparency and participatory interventions can indeed—under the right circumstances—add very substantial value. As a result of the Ugandan PETS initiative, the share of allocated resources going to schools rose rapidly; the Pakistani, El Salvadoran, and Kenyan initiatives resulted in substantial declines in teacher absenteeism and in student performance on test scores; El Salvador's EDUCO program sharply reduced drop-out rates. But there are some important gaps to be considered before these results can be embraced as strong evidence affirming the value of bottom-up initiatives.

First, in advocating for bottom-up initiatives, we would want to know something about the likelihood of their effectiveness—but the results offer no indication on this score. (I selected the studies reported in Table 9.1 to illustrate the possibilities, not to be "representative," which, given that the available research comprises a small number of case-specific impact evaluations, is an unachievable goal.) A priori, whether the result of a particular intervention is positive depends partly on the intervention itself and partly on the relative strength of developmentally oriented and predatory influence networks in the relevant locales. In some countries, predation will surely dominate, and bottom-up initiatives will not work. But even in countries where bottom-up initiatives are worth trying, the expectation is not that they work everywhere—but rather that they sometimes work and that something systematic can be said as to the circumstances under which different types of initiatives might work and why. (I included the results from India as a reminder that in any given setting the returns from bottom-up initiatives are uncertain.)

More fundamentally, to advocate for bottom-up approaches—and to better design and target these approaches to enhance their effectiveness—we need to understand better the transmission mechanisms through which they are effective. At what point in the vertical chain that links politicians, policymakers, and frontline providers did the successful transparency and participatory initiatives reported in Table 9.1 have their impact? At the service provision front-line, as per the logic of the "short route"? By affecting the incentives and behaviors of politicians and policymakers, as per the long route? Or by influencing the many in-between spaces that link top-down policymaking and the service provision frontline—district government offices, politically influential local actors, and the like? To put the question differently, are the successes in Table 9.1 a result of the second transmission mechanism for transparency and participation in action or a disguised variant of the first mechanism? Again, the results fall short of providing a clear answer.

Consider the Ugandan PETS and El Salvador's EDUCO program—both of which achieved impact on a large scale. At first glance, their performance gains indeed came via the short route. In both, the locus of interaction of service users was with frontline providers, not via "voice" interactions with politicians nor by changing the hierarchical relationships between policymakers and providers. However, a closer look suggests that the interventions were associated with complex (but underanalyzed) changes in the interactions among service users, service providers, and higher-level political and bureaucratic actors:

• Uganda's PETS was reinforced by complementary commitments from Uganda's central government to improve education-sector performance—part of a broader political commitment by the country's president, initiated in 1996, to provide free education for all. In other countries where the top-down commitment was weaker, public expenditure tracking initiatives were not as successful.[10]

- Similarly, EDUCO's success did not take place in a political vacuum. The initiative was begun in the aftermath of a decade-long civil war. But the country was deeply polarized, with the rural-based Farabundo Marti National Liberation Front putting down its arms without a decisive military outcome, and with continuing deep distrust in the countryside of both the military and the urban-capital-based civilian government apparatus. There was an urgent need to demonstrate that government could respond to broader social concerns—but without imposing its will in its usual top-down ways.

Now consider the Pakistani and Kenyan examples. Again, at first glance their very strong results seemingly signal straightforwardly that bottom-up approaches can be effective. Both were explicitly targeted at local levels, with no engagement from the center. But, again, it is not that simple. Both are randomized control trials. Randomized control trials comprise experiments managed by expert teams, with very specific (evaluation-driven) objectives to implement the "treatment" as systematically as possible. The team inevitably itself becomes part of the external environment: By parachuting in an external, artificial transmission mechanism, it short-circuits the political dynamics that otherwise would surround reform. There is no way of knowing who, absent the experiment, would take the lead in fostering the initiative, whether they would exhibit the same diligence in their follow-through—and whether they would have the authority to act.

In sum, while there are some empirical grounds for encouragement as to the potential for bottom-up approaches to improve school performance in difficult environments, the findings remain ambiguous. Research has been preoccupied with measuring impact, with an implicit presumption that what matters are the specific ingredients of a treatment's design rather than its interaction with the broader environment. Consequently, vast knowledge gaps remain as to what are the transmission mechanisms through which bottom-up interventions work, how threat-trumping dynamics play out in practice, to what extent (and how) new initiatives can be injected into the mix, and how any new initiatives might affect the threat-trumping dynamics. Framing the current state of knowledge from a "glass half-full" perspective, the gaps point to an exciting and practical frontier research agenda, one that would best be carried out in a multidisciplinary way—with much more collaboration between educationalists, economists, and other social scientists than has so far been the case.

Policy possibilities.   Insofar as transparency and participatory initiatives indeed have the potential to achieve significant gains in learning outcomes, how might they be pursued? At one end of the spectrum, prevailing educational policies and vested interests might be so constraining that only systemic political reforms, reaching beyond the education sector itself, will be capable of opening up the space for bottom-up initiatives to move forward. At the other end, the formal requisites for bottom-up engagement may indeed be present; what is needed may be more direct engagement with frontline stakeholders to leverage the latent potential. In between, as per Figure 8.2 in the previous chapter, it may be possible to work with committed public officials at middle levels of the education-sector bureaucracy to open-up space to experiment with potentially promising ways forward.

Three complementary transparency and participatory entry points are especially noteworthy. The first two comprise:

- Self-standing initiatives along the lines outlined above—expenditure tracking, school performance scorecards, capacity-building support to better enable parents and communities to take on a governance role, and the like.
- Initiatives to strengthen the enabling environment for participatory governance at the school level by, for example, promulgating enabling legislation that decentralizes responsibility for education, and empowers multistakeholder school governing bodies.

Though familiar, standard practice among protagonists of bottom-up approaches, the above two entry points can be politically difficult to implement. As Merilee Grindle explores in detail for five Latin American countries, they often are perceived to be directly counter to the interests of powerful, centralized education bureaucracies within the public sector, and of union organizations (often themselves highly centralized) which represent the economic interests of teachers. Yet for all of the difficulties—and as per the title of her book—Grindle shows how, 'despite the odds,' educational reformers in Brazil, Mexico, and Bolivia were able to align with influential allies, and thereby navigate political obstacles and move forward with reforms which shifted responsibility downward toward the school level.[11]

The third entry point for strengthening transparency and participation is more directly bottom-up; it builds on whatever arrangements might already exist formally for engagement by parents and communities at the school level. It comprises:

- Initiatives to strengthen networks of support for participatory school-level engagement (school governing bodies, parent councils, and the like).

The logic of this entry point follows directly from the approach to multistakeholder engagement laid out in chapter 8. A focus on network strengthening could help build the capacities of school governing bodies, and other mechanisms for engaging parents and communities. Additionally, and perhaps more importantly, it could also help link governing bodies and parent organizations in more politically vulnerable (likely poorer and more rural) communities with influential allies—thereby potentially reshaping local threat-trumping games in favor of more developmentally oriented outcomes. As with the other entry points, it offers a "wholesale" way of working from the bottom up—via an intervention that potentially can reshape threat-trumping dynamics across multiple locales.

As the above discussion signals, especially in difficult environments where there are high levels of discretion and personalized decision-making, technocratic interventions will yield results only if they are aligned with the incentives of the principal actors. Coming to grips with these incentives will require a new wave of learning—one that goes beyond the more narrowly technocratic focus of most recent research on basic education and explores more directly the political and institutional channels through which specific interventions can be promulgated and implemented, and then (perhaps) alter school-level behavior.

Parallel Initiatives—Community-Driven Development

Now let us turn to an example of the third transmission mechanism introduced at the outset of this chapter—CDD. In no area has the enthusiasm among donors for bottom-up initiatives gone as far—and induced as much vociferous counterreaction—as in CDD. From small beginnings in the early 1990s, as of 2011 the World Bank had approximately 400 active CDD projects, valued at almost $30 billion, on its books. For advocates of bottom-up development, this is a remarkable triumph. For champions of long-route approaches to institutional development, the mushrooming of CDD warrants a special place in hell.

Here, drawing loosely on the example of Indonesia's Kecamatan Development Program (KDP), is how a typical CDD project works[12]:

- Bloc grants are transferred from a central unit (which could be a line agency within government or a self-standing project implementation unit, supported by donors) to multistakeholder local committees, which represent a group of villages.
- External facilitators work directly with villages to identify, via a participatory process, priority local needs—generally but not always focusing on local infrastructure investments.
- These multistakeholder committees then decide which of the village submissions to fund. The deliberations of the committees are held in public and the outcomes made public.
- Implementation and procurement is undertaken by an elected village-level team; disbursement to the team is in tranches; in order to access each additional tranche, the implementation team is required to report to an open village meeting on how funds received to that point had been used.

CDD projects are thus organized around "islands of effectiveness," which bypass the public sector entirely and embrace parallel, participatory arrangements for service provision. Decisions as to which investments deserve priority are made at local levels by communities, not from the top down. The task of overseeing how resources are used, including being vigilant against corruption, also involves the beneficiary communities, leveraging their incentives to achieve the collective result. Interestingly, for all that standard public-sector institutions are bypassed, some CDD features are beginning to be incorporated into nationally financed and implemented poverty alleviation programs: India's Mahatma Gandhi Employment Guarantee Scheme and South Africa's Community Works Programme comprise two examples.

CDD thus illustrates powerfully the multistakeholder, principal-to-principal approach to service provision that was highlighted in chapter 8 as an alternative to the long route. Its mushrooming provides a perfect arena for exploring empirically some of the fundamental questions and concerns raised by this multistakeholder alternative: How well does it deliver local services? How does it interact in practice with local social dynamics? What are its implications for longer-run institutional strengthening? Each is considered in turn.

CDD as a channel for service provision.   There is an underlying issue that runs through the assessment of CDD and needs to be noted up front. What is the appropriate counterfactual against which it should be assessed? As per the quotes at the beginning of this chapter, many critics of CDD presume that the alternative to its enclave approach is a better-performing public sector. In practice, many (though not all) CDD projects have been implemented in situations of crisis, where top-down public administrations have either been missing or have stopped functioning.

Two of the earliest projects were initiated in Latin America in the immediate aftermath of economic crisis (in Bolivia in 1987 and Peru in 1991). Afghanistan's National Solidarity Program and Nepal's Poverty Alleviation Fund both were begun in the immediate aftermath of war. A series of projects were begun in Indonesia during the political turmoil of the end of the Soeharto dictatorship and the emergence of democracy in the late 1990s. The Indonesian projects are far and away the largest and most extensively studied CDD initiatives in the world; research on the KDP in particular offers a rich set of insights on which we draw extensively in the discussion that follows (with due caution not to read too much into findings from a single initiative, undertaken in a distinctive setting).

Given these difficult contexts, the gains in service provision that came from CDD initiatives, as reported in a comprehensive review of the performance of seventeen of these initiatives (including the ones above) for which robust impact evaluations had been undertaken, were remarkably positive[13]: Seven of nine projects for which information was available achieved statistically significant positive impacts on household living standards and welfare. Many more provided gains in access to and use of education, health, water, and roads. For example:

- In Afghanistan, there was a 20-percent increase in the use of protected water sources in villages supported by that country' $120 million CDD National Solidarity Program.
- Interventions supported by Nepal's $110 million CDD Poverty Alleviation Fund led to a 14-percent increase in participation in school among children ages six to fourteen.
- The Philippines $182 million KALAHI-CIDSS CDD program resulted in a 6-percent increase in the proportion of households whose homes were accessible year round by roads and a significant increase in the proportion of households visiting a health facility when ill.

In at least six countries (Bolivia, Honduras, Indonesia, Nepal, Nicaragua, and the Philippines), the unit costs of providing small-scale, public infrastructural facilities were 13 to 40 percent below the equivalent cost of service provision by government.

For a more in-depth sense of the benefits, consider the KDP. By 2008, a decade after start-up, it had projects underway in over 34,000 villages, about half of Indonesia's total. By that time, it had built or rehabilitated 40,000 kilometers of roads; 11,000 irrigation systems; 10,500 clean water supply units; 3,800 health posts; 6,700 schools 6,500 bridges; and 2,900 sanitation units. A 2005 impact evaluation reported internal rates of return to KDP investments of 39 to 68 percent. A 2008 evaluation found that controlling for other variables household consumption in KDP villages was an average of 9 percent higher than in a control group. Government subsequently adopted the KDP as its own flagship National Program of Community Empowerment. By 2011, the cumulative budget that had passed through the program was in excess of $3 billion.[14]

To be sure, not all CDD initiatives are as successful in providing services as the ones highlighted above. Some are ill-designed and hastily prepared; others are introduced in environments with too much instability or (as discussed further below) too much local dysfunction to be effective, regardless of the quality of design and implementation efforts. Even so, the results reported here surely offer at least some intriguing sense of possibility in settings where more conventional approaches to the provision of public services will not work.

Local-level dynamics and the challenge of capture. How do local power dynamics affect CDD initiatives? Again, as with so much of the discourse of CDD, stereotypes dominate—be they the romantic stereotypes of harmonious, egalitarian, and democratic local village cultures or dark stereotypes of predatory elites who capture for themselves resources intended for the poor. Evidence as to who in practice are the beneficiaries of CDD initiatives can help us get a more empirically grounded view.

Specifically, are the benefits of CDD captured disproportionately by elites? A large number of studies, from over a dozen countries, address this question.[15] In this work, the dilemma of the counterfactual again looms large: captured, relative to what benchmark? One option is to use a benchmark of perfection. This is the approach taken by many of the studies summarized here—they assess capture relative to perfect targeting of the poorest and most marginalized groups.

However, viewed through the lens of the threat-trumping perspective laid out in chapter 8, perfect targeting is not the appropriate benchmark. From a threat-trumping perspective, in order for a participatory initiative to be effective, it needs to be embedded within a coalition that is sufficiently robust to fend off predators. This almost certainly will require low-income beneficiaries to be aligned with powerful allies. Sometimes these allies may be found among nongovernmental organizations or government officials genuinely committed to pro-poor policies. But often influential allies will only come on board if they are able to reap some benefits for themselves. Whether the share of benefits "captured" by elites is so large that one might describe the initiative as a failure thus involves a combination of evidence and of judgment.

Unsurprisingly, almost all of the CDD programs for which results on the distribution of benefits are reported fall short of perfect targeting. But almost all also turn out to be pro-poor in the distribution of their benefits.

Studies from Bolivia, Burkina Faso, Indonesia, Jamaica, Pakistan, and Senegal all find that local-level deliberations are dominated disproportionately by wealthier and better-educated residents. But for the most part, this has not prevented a general progressive distribution of benefits. In Indonesia's Urban Poverty Project, the poor actually did better in community boards that were dominated by elite groups than those that were more egalitarian in their composition. In Jamaica where funding decisions seemed to reflect more the preferences of elites than the majority, overall satisfaction with CDD projects remained high.

Even the more critical findings signal that capture is constrained. A review of who benefited from village infrastructure projects in Pakistan found that the distribution of benefits was similar to what was achieved in a comparator government project. India's Mahatma Gandhi Employment Guarantee Scheme was successful in providing low-wage jobs to the poor—even though the more unequal a village, the less likely its most marginalized were to participate in the scheme. And in Senegal, though village chiefs and membership of the ruling political party disproportionately influenced which villages received CDD resources, overall the poor were the biggest beneficiaries of the program.

In sum, the reported results offer cause for optimism that in very many settings, even if those most active in CDD-style participatory processes are disproportionately better off, developmentally oriented influence networks can hold their own against predators. Even taking the risks of capture into account, it seems that sometimes CDD indeed can provide a practical means of providing resources in ways that can help alleviate poverty—even in the most difficult governance environments.

Broader effects on institutional development.   A final common critique of CDD initiatives is that, even if they indeed can successfully support the provision of services to a broad range of citizens, they bypass and undercut state institutions and thus have negative long-run consequences for development. As a counterpoint to that view, consider the following description of Indonesia's KDP initiative:

> *The program is in many ways a democratization initiative masquerading as an anti-poverty project. It aims to deliver small-scale infrastructure to marginalized communities, but the mechanisms it uses are aimed at empowering communities, socially and politically as well as economically.*[16]

Viewed from this latter perspective, CDD has the potential to help nurture a culture of citizenship and civic engagement and thereby over the longer term help build democratic state institutions, both at local levels and more broadly. Two sets of evidence potentially can clarify which of these competing views is closer to the truth.

A first set of evidence explores whether involvement in CDD initiatives leads to a broader willingness to engage in participatory democratic processes. Three robust impact evaluations found evidence of positive spillovers:

- Afghanistan's National Solidarity Program stimulated participation in local governance by increasing both the frequency of village assembly meetings and attendance at the meetings.
- A community reconstruction project in northern Liberia resulted, according to survey results, in a reduction in social tension, an increase in trust in local leadership, and an increase in participation by marginalized groups in community decision-making activities.
- A final evaluation of the Philippines KALAHI-CIDSS program (measured after seven years of project interventions) found a 12-percent increase in the proportion of respondents indicating that most people in their village can be trusted—and a smaller, but still positive, impact on trust in local and national officials.

By contrast, impact evaluations in Nepal and Sierra Leone found no evidence of positive spillovers from CDD to local democratic participation more broadly.[17] (By now, the reader should expect this type of variation, insofar as the impact of CDD almost certainly depends on country- and local-level political dynamics).

A richer story emerges from in-depth quasi-anthropological research of Indonesia's KDP project, carried out in forty-one villages located in two of the country's thirty-four provinces. Interviews with key village-level informants suggested that sustained engagement with KDP processes indeed had contributed to the emergence of more participatory and peaceful political interactions at the local level, beyond the KDP itself. As Table 9.2 summarizes, a substantially higher proportion of key informants reported increases in attendance in village meetings, improvements in democratic processes, and reductions in ethnic tensions in villages where KDP was implemented than in villages where there had been little or no KDP activity, with the effect especially large in villages where KDP had been active for four years.[18]

The second set of evidence focuses on the effect of CDD on the evolution of formal institutions—specifically whether the presence of CDD hinders or accelerates the emergence of participatory and accountable local governments. Here what seems to matter most are not so much the specifics of CDD design as the broader country commitment to decentralized governance.

Table 9.2 **Interaction Between KDP and Participation in Selected Indonesian Villages**

	Non-KDP Villages (%)	*1-Year KDP Villages (%)*	*2- or 3-Year KDP Villages (%)*	*4-Year KDP Villages (%)*
More groups come to village meetings	42	62*	62*	75
Decision making is becoming more democratic	46	n/a*	n/a*	67
Interethnic relations have improved	n/a	38	50	69

Notes: KDP = Kecamatan Development Program; n/a = data not available. *= This percentage is calculated for the full set of 1–3–year KDP villages.

Source: Barron, Diprose, and Woolcock (2011), pp. 177, 189–191.

Indonesia's KDP initially was designed as a wholly parallel initiative—but in 2001, for reasons that were rooted in the country's broader political transformation and had little if anything to with the KDP, Indonesia embraced a far-reaching program of political decentralization. To align with this commitment, the second and third phases of KDP incorporated greater oversight from district parliaments, government monitoring, links with sectoral agencies such as education and health, and expanded use of matching grants from district governments. So in Indonesia CDD and decentralization turned out to be synergistic. By contrast, in Malawi and Zambia a broader commitment to decentralization was lacking, so determined efforts by CDD teams to forge links with local governments made little headway.

A final example, Peru's social fund FONCODES, illustrates powerfully how broader political dynamics shape the institutional impact of CDD.[19] FONCODES, begun in 1994, was a flagship project of the country's populist president Alberto Fujimori. FONCODES was indeed well targeted to low-income communities: 80 percent of FONCODES' over $900 million of resources (including strong support by the World Bank) went to the poorest 40 percent of municipalities. However, notwithstanding this effective targeting, it also increasingly became apparent that FONCODES was being used as a source of patronage and popularity. Disbursements increased in the months directly preceding elections, and while poorer areas were more likely to get funding, those poorer areas that were "swing voters" were favored in resource allocation.

When the Fujimori government fell, the expectation was that, given FONCODES' close identification with Fujimori, the program would be shut down. But its skills turned out to be too valuable to lose. The governments that came after Fujimori did not close FONCODES but restructured it to become a mechanism to support a program of political and fiscal decentralization—a program that leveraged the bottom-up capabilities built by FONCODES in its earlier incarnation. By the end of 2005, about one-fifth of Peru's district governments had been accredited to manage FONCODES transfers; conditions for accreditation included the formulation of participatory municipal development plans and fulfillment of fiscal transparency regulations.

Institutional Incrementalism as a Process of Search

The goal of this chapter has been to explore whether transparency and participatory initiatives can help improve public service provision even in settings where the long route does not work well and where political economy realities are such that it is unlikely to improve. The focus has been on arrangements that leverage multistakeholder governance to strengthen service provision—perhaps (as in the example of basic education) via complementary forms of engagement that compensate for public-sector weaknesses, perhaps (as in CDD) by supporting islands of effectiveness that worked around absent or dysfunctional public organizations.

The evidence is incomplete but encouraging. Initiatives to improve basic education via the intensive use of transparency and participation sometimes can indeed achieve strikingly large gains—though the results vary across settings and the available research offers at best limited insight into the transmission mechanisms through which these positive results are attained. Indeed, because of its neglect of the broader context, the recent preoccupation with robust impact evaluation has distracted attention from understanding better the practical challenge of identifying potential entry points for change, and thereby actually making reform happen—seeking out options, at a variety of different levels, where champions of change might have the space and influence to move forward even in the face of opposition.

CDD also sometimes results in major gains for poor communities. To be sure, elites play a disproportionately large role in CDD projects—but this does not seem to prevent a substantial share of benefits going to poor people. And while the institutional mechanisms for CDD indeed often bypass rather than strengthen public institutions, there are intriguing signs that there can nonetheless sometimes be valuable gains in organizational learning and, more broadly, in deepening a culture of citizenship.

Future research could thus usefully go beyond the examples in this chapter of basic education and CDD and explore across a much broader swathe of activities the potential of transparency and participation to improve public service provision even in difficult governance environments. Promising areas of application might include other public services supplied by government, multistakeholder arrangements for the governance of state-owned enterprises, and participatory approaches to the governance and oversight of public procurement.

Yet for all of the potential, it is important not to fall into the trap of the conflicts over first principles described in chapter 8—and end up replacing one comforting but illusory set of false certainties with another. The evidence that in settings where top-down approaches will not work, bottom-up approaches can sometimes add value remains partial—intriguing, but not yet decisively compelling. Already, though, it is clear that positive results may be achieved in some settings but not others, and that the result will depend on the balance among threat and trumping influence networks. Also clear is that in cases where bottom-up approaches can add value, the gains are incremental and their cumulative consequences uncertain—although the cumulative consequences of what seem to be partial and in some ways even counterproductive interventions can play out in surprising ways.

Here, Bill Easterly's distinction between "planners" and "searchers" and Matt Andrews' "problem-driven iterative adaptation" are useful.[20] Planners look for the "best practices" that, once identified, can—given "political will"—be adopted the world over, cookie-cutter-like, as *the* solution to the development problem. By contrast, searchers seek out answers through trial-and-error experimentation. For all of the current limits of our knowledge as to the efficacy of bottom-up approaches, it was the recognition that in many settings the public sector does not, and will not, function well that occasioned the search for the alternatives in the first place. There is no point in looking where the light is best, if we know that is not where what we are seeking is to be found. We must learn to look where the target of our search may in fact be located, even if the light there is not that good—even if, that is, our knowledge as to the strengths, weaknesses, and range of application of the various options remains incomplete.

CHAPTER 10

Multistakeholder Governance and the Private Sector

Over the past dozen or so years, spurred by the inclusion in the United Nations Millennium Development Goals of global targets to enhance access to education and health services by the poor, the provision of basic services moved to center stage in the development discourse. Yet for all of the global preoccupation with meeting the Millennium Development Goals, over the long run, sustained economic growth (not one of the goals) is the principal driver of poverty reduction—and the active engagement of the private sector is key to growth.

The standard policy prescriptions for private-sector development have mirrored closely the good governance prescriptions and, unsurprisingly, they come up against the same limitation. They presuppose a set of background politics and institutions that do not exist in many low-income countries. By contrast, this chapter takes weaknesses in governance as its point of departure and explores the development potential of an alternative institutional agenda for engaging the private sector, one that potentially is better suited to these more difficult environments. Consistent with the approach laid out in chapter 8, the focus is on principal-to-principal multistakeholder initiatives.

The Chad–Cameroon Pipeline project provides a powerful illustration of the opportunities, challenges, and controversies surrounding a multistakeholder approach to private-sector development. The project began in 1994 with an unusual approach by the Exxon Corporation to the World Bank. Exxon had discovered vast oilfields in the Sahelian African country of Chad and was contemplating investing upward of $6 billion to extract the oil and ship it over 3,000 kilometers by pipeline to Douala in Cameroon and thence to world markets. There were so many things that could go wrong with this investment, each entailing such high costs, that in retrospect it is astounding that Exxon was willing to entertain the venture.

There were the environmental risks of a pipeline that traversed desert, communal farmland, and tropical forest—and Exxon, of course, knew something about this type of risk and its reputational consequences, from the 1989 saga of the Exxon Valdez oil spill in coastal Alaska. There were the risks of sabotage from militias opposed to the Chadian government: In the three decades since independence, Chad had been chronically unstable, its population subjected to a long cycle of coups and civil war, which had ended only in the early 1990s, with a military victory by General Idriss Deby, which he punctuated by winning 69 percent of the vote in 1996 in Chad's first ever democratic election.

And, perhaps most unpredictable of all, there were the implications of making a $6 billion oil investment in what was then among the poorest countries on earth—a country of about 8 million people with an average per-capita income of close to $200 per person. Across the globe, the natural resource "curse," as it has come to be known, has had a long and dismal pedigree of fomenting not rising levels of living for the citizens of resource-abundant countries but inequality, corruption, strife, and, at the limit, civil war.

Natural resource bonanzas create the opportunity for both private investors and the elites who control the levers of power (and thus access to the resources) to reap huge financial rewards, without any need for accountability to a country's citizens ('No representation without taxation' is the evocative way in which the problem sometimes is described by governance practitioners.) All too often, as we saw in the example of Zambia's copper privatization in chapter 5, the result can be an agreement among opportunistic global private firms and cynical domestic political elites—with no fiscal benefits accruing to citizens.

But then there is the "other hand": Chad's landlocked, semidesert geography had seemingly consigned the country's people to poverty without end. The discovery of oil offered the prospect of a different future. By what right should non-Chadians make the decision that this door of possibility should remain shut? This is where the World Bank came in. It wasn't the Bank's money that Exxon was after—the proposed contribution by the Bank was $340 million, just under 5 percent of the total project cost of $6.5 billion. What the Bank could bring was the imprimatur of development respectability.

As a member of the Bank's Africa regional management team, and as the manager responsible for some Bank staff who participated in the governance dimensions of the resulting operation, I was party to the controversy occasioned by Exxon's audacious request. Should the Bank expose itself to the reputational risks? Did we have sufficient confidence that positive development results could follow from this type of investment in this type of setting?

In the end, the Bank decided to go forward. But it did so in a novel way: It conditioned its involvement around a wide variety of unusual institutional arrangements to address the 'resource curse' fiscal hazards that all-too-often accompany natural resource investments in settings with weak domestic governance. These included commitments from the Chadian authorities that:

- Each year 10 percent of oil earnings would be set aside for a future generations fund.
- No less than 85 percent of the remaining oil revenues received by the Chadian authorities would be spent on a set of priority sectors, as agreed by the government, the World Bank, and other development partners. These comprised the bulk of economic activity: education, health, transport, housing, civil works, social affairs, rural development, mining and energy, justice, and telecommunications.
- The Chadians would support the establishment of a local multistakeholder group to provide input on the allocation of these revenues and to oversee that the money indeed was spent as intended.
- Exxon would make all payments earmarked for the Chadian government into an international escrow account—with an international oversight group monitoring all revenues that went into the account and where they all subsequently went.

In addition, by committing to support implementation, the World Bank put itself on the line as part of the oversight structure. The totality of these institutional arrangements aimed to achieve the improbable: a positive development result from a large-scale oil investment in an especially unpropitious setting.

* * * *

The Chad–Cameroon project was an early recognition that, in difficult governance settings, conventional prescriptions for getting the business environment right were an ill fit for the task at hand. Using as a point of departure the distinction highlighted in chapter 8 between function and form, this chapter focuses on three familiar pillars of private-sector development and explores for each alternative ways forward—focusing on the potential and limits of multistakeholder approaches that support islands of private-sector effectiveness within a broader sea of dysfunction in the business environment.

The first pillar comprises the challenge of providing the credible commitment necessary to attract private investment. Credible commitment matters because an investment is a bet on the future. In part, it is an entrepreneurial bet that the activity being pursued has the potential to yield a lucrative stream of profits over time. But it is also an institutional and political bet that the rules of the game will remain stable. The standard prescription for providing credible commitment is to have a strong, impartial judiciary, capable of protecting property rights and mediating disputes between firms. But what if the justice system and other formal checks and balances institutions are weak? The next section of this chapter explores whether and how multistakeholder, principal-to-principal arrangements can provide credibility in these more difficult governance settings.

Second is the challenge of providing the support services needed by private business. In part, this is the agenda of public-service provision explored in chapters 8 and 9. But there also is an additional, more controversial dimension—namely proactive support to firms and farmers. In the conventional discourse on private-sector development, there are divergent views as to the appropriate scope for proactivity on the part of government. For agriculture, it has long been recognized that government has an active role to play in supporting small farmers, through extension services and (more controversially) the provision of credit. For manufacturing, the notion of an active role has been more controversial—though it is broadly understood that manufacturing firms cluster in groups, with strong interfirm spillovers, joint gains from shared, quasi-public-good facilities and services, and thus, at least in principle, some role for collective support systems.[1] But regardless of one's a priori view as to the desirability of public provision of these support systems, in settings where governance is weak there is little likelihood that the support systems can be provided effectively via top-down, long-route mechanisms. The second section of this chapter explores the potential for providing proactive support via collective arrangements anchored within the private sector.

Third is the challenge of aligning private and social benefits and costs. In the conventional approach to private-sector development, this is the domain of economic regulations (and law more broadly) that govern the environmental, labor, social, and ethical practices of firms—and of fiscal policy (including an efficient corporate tax regime), which ensures that an "appropriate" share of profits is used for achieving social goals. But what if—as with the example of oil investment in Chad—neither regulation nor fiscal policy is effective? The third section of the chapter explores the potential for filling this gap via multistakeholder initiatives to forge new global rules, led by global civil society and corporate actors.

But before proceeding, a cautionary note is in order. An important distinction in the development literature is between investment-driven and productivity-driven growth.[2] In earlier stages, development is driven principally by investment that leverages a low-income country's comparative advantage in the costs of factors of production (abundant natural resources, for example, or low-wage, unskilled labor) or that produces manufactures for a protected domestic market. In later stages, an ongoing capacity to adapt and innovate becomes more important.

The conventional prescriptions for improving the business environment in principle provide a platform that addresses both investment and productivity. Protections for property rights provide the credibility needed to attract investment. Providing a level playing field for all private firms enables markets to operate smoothly, facilitating ongoing economic adaptation. But when weaknesses in formal institutions render the conventional approach ineffective, a new dilemma arises: As we shall see, institutional alternatives capable of addressing the challenge of credibility risk introducing rigidities that inhibit the capacity to adapt down the road. Finding ways of reaping the benefits of credibility without paying too high a price of loss of flexibility turns out to be a difficult challenge, one with no easy answers.

Attracting Private Investment

Investments often involve irreversible decisions (to, say, drill an oil well, sink a mine shaft, or invest in a large-scale steel plant), so the risk of opportunism looms large. Governments and political leaders have a strong incentive, ex ante, to declare their support for a new investment so as to ensure that the activity gets underway. But ex post, once the activity is up and running, their incentive can be strong to renege on the deal and capture the benefits of the upfront investment for themselves.[3] Insofar as these risks loom large, private investors will stay away.

We began exploring how to reduce these risks in chapter 5, with the examples of Zambian copper and Bangladeshi garments. For Zambian copper, the answer was straightforward but disconcerting: Provide a sufficiently high return, and thus sufficiently rapid payback, that makes the opportunity to proceed, almost regardless of risk, too compelling to pass up. For Bangladeshi garments, the answer had more to do with the balance of forces. The country's garment manufacturers had a compelling shared interest in assuring that Bangladesh was viewed by global buyers as a reliable, hassle-free export platform—and their political connections were sufficiently widespread to assure protection against predation, regardless of which political party happened to be in power.

The role of personalized relationships between private firms, government officials, and political leaders in underpinning investment also emerges strongly in comparative studies conducted in China and Indonesia by the Centre for the Future State at the University of Sussex's Institute of Development Studies[4]:

- In Indonesia, a comparative assessment of two municipalities (Solo and Manado) found that in both, strong relations between local authorities and businesses were important drivers of private investment. In Solo the relations were more transparent and inclusive, organized around a wide range of business associations; in Manado, the relations were more individualized, with specific favors going to individual firms. But the authors concluded that it was the closeness of the relationships and the sense of security they provided—not their "quality" from a good business environment perspective—that was decisive in attracting investment. (The authors suggest, though, that the Solo-style relations are more likely to provide the kind of support that can facilitate far-reaching economic transformation.)

- In China, the research goal was to explain why the Tianjin Economic-Technological Development Area was successful in attracting foreign investment, while the immediately neighboring Dongli Economic-Technological Development area was not. The key difference was that the former was more able to make, and deliver on, promises to provide infrastructure and other ongoing support. In turn, the reason for this difference was that Tianjin Economic-Technological Development Area was very well connected through personal networks of officials of the Communist Party of China at subnational and national levels—including high-level support from Tianjin-born former Chinese Premier Wen Jiabao.

In their classic book, *The Politics of Property Rights*, Stephen Haber and associates suggest an analytical insight that links the Bangladeshi, Chinese, and Indonesian examples. They highlight the central role of property rights in assuring credible commitment—but, contrary to the dominant view, they argue that property rights are not necessarily a public good, dependent on the full panoply of a justice system. Rather, they can be constructed in an ad hoc, targeted way—that is, they can be "privatized." Key to the successful privatization of property rights is to structure private investments in such a way that they will be buttressed by a "trumping" coalition that is sufficiently robust to deter any effort by potential predators to capture the investment's returns for themselves.[5] Haber et al. illustrate their insight via an in-depth and original analysis of Mexican economic history.

Mexico's first six decades subsequent to its 1821 independence from Spain were difficult, with a total of seventy-five governments, none lasting more than three years. But the coming to power in 1876 of General Porfirio Diaz ushered in three decades of political stability and rapid economic growth. In the conventional reading of Mexican history, the basis for this prosperity was the Porfiriato's embrace of laissez-faire capitalism. But, as Haber et al. show, this was not the right explanation. General Diaz inherited a desperately poor, bankrupt country, with many well-armed warlords scattered across the landscape; his control over Mexico's territory was very uneven. To consolidate control, he desperately needed revenues; to get these, he needed to get the economy moving—and this would take private investment. But how could he provide investors with the credible commitment they needed as to the stability of the rules of the game?

The example of the cotton textile sector illustrates how privatized property rights worked during the three-decade-long "Porfiriato." To attract investment into cotton textiles, General Diaz offered a protected domestic market. And to provide assurance that the protection would remain and that investors would retain the fruits of their efforts, he encouraged some of the new textile operators to locate in territories controlled by rival warlords—with the rival warlord families themselves becoming coprincipals, as equity owners in the new operation. He thereby achieved a double gain: He gave the warlords a stake in continuing political stability—and he provided investors with assurance that he would not renege on his commitment to protect the local market. Changing the rules would not only be an attack on defenseless businessmen; it would be incurring the wrath of ruthless armed warlords. The results were remarkable: The real value of textile output rose almost tenfold—from 8.5 million pesos in 1883 to 73 million in 1912.[6]

Subsequent to General Porfirio's rule, and following a period of civil turmoil, there was a radical change in the composition of the multistakeholder coalition that provided the platform for Mexico's investment-driven growth. Mexican politics restabilized under the umbrella of the ruling Party for Institutionalized Revolution (PRI), an alliance between organized labor, peasants, and the public bureaucracy. As coprincipal, organized labor took on the credibility-enhancing role that hitherto had been played by warlords. Businessmen may have resented having to share the rents that came from a protected domestic market in the form of new minimum labor standards and higher minimum wages—but they surely understood that this was part of the deal through which their property rights remained protected. The PRI system ushered in almost a half-century of steady growth and reduction of poverty.

By the 1980s, sustained growth had led to the emergence of a strong middle class and a sustained effort to move Mexico toward a competitive polity anchored in the rule of law. But the sought-for institutional arrangements were entirely at variance with the discretionary (and often corrupt) allocation of benefits that lay at the heart of PRI governance. Dismantling the culture of corruption that had become deeply entrenched during a half-century of PRI rule and locking in impersonal rule of law institutions has proven extraordinarily difficult.[7] This raises a broader issue.

The insights of Haber and the experiences described above of Bangladesh, China, Indonesia, and Mexico are all variations on the general theme of how to provide the credible commitment needed to attract private investment in settings where politics and institutions are personalized. Each depends for its effectiveness on the intertwining of economic and political power in ways that can be an invitation to predatory corruption. Hence the question: Do these insights and experiences point to a way forward for countries with weak institutions—or do they illuminate crime scenes? (Or both?)

A preoccupation with getting the business environment right combined with blanket condemnation of corruption sweeps the question under the carpet. But the analysis laid out here suggests that there is no getting away from it: In the many settings where institutions are personalized, locking in the credible commitment needed to attract private investment will almost always be organized around targeted, principal-to-principal agreements that share rents between entrepreneurs and other powerful actors. One way to proceed is to make personalized deals with powerful, politically connected individuals. But there are also other options, including:

- linking investment to policies that provide privileges and create rents that are shared with organized interests, giving them a stake in the status quo. Protectionism (as in Mexico) is one example; the conferral of monopoly privileges is another;
- equity-sharing arrangements with investment vehicles set up by one or another organized interest (perhaps a labor union, perhaps a political party);
- partnerships with government entities—for example with local government (as in the classic example of China's township and village enterprises[8]), or perhaps by providing a minority equity share to a holding company for state-owned enterprises (common in China, Brazil, Russia, and many other countries).

In the usual development discourse, each of these is condemned equally. But the analysis laid out in this section suggests that there potentially are important differences in their implications for development. Which among the range of credibility-enhancing rent-sharing arrangements is less likely to descend into kleptocracy and more likely to provide a platform for productive investment? Or, taking a longer-run perspective (and recalling the distinction at the outset of this chapter between investment-driven and productivity-driven growth), which among the credibility-enhancing alternatives has a lower risk of locking in rigidities and thus is better placed to facilitate continuing adaptation as the economy evolves? Plausibly, the answers could vary across countries, depending on their background political, social, and institutional characteristics. The practical benefits for low-income countries of research that explores these shades of gray could be very high.

Support Systems for Firms and Farmers

Let us now turn to a second pillar of private-sector development: proactive support for firms and farmers. While private investment can enable a country to take advantage of its comparative advantage in, say, natural resources, development involves a more profound transformation in a country's economic structure. The challenge is formidable: Complex market economies are underpinned by a variety of market-enhancing institutional, organizational, and infrastructural supports. In low-income economies, the requisite markets, institutions, organizations, and infrastructure are all missing. Protagonists of developmental states have long taken the view that strong, top-down government is needed to make the transformation from a simple, low-income to a complex, higher-income economy. The examples in chapter 4 of Korea and Ethiopia illustrate this dominant trajectory in action.

While initially the focus of the literature on developmental states was on the need for a bureaucracy that was insulated from the pressures of politicians and other powerful economic and social interests, in a more recent strand it shifted to (as per the title of Peter Evans classic book on the subject, *Embedded Autonomy*) how activist public officials might leverage alliances with forward-looking private firms to press forward with an agenda of economic transformation.[9]

As with Evans' work, this section explores whether and how multistakeholder governance might be leveraged to foster economic transformation and enhance the productivity of firms and farmers. But in contrast to Evans, here there is no presumption of an activist government that drives the process forward. The focus is on settings where the goals, authority, and incentives of political and bureaucratic actors are much more ambiguous than is presumed by Evans (or, for that matter, by advocates of the view that governments should remain at arms-length from business and focus on providing a level playing field). Some public actors may indeed seek to partner in pursuit of a developmental goal, but others are as likely to lend their weight to predatory as much as to developmentally oriented purposes.

In such settings, can multistakeholder initiatives organized around specific islands of collective action (ones in which the private sector and other nongovernmental actors play leading roles) help address the gaps in support systems? For such initiatives to be successful, they will need to address both of the challenges identified in chapter 8—the challenge of facilitating cooperation among the participants and the challenge of fending off others who are less supportive of the effort to create new value. Zambia's cotton and South Africa's garments and textiles sectors offer rich examples of these dynamics in action.

Cotton outgrowing in Zambia.   As described in chapter 5, Zambia's cotton exports have surged since the mid-1990s—with the expansion based on innovative arrangements that link cotton ginners and smallholder farmers. But the expansion has been very uneven—punctuated by repeated crises that can be traced back to gaps in the institutional arrangements. What have been the institutional underpinnings of this expansion—and of the repeated setbacks?[10]

The story begins in 1994 when, as part of the broader effort at economic liberalization in the first term of President Chiluba's presidency, Zambia embarked on a far-reaching restructuring of its cotton sector—selling its hitherto state-owned ginneries to two private companies, Lonhro and Clark Cotton. In the 1980s, farmers growing cotton had received support from public extension and credit services, but these services became increasingly ineffective in the face of Zambia's public sector's cumulative loss of capacity and of resources. Clark Cotton and Lonhro provided a nongovernmental institutional alternative: They organized their Zambian cotton ventures around outgrower schemes with smallholder farmers—wherein the ginners provided packages of seed and fertilizer on credit and the small farmers, in return, agreed to sell their cotton crop to them at an agreed-upon price.

These outgrower initiatives seem, at first glance, to have been spectacularly successful. Production rose from an annual average of under 60,000 tons per annum in the early 1990s to over 100,000 tons in 1998 and close to 200,000 tons in 2005. Eleven percent of all Zambian smallholders were active in cotton growing. But these aggregates mask dramatic year-on-year fluctuations. Production in 1999 fell back to 50,000 tons, less than half that of 1998. Though it subsequently recovered, there was another crash after 2005—with levels again falling by close to half, back down to a little over 100,000 tons in 2007.

The reasons for these cycles can be found in the weaknesses in the collective arrangements that linked the ginners and smallholder cotton farmers. The relationship between ginners and smallholders farmers is a quintessential example of a transaction separated in time. Ginners provide inputs up front; farmers deliver when the crop is harvested. Ginners thus confront the risk that farmers will "side-sell" to independent buyers who, not having paid input costs up front, can offer farmers a better net price. In a well-functioning market economy with strong institutions, a formal legal contract can provide credibility for the transaction. But when institutions are weaker, as in Zambia, ready recourse to the rule of law is not available. Indeed, both the 1999 and 2006 crashes had their roots in institutional failures:

- In 1999, a group of independent traders emerged, purchasing and reselling cotton, without providing any inputs themselves; a year later they had left the market but not before Lonhro, citing input credit losses, withdrew from the scene. Cotton production temporarily plummeted, until a new ginner took over Lonhro's assets.

- In 2006, between the time of planting (when the ginners announced their purchase price) and of harvest, Zambia's currency, the kwacha, had appreciated by a third. The ginners unilaterally announced a corresponding decrease in what they would pay to farmers. Meanwhile, a new generation of ginners had come on the scene—and took advantage of farmer discontent with the unilateral actions of the established ginneries to buy cotton when it came onto the market. Again, production levels collapsed.

Table 10.1 overleaf uses Ostrom's good-practice principles, introduced in chapter 8, as a benchmark to clarify where the institutional weaknesses in Zambia's cotton sector were to be found. As the table signals, the underlying failure was the unilateral nature of the effort. Ginners made little if any effort to actively engage farmers. As a result, there was little sense of obligation to practice restraint when independent buyers came onto the scene and encouraged farmers to sell to them on more advantageous terms and default on their repayment obligations to the input-providing outgrower-ginners.

As of 2012, the outgrower schemes continued to operate, but the relationship remains fraught, with continuing conflict over how to share unexpected windfalls and losses in the face of market downturns.[11] The good-practice principles offer some pointers for making more robust the collective action arrangements that link outgrowers and small farmers. These could include:

- an up-front effort to help establish an association of smallholder farmers and a corresponding association of outgrowers;
- more participation of the farmers, via such organizations, in agreeing on the out-grower rules of the game; plus
- direct involvement of the associations in monitoring the behavior of farmers and outgrowers vis-à-vis the agreement and in enforcing compliance.

But collective action does not happen automatically. It takes leadership to set a cooperative endeavor in motion; it takes ongoing mutual learning to facilitate cooperation among participants who (as in the Zambian example) have little history of working together as coprincipals. It takes an organizational structure to sustain cooperation over time.

In principle, the initiative to establish institutional arrangements of cooperation could come from government. But to be effective, government involvement would need to be flexible and differentiated, sufficiently agile to respond to the specific needs of the "island of effectiveness" being supported. Further, as research evidence on cooperation underscores,[12] the

Table 10.1 **Governing Markets—The Performance of Three Private-Sector-Led Initiatives**

Types of Rules	Zambian Cotton Outgrowing	The Cape Clothing Cluster	South Africa's National Garments Initiative
Rules governing eligibility	*Partial*—Failure to exclude side sellers	*Good practice*—Members are formally registered, and the induction of new members is publicly announced	*Unclear rules*—Throughout the process labor remained outside the participatory effort and made its influence felt through back channels.
Operating rules	*Weak collaboration*—Rules set by ginners, with little effort to incorporate small farmers in the process; no agreed mechanism to modify prices in face of exogenous shocks	*Good practice*—The organization runs along lines laid out in its founding agreement	*Unclear rules*—No consensus as to the role of labor, no mutually respected, neutral mechanism for addressing conflict among the participants.
Rules governing monitoring	*No collective monitoring mechanism*	*Good practice*—Systematic monitoring is undertaken by an organization contracted to provide services to the cluster and accountable to the cluster for performance	*Not applicable.* (The initiative never reached implementation stage.)
Rules governing delegation	*Partial*—Outgrowing supported by policy, but ambiguous intervention	*Good practice*—Provincial authorities recognize the rights of the cluster participants to organize, as well as a clearly defined autonomous area for decision making.	*No autonomous domains of decision-making*—Seeming agreements negotiated among private-sector actors, and with government, repeatedly overturned.

public officials involved would need to understand their role to be one of coprincipal—facilitating rather than substituting for cooperation. So far, in Zambia's cotton sector, there has been little sign of such an approach to government engagement.[13]

But, as noted at the outset of this section, supportive government involvement, though desirable, is not necessary for success. One of the strengths of a multistakeholder approach is that leadership to facilitate cooperation could come from any of the stakeholders involved. It could come from farmer organizations or nongovernmental organizations that work with small farmers. It could come from donors, or even from outgrowers themselves. But regardless of who leads, the key to success is a readiness to forego pressing for a short-term advantage and to recognize that the long-run interests of all participants lie in institutional arrangements that are perceived to be fair and, hence sustainable.

South Africa's garment sector.   This offers a second example of the potential and limits of multistakeholder initiatives to provide collective services. Domestic manufacturers, located principally around the cities of Cape Town and Durban, had long been the dominant suppliers of garments to South African consumers—initially behind strong protection against imports, but post-1994 in more liberalized markets. By the mid-2000s, though, they were coming under increasing pressure from Chinese imports.[14] Between 2004 and 2007, over one-quarter of formal sector jobs in garment manufacturing were lost.

Stakeholders in the sector responded with a variety of collective initiatives at both local and national levels with the aim of strengthening the productivity of the domestic "value chain" that linked retailers, garment producers, and textile manufacturers to one another. The results of these efforts were mixed— and the good-practice principles again offer a useful lens for assessing what worked, what did not, and why.

One local initiative was the Cape Clothing Cluster, a private-sector membership-based (and membership-driven) organization of firms. Its members (forty-six firms as of late 2011) comprise a critical mass of the leading garment and textile firms in the province, plus the major retail chains. It is financed through a combination of annual member fees, plus financial support from the Western Cape provincial government—but other than providing some financial support, the provincial government remains at arms-length. The cluster organizes training workshops and seminars, joint visits to member factories, industry-wide gatherings, and study tours. Sectoral newsletters are distributed (both to members and on the cluster's website) every quarter. Each member's operational performance is benchmarked against aggregated performance indicators of South African and international competitors. As Table 10.1 summarizes, the institutional arrangements that underpin the cluster benchmark well against Ostrom's good-practice principles.

While the Cape clothing cluster illustrates how a private sector led collective initiative in manufacturing can add value with very limited involvement on the part of government, efforts at collaboration played out very differently at the national level.[15] The national process was set in motion in 2004, when South Africa's Department of Trade and Industry began to produce customized plans for a variety of sectors, including clothing and textiles. At first, all seemed to go smoothly; indeed the customized sector planning process looked to have the potential to be a model of the "embedded autonomy" approach to industrial development advocated by Peter Evans.

By mid-2005, the key elements of a plan for garments and textiles had been thrashed out among private sector, government, and parastatal stakeholders. At the heart of the plan was a Textile and Clothing Development Council where industry and government stakeholders would come together to advise, develop, and ensure implementation of a series of proposed interventions. The plan also included loans to upgrade manufacturers' technology and capital; roll out of a national subsidy for upgrading operational production activities in line with world-class manufacturing standards; action to stop illegal imports of clothing; and scaled-up national training initiatives to create sustainable skills in the workforce.

But a key player—the South African Clothing and Textiles Workers Union—though invited to participate, had remained aloof from the collective endeavor. Instead, it used its political connections with senior government officials[16] to try and reshape the design of the sectoral plan. Thus, rather than the formal signing off of the sector plan expected by business, the Department of Trade and Industry called a meeting at which a revised plan was presented. The revised plan proposed a shift in focus from creating competitiveness to mandatory requirements that retailers source locally, enforced through quantitative restrictions; prohibitions on retailers from sourcing clothing from manufacturers whose compliance with formal agreements between business and labor on industrial relations was in dispute; and a restructuring of the Textile and Clothing Development Council as a tripartite body, with equal representation from business, labor, and government.

Subsequent months saw extended shuttle diplomacy, involving repeated bilateral negotiations between government and business and then government and labor—each round producing a new iteration of a draft plan. More than a year after the "finalization" of the initial version, after many protracted meetings and clause-by-clause negotiations, the negotiations resulted in a revised document. But by then much damage had been done, and the agreement that was made was largely pro forma. The proposed tripartite body never met.

As the last column in Table 10.1 underscores, South Africa's national-level garments initiative fell short of almost all of Ostrom's good-practice principles for collective action. Sectoral stakeholders, though able to organize collectively at local levels, proved unable to orchestrate an equivalent process on a national scale. Politics turned out to be trumps—and in this instance the developmentally oriented influence networks were not strong enough for a collaborative initiative to work.[17] The very large differences in the interests and perceptions of their relative bargaining power, combined with a failure of government to effectively balance and mediate, left the stakeholders unable to achieve the win-win, multistakeholder way forward that seemed so tantalizingly within reach.

External Anchors

Now let us turn to the third pillar of the private-sector development agenda considered in this chapter—aligning private and social benefits and costs. Conventionally, this is the domain of regulatory and fiscal policy—but in settings where governance is weak, neither is likely to be effective. This section explores the potential and limits of an alternative, multistakeholder approach—namely initiatives led by global civil society and corporate actors to forge new global rules for governing environmental, social, and ethical practices in low-income developing countries with weak formal institutions.[18]

From the contemporary use of New York statutory law as a basis for adjudication of international business disputes to, at the limit, the imposition of colonial authority over vast swathes of the world, there is a long history of using the institutions of one part of the world as a platform for resolving disputes—or otherwise asserting authority and control—in another. But within the past two decades, something new has begun to emerge.

Accelerating globalization has brought with it intensified scrutiny by civil society activists of the governance standards of global private firms and of their impact in low-income countries. One intriguing response has been a series of multistakeholder initiatives that bring together public, private, and civil society actors in a participatory effort to forge new global rules, plus new ways of monitoring and enforcing them. These initiatives span a broad range of focal points for activism—from labor standards, to the environment, to anticorruption. Here we focus on three illustrative examples:[19]

- the use of standards to support environmental sustainability—as exemplified by the role of the Marine Stewardship Council (MSC) standard in South Africa;
- the Extractive Industries Transparency Initiative—as an illustration of a global effort to reduce corruption by making the arrangements between globalized businesses and developing countries less opaque; and
- the Chad–Cameroon Pipeline Project (the example with which we began this chapter and with which we shall end), as an effort to provide a global anchor to enhance the developmental benefits of oil extraction.

Sustainable fishing—Hake in South Africa.   The deep-sea hake fishery off South Africa's west Atlantic coast is the largest of the country's fisheries, with revenues in excess of $150 million per annum.[20] Governing any high-value fishery poses a formidable challenge. A fishing operation's short-run incentive is to fish as much as possible—but, in classic "tragedy of the commons" fashion, the inevitable result would be destruction of the fishery.

Under any circumstances, putting in place rules of the game that assure sustainable fishing is difficult—but it is especially difficult in settings where the political and bureaucratic incentives are overwhelmingly short-run, personalized, and clientelistic. All too often, the result the world over has been chronic corruption in fisheries regulation—with repeated instances of government officials turning a blind eye to overfishing or even regularizing it by giving (for a price) rights of access beyond sustainable levels.

Contemporary fisheries governance in South Africa confronts an added difficulty. The incumbent fishing companies had come to their dominant positions through the preferential access to fisheries, which they had been granted by that country's apartheid government. So, unsurprisingly, the past two decades have witnessed repeated rounds of conflict between the post-apartheid elected leadership of the country and incumbent fishing companies. In some cases the result has been disastrous, leading to the near destruction of the fishery.[21] But the hake fishery has, so far, been a success story. Hake fishing has remained highly profitable, with sustainability protected. How was this achieved?

Part of the answer lies in the economics of the fishery: The quite large minimum efficient scale needed to participate in deep-sea fishing meant that new, undercapitalized participants could not easily enter. There was, though, no shortage of potential foreign entrants, who would have been all too happy to share fishing rents with politically connected local partners. But the more interesting part of the answer lies in the efforts of the two dominant incumbent companies to build new multistakeholder influence networks capable of trumping threats to sustainability (and, it must be noted, to their privileged positions). One of their tactics was widespread across post-apartheid South Africa—bring politically connected black partners into established businesses.[22] The second was to incorporate a global anchor into the institutional arrangements for governing the fishery.

Working through the South African Deep Sea Trawling Industry Association, the incumbent firms applied to the MSC for certification that the fishery was being sustainably managed. (The MSC is a global, multistakeholder nongovernmental standards organization, which enjoys high credibility internationally among nongovernmental organizations, consumers, and the private sector.) In 2005, subsequent to a robust evaluation process, South Africa's hake fishery was certified for the first time. The MSC recertifies fisheries, using independent third-party verifiers, every five years for the right to continue to use the MSC eco-label. In 2010, South Africa's hake fishery was recertified.

Certification has commercial advantages: Some of the major customers of South Africa's hake suppliers had committed to source its fish products only from sustainably managed fisheries. But MSC certification also had a powerful impact on the regulatory environment. The presence of the MSC as part of South Africa's regulatory process meant that there was now a new signal—one that was highly visible and highly credible internationally—as to whether the fishery was being sustainably governed.

Though regulators retained the authority to reallocate quota over the long-run, MSC certification—and its signal that South Africa's hake fishery was a global exemplar of sustainability "best practice"—served to constrain the room for maneuver of any future regulators (and their political masters) who might threaten to destabilize the governance of the fishery for political purposes. Whether, over the long run, these institutional arrangements will continue to trump new threats remains uncertain. But so far, even in the face of some difficult political challenges, they have prevailed.[23]

The Extractive Industries Transparency Initiative (EITI).   In 2002, then British Prime Minister Tony Blair announced the multistakeholder EITI initiative at the World Summit on Sustainable Development. A key precursor to the establishment of the initiative was the release in 1999 by the international nongovernmental organization Global Witness of the study "A Crude Awakening," which documented the links between oil, banking, and corruption in Angola. Immediately following the release of this report, a coalition of global nongovernmental organizations launched a campaign to pressure global oil and mining companies to "Publish What You Pay."

Membership of EITI's twenty-person board is distributed among each of four categories: implementing countries (i.e., exporters of natural resources whose governments have chosen to participate in the initiative), supporting countries (i.e., government champions from developed countries), civil society organizations, and the private sector. As of late 2010, thirty-three country governments had signed up as "candidate" countries for EITI implementation. The governments of high-income democracies also signed up as EITI "supporting" countries.

The EITI is organized around three sets of institutional arrangements that aim to lock in incentives for enhanced transparency and oversight over oil revenues. They comprise:

- Rules that aim to make transparent the transfers of finance between governments and energy and mining companies. The rules require governments to provide information, audited according to international standards, as to what payments they have received from these companies—with parallel information from the companies themselves, also audited according to international standards, as to what payments they have made.[24] Further, the rules require that an organization be contracted to reconcile these figures and that the report containing the various sources of data, any discrepancies uncovered, and their reconciliation be made public.

- Rules that mandate the establishment at country level of a multistakeholder group, with "adequate representation" of major civil society, private sector, government, and other stakeholders, to oversee the country's EITI implementation.
- Rules that require an external validator, selected from a list of validators accredited by EITI, to assess whether an EITI "candidate" country has met all the EITI criteria and so is EITI compliant. The validator's report needs to be viewed as broadly acceptable by the country-level multistakeholder group—with the final decision on compliance made by the global EITI Board. All candidate countries are required to conduct a validation exercise within two years of having signed up (and hence having met the sign-up criteria) for EITI, or else their candidacy will be suspended.

While the EITI continues to evoke widespread enthusiasm, it is too early to declare it a success. For one thing, it is not really clear what the built-in incentives for self-regulation are. To be sure, international oil and mining companies subject to legal prohibitions against corruption at home or abroad, and vulnerable to shareholder activism, had a clear incentive to promote the EITI as a way of avoiding a no-win (for them) "race to the bottom" with international companies less restrained by such strictures. But the incentives for exporting country governments to voluntarily agree to hold themselves accountable to the global community are less clear. In the short run, a combination of principled leadership in some countries, plus encouragement by donors, has proven sufficient to induce an initial round of exporting countries to sign up. But some major oil-exporting countries remained outside of the EITI process, and none of Brazil, Russia, India, China, and South Africa (the BRICS countries) have signed up as either supporters or members.

Even more fundamentally, it remains uncertain whether the simple, consensual rules that are the foundation of the EITI are sufficiently robust and demanding to achieve more than modest results. Thus far the EITI has focused single-mindedly on a narrow goal—assuring that accurate audited information on payments between governments and international oil and mining companies is put into the public domain. The hope is that transparency and civil society engagement can be a springboard for broader accountability over how public resources are used, and hence gains in both governance and poverty reduction. Whether these dynamics will play out along the lines hoped by the EITI in more than a modest number of countries remains uncertain—although the example of Chad, to which we shall return shortly, is an intriguing one.

A Glass Part-Full?

The options for private-sector development explored in this chapter depart in fundamental ways from the familiar templates for good governance and getting the business environment right. The usual focus is on systemic strengthening of formal rules and of the principal–agent relationships that hold bureaucrats accountable. By contrast, the logic of change laid out in this chapter is very different. The focus is on using microlevel institutional initiatives to support the emergence of islands of effectiveness within a broader sea of dysfunction— and doing so via very specific, often personalized, principal-to-principal multistakeholder arrangements that follow the logic laid out in chapter 8. The arrangements have included: alliances that link powerful economic and political actors in order to provide the credible commitment needed to foster private investment; stakeholders working together to provide local public goods from which they can benefit jointly; and voluntary, multistakeholder, issue-specific global networks organized around collectively agreed-upon rules and mechanisms for enforcing them.

Many readers will, I suspect, feel deeply ambivalent about where the exploration in this chapter has led us; I know that sometimes I do. The approach to attracting private investment can come perilously close to condoning corruption. The perspective on proactive support for private-sector development may seem frustratingly ambiguous in its advocacy for multistakeholder cooperation to support islands of effectiveness on the one hand and, on the other, its cautionary tales as to the practical difficulties of making such cooperation work. And the discussion of global anchors can be read as an embrace of feel-good, Northern romanticism, which falls way short of the magnitude of the challenges of a globalized world.

Indeed, the results achieved by these institutional substitutes are themselves ambiguous. Did Zambia accelerate investment in copper mining by creating robust alliances, or by succumbing to predation in the form of too-sweet deals? How much genuine value was created by the multiprincipal initiatives in the Zambian cotton and South African clothing sectors? Does the EITI genuinely enhance the developmental benefits of natural resource extraction, or does it amount to little more than a set of feel-good rules with little practical consequence? More broadly, to what extent do the solutions to the problem of credibility create rigidities that can forestall further development down the road?

Certainly, the options laid out in this chapter fall very, very far short of what chapter 4 described as possible in a proactive developmental state—a high-performing, proactive one such as Korea, or a nascent one focused on more basic development tasks such as Meles Zenawi's Ethiopia. And they lack the beguiling straightforwardness, and adaptive capability, of advocacy for a level playing field with identical rules for all participants. The glass is only part-full (perhaps not even half-full). But what is the practical alternative against which to benchmark? As earlier chapters—and, importantly, the cross-country data laid out in chapter 7—underscore, for many (perhaps most) low-income developing countries, these "high road" options are not feasible.

For very many countries, the relevant counterfactual to the messy options laid out in this chapter for getting growth moving may not be one or another "high road" path of development but stagnation—accompanied by deepening despair and a downward pull toward disaster. We do not live in the world of what economists call "first best" options, not even their "second best"—we live in an "n-th best" world. In this real world, nothing practical is achieved by the endless refinement of unachievable visions of the way we want things to be. Acknowledging as the point of departure the difficult challenges posed by weaker governance, we need entry points capable of moving development forward.

*   *   *   *

Consider again Exxon's Chad–Cameroon oil project. The unusual institutional arrangements described at the outset of this chapter aimed to defy the natural resource curse—to lock in development results from oil revenues, even in the face of strong political pressures to the contrary. The World Bank was invited into the deal as the third-party enforcer—on the presumption that the costs to the government of Chad of reneging on an agreement struck with an official multilateral organization like the World Bank were higher than the costs of reneging on Exxon. The trouble was that the calculus was incomplete.

By 2005, the government of Chad found itself confronting a new insurrection and wanted to use its oil money to scale up its army. Where was this money? In an international escrow account monitored by an international, multistakeholder Board of Overseers—to be released only against a pre-agreed set of spending commitments, with over 80 percent committed to be used for social expenditures. Unsurprisingly, the Chadians began to unilaterally break the agreement. Paul Wolfowitz, then president of the World Bank, sprang to the rescue. In early 2006 he returned from Ndjamena, Chad's capital, with a new agreement that modified somewhat the share of expenditures going to priority sectors. But this agreement rapidly fell to the wayside in the face of continuing military troubles.

I stopped tracking this saga in detail in 2007, when the Chadian authorities used their growing flood of oil revenues to immediately repay in full the World Bank, and the Bank pulled out of the country. Meanwhile, Chinese oil companies had become increasingly active in Chad. By 2008, rebels had made their way to the gates of Ndjamena. So, when I decided to include the Chad project as a cautionary tale in my 2010 graduate seminar at Johns Hopkins University's School of Advanced Studies, I fully expected to find that the government of Chad had fallen; that Exxon had pulled out; and that, with the resource curse having asserted itself in its most malign form, the commitment to social expenditures had collapsed. I was surprised by what I found.

General Deby's government had not fallen—though it had taken intervention by French troops to help it survive and the veneer of democracy had been stripped away. Exxon had not left; indeed it continued to describe its Chadian venture as an example of good development practice. And, though the country was hardly an exemplar of probity and productivity, the development gains being achieved were not insignificant:

- Chad's per-capita income doubled between 2000 and 2005;
- annual fiscal revenues received by government rose from $112 million in 2000 to upward of $2 billion by 2008;
- by 2008, the oil sector had purchased $1.2 billion of goods and services within Chad;
- between 2000 and 2008, the quantity of paved roads in the country rose from 300 to 1,200 kilometers; the primary-school enrollment rate rose from 61 percent to 88 percent of the relevant age cohort; and the percentage of the urban population with access to clean water rose from 34 percent to 48 percent.

On the governance and accountability front, the allocation of oil revenues remained geared quite strongly toward social expenditures, and the budget processes remained transparent. An otherwise critical report of the World Bank's Independent Evaluation Group reported that:

> *Chad achieved a level of revenue transparency nearly unique in Africa and nearing international best practice. Equally important, during the past several years habits have been built in the direction of openness rather than secrecy.*[25]

Indeed, after the World Bank's involvement in the sector ended, Chad reaffirmed its commitment to transparency by applying to join the EITI and was accepted as a candidate country in 2010.

None of this is to suggest that Chad is a paragon of good governance—indeed, it perhaps points to the narrowness of the EITI's expectations on its member countries. And the costs of Chad's school and road infrastructure (including corruption via overinvoicing) made them among the most expensive in the world. But the combination of new institutional arrangements and development gains suggests that the determined efforts to strengthen institutions of oversight and accountability at the outset of the oil venture were not without consequence.

There is one final question to be considered vis-à-vis the Chad oil deal. Given all that subsequently transpired, was it worth pursuing in the first place? When I confronted my students with this question, I was surprised by their response. Close to 90 percent of them thought that the World Bank did the right thing by going into the deal. And even knowing what actually happened, over 80 percent still thought that the effort was worth the risk. In an imperfect world, the half-loaf of what was achieved—in all its messiness and all its continuing uncertainties—seemed to them to be preferable to resigned acceptance of Chad's otherwise desperately poor, pre-oil reality.

PART

DEVELOPMENT STRATEGIES—THE GOVERNANCE DIMENSION

Parts I and II of this book laid out some dynamic trajectories along which countries can make the journey from a point of departure of low incomes and weak institutions to a destination of high incomes and robust sustainable institutions. Part III examined some options for countries to better address specific governance constraints that threaten to block the way forward. Part IV explores how the effort to build governance institutions capable of supporting ongoing development momentum might be approached strategically. The aim is to identify an initial round of actions that opens up the path for later stages of the journey, to assess constraints that might inhibit this initial round of actions, and, as needed, to identify alternative pathways that get around those constraints—to help clarify what is to be done, how, and by whom. But before scoping out the contours of the way forward, more needs to be said about how the governance and development discourse has evolved.

CHAPTER 11

Governance and Development—
Deconstructing the Discourse

Words are ambiguous things. They can clarify or they can obfuscate—and sometimes it is not easy to tell the difference. This ambiguity has been especially acute in the discourse on governance and development.

As governance moved to the forefront of the development discourse, it posed a series of difficult challenges for the World Bank and other multilateral and bilateral development agencies. These agencies have played a major role in shaping the way in which governance has been integrated into development work. So understanding better how governance challenges interacted with the agencies' organizational incentives and constraints offers important insights into how the governance agenda gained traction, how it came to be framed, and how it was incorporated into operational work.

* * * *

As I described in the first pages of this book, the end of the Cold War seemingly was something of an intellectual liberation for the aid endeavor. A consequence of Cold War geopolitics was that failures in the ways in which governments used aid could not be spoken about directly. Instead, aid was framed exclusively in economic terms—the combination of money, good technical advice, and evident goodwill would take care of all. Now these strictures could be eased, and governance could become part of the discourse. But what followed, though very different in content, again sacrificed the effort to address some deeply rooted obstacles to development on the altar of political and organizational imperatives—this time via the embrace of a type of high-mindedness that was unconstrained by difficult realities.[1] The result was a new series of impossible expectations.

In 1994, at a high-level meeting in Madrid, the incoming president of the World Bank, Jim Wolfensohn, found himself confronted by a chant from demonstrators that "fifty years is enough." In their view, a half-century after the signing of the Bretton Woods agreements, the world no longer had any use for the institutions it created. Over the next few years, in his inimitable, passionate way, Wolfensohn went on the counteroffensive.

The challenges of implementation, accountability, and corruption—all governance issues—became increasingly central to the World Bank's agenda. Weaknesses in implementation had emerged as a popular explanation for weaknesses in the performance of development aid. So, as explored in chapter 8, "fix public management" was given new priority in the development agenda. But then came the critique (also laid out in chapter 8) that underlying weaknesses in public management lay weaknesses in accountability—and that underlying these lay weaknesses in the quality of checks and balances institutions. "Fix these too" was the seemingly logical response.

Then there was the challenge of combatting corruption. In 1996, when Wolfensohn made a major speech signaling the World Bank's determination to fight the "cancer of corruption," he was breaking a decades-long practice of avoiding any explicit use of the C-word. But what unfolded over the subsequent dozen years (including during the tenures as World Bank president of Paul Wolfowitz and Robert Zoellick) went beyond recognition of the importance of the challenge. Corruption became something for which the Bank would have "zero tolerance."

At first sight, "zero tolerance for corruption" is unambiguously the right thing to do. But what exactly does it mean? Certainly it means a determined commitment to the highest standards of probity among Bank staff—something for which the organization continues, rightfully, to pride itself. It also means (again, appropriately, and an area where the Bank made a major push) a commitment to act on allegations of corruption associated with Bank-funded development projects—and the creation of mechanisms through which suspicions of malfeasance in development operations could easily be reported. And it can also mean, as per the discussion in chapters 9 and 10, the incorporation of transparent, third-party mechanisms for monitoring the implementation of efforts to improve service provision—something that increasingly has become a mainstream part of practice within the Bank.[2]

But "zero tolerance" can be taken to impossible lengths. As we have seen, corruption is endemic in many parts of the world. Indeed, the analysis in this book suggests that personalized deal-making organized around the sharing of rents is central to the logic of political order in many developing countries with weak formal institutions. Does "zero tolerance" imply that the World Bank and other donors should not work in these countries—even though this is where a large proportion of the world's poor live? Evidently, unless the intent is to end the aid endeavor almost entirely, the answer must be "no."

Holders of the purse-strings of foreign aid—the US Congress and parliaments throughout Western Europe, Japan, and elsewhere in the democratic, industrialized world—surely recognized the challenging realities. It is hardly as if their countries, where checks and balances institutions are strong, are entirely corruption free. But in the face of widespread skepticism among voters in "northern" countries as to the benefits of aid, they had little appetite for explaining these complexities to their constituents. On the contrary, in the polarized politics that increasingly prevailed within some donor countries, any effort to address complexity—indeed, any acknowledgment that results might fall short of perfection—risked playing into the hands of opponents, who were all too ready to characterize aid as wasteful support for "corrupt dictators."

In consequence, instead of an engagement with complexity, the mainstreaming of governance into the development discourse resulted, for the most part, in a "doubling down" on simplistic responses. The response of the development community to governance-related criticisms of its effectiveness was to say "yes":

Yes—public management will be fixed;

Yes—behind shortfalls in public management are weaknesses in accountability, and behind these are failures of checks and balances institutions—good governance will take care of these, and

Yes—corruption is a cancer, for which there will be zero tolerance.

Yes: Insofar as there was not already a perfect world, the efforts of the World Bank and other donor organizations (working in partnership with people of goodwill everywhere) would make it so.

In the immediacy of efforts to combat crises that threatened the legitimacy of the aid endeavor, high-minded affirmations serve as a firewall. But in the long run the consequences have become increasingly corrosive. Development unfolds in difficult environments with weak institutions; the outcomes even of the best efforts are inherently uncertain. Maximalist promises, for all of the immediate relief they provide, are inconsistent with both the substance and spirit of the task at hand.

To be sure, some teams of Bank staff members and their country counterparts remained strongly committed to their development mission—and quite often were able to do excellent work. And under the overall umbrella of the governance agenda, some staff within the World Bank and other development agencies pressed determinedly to incorporate political economy realities into development work, with some success.[3] On the anticorruption front, consensus was indeed reached that zero tolerance would not be taken to its absurd limit—the Bank would remain engaged even in the most difficult governance environments. But from the perspective of Bank staff, the message sometimes seemed ambiguous. (I still remember vividly the sense of crisis that pervaded the Bank's team working in Kenya when the media reported one of the country's endless scandals du jour—in this instance a corrupt deal on oceanfront real estate in a tourism project with which the World Bank Group had no involvement whatsoever.) Among staff who were unwilling to put their jobs on the line, the natural response to the anticorruption crusade was extreme aversion to risk. This reached its absurdist limit in an investment project in India that incorporated into its design the recruitment of close to 300 internal financial auditors to monitor how the money would be spent.

In the difficult environments where most poor people live, development work necessarily involves eyes-wide-open risk taking. However, in the culture that had taken hold within development agencies, mirroring back challenging uncertainties, and confronting fundamental dilemmas and trade-offs had in practice all-too-often become unacceptable. Viewed from the perspective of the immediate organizational imperatives of donors, what mattered most was the short-term impact on external constituencies of the words surrounding the governance and anticorruption agenda (GAC, in its unlovely acronym). But against a backdrop of maximalist, unachievable rhetoric, failure becomes the only plausible outcome.

*   *   *   *

There is a further pernicious consequence to this embrace of high-minded rhetoric, empty of meaningful content. Within developing countries, too, the governance agenda often turned into a preoccupation with form rather than an effort to achieve concrete development results. Matt Andrews and colleagues have usefully described this preoccupation with form as "isomorphism":[4]

> *the propensity for organizations to pursue change to get greater legitimacy, rather than better performance. . . . It commonly is seen as explaining change in contexts where entities are highly dependent on external con-stituencies in which more appropriate best practices are highly defined. . . . Organizations that do not yield to isomorphic pressures to adopt these best practices face losing legitimacy and external support.*

The good governance agenda comprises a powerful example of isomor-phism in action. It comes complete with powerful normative standards with a strong moral content and a variety of increasingly sophisticated scorecards for assessing how countries perform in relation to the standards.[5] The result, Andrews shows, is a repeated pattern of efforts to improve a country's perfor-mance vis-à-vis one or another of these scorecards—with a de facto emphasis on legislative and other "stroke of a pen" reforms that can achieve rapid de jure gains in performance. The aim is *"to earn governments in developing countries short-term credit from outsiders on whom they depend"*[6]—but all too often without anything of significance actually changing on the ground.

*   *   *   *

For all of the (false) comfort that it offers, it is time to put the good governance discourse behind us—it has become counterproductive in its consequences for development practice. This book is one of a series of recent contributions that explore practical alternatives.[7] While they vary in their details, all share the following features:

- an insistence that the appropriate point of departure for engagement is with the way things actually are on the ground—not some normative vision of how they should be;
- a focus on working to solve very specific development problems—moving away from a preoccupation with longer-term reforms of broader systems and processes, where results are long in coming and hard to discern, and where the temptation to engage in isomorphic mimicry is correspondingly large; and
- an emphasis on ongoing learning—in recognition that no blueprint can adequately capture the complex reality of a specific setting and thus that implementation must inevitably involve a process of iterative adaptation.

The distinguishing feature of this book is its extended exploration of "good fit." "Good fit" offers an initial orienting framework, as a guide for helping to identify which of a broad array of alternative interventions potentially are most relevant as points of departure, across a parsimonious set of divergent country settings. The intent is not to prescribe some mechanical formula but to provide a platform for subsequent learning. Chapter 12 provides more detail as to how this might work.

CHAPTER 12

Navigating the Development Knife-Edge

When we look beneath the rhetorical discourse and focus on the realities of governance, what we see can be startling, even dispiriting. But this should not come as a surprise.

The goal of governance reform is to establish the institutions, the rules of the game, within which economic and political processes play out. When the rules are clear, and their monitoring and enforcement mechanisms are in place, they can recede into the background, and the focus can be on the game itself. But when the rules themselves are contested, and there is as yet little mutual agreement as to how they will be enforced, then what can more often come to the fore are the most unruly and difficult dimensions of human nature.

Consider the way in which two Nobel Prize-winning economists, Douglass North and Oliver Williamson, define institutions and governance. According to North, institutions are "humanly devised constraints which govern human interaction." Williamson builds on this, suggesting that "governance is an effort to craft order, thereby to mitigate conflict and realize mutual gains."[1] In focusing on the governance dimensions of development we are thus, by definition, seeking mechanisms of addressing a struggle between our better and our baser natures in a manner that facilitates cooperation. So it is unsurprising that when we look closely—and especially when we look at settings where the restraints themselves are still being contested—we see this struggle in action, with the outcome profoundly uncertain.

Sometimes we see an ongoing struggle between enforcing and reneging on agreements. Sometimes we see an effort to bring order by appealing to self-interested, self-seeking motivations that, if not addressed, threaten to bring down the entire edifice of cooperation. And sometimes we see the lust to dominate—or, perhaps, the effort to fight fire with fire by repressing opponents whose perceived desire to dominate is what we fear.

Confronting such primal uncertainty is profoundly discomfiting, in all of its messiness and all its ambiguity. So, instead, we embrace ways of escape. One escape route is to neuter this struggle behind a veil of bloodless technocracy. Another (less bloodless but perhaps no less effective as a way of evading the messiness and complexity) is to frame a fight to the finish between all that is noble ("us") and all that is base ("them")—and then to advocate high-mindedly for "best practices" that somehow assume away, or decisively defeat, all that stands in the way of their achievement.

This book, by contrast, offers neither the false comfort of assuming away the more difficult realities of human nature that are at the heart of the challenge of improving governance nor the false certainty of ready-made solutions. Rather, its central tenet is that to achieve progress we need to begin by seeing things as they are and to work from there. If we do that, we have the possibility of initiating and sustaining forward movement along the development knife-edge. That is the essence of what I mean by "working with the grain."

Integrating Governance into Development Strategy—A Multilevel Approach

Governance shapes development strategy at multiple levels. At the most fundamental level are the ways in which the prevailing institutional and political arrangements shape incentives and constraints—and the strategic decision as to which of these arrangements should be accepted as given and which should be the focus of efforts at reform. One level down are questions of how to prioritize and sequence governance reform. At a more microlevel are questions of the design of specific, focused efforts to address specific governance and policy challenges within specific sectors. Each is considered in turn.

Which trajectory?—An agnostic approach.   In writing this book, one of my goals has been to try and win some space for the effort to nurture sustainable democracy from its more grandiose champions. Advocacy of democracy has been maximalist, shrill, its pendulum swinging repeatedly from euphoria to outrage, with disappointment along the way. Taking a long-run perspective, my deepest governance commitment is to support the emergence of sustainable democracies. But, as we have explored, the paths to sustainable democracy are circuitous, roundabout. For this reason, I have come to the view that, taking a decade-or-so horizon for decision making—the time horizon of even relatively far-sighted leaders and the focus of this book—the appropriate point of departure for devising a development-friendly governance strategy is agnosticism as to which trajectory offers the better way forward.

This case for agnosticism rests on the desirability of sustaining the momentum of the virtuous circles that, as laid out in chapter 6, link inclusive growth, positive expectations, and institutional improvement—irrespective of the country's point of departure. The argument has three steps: that feasible options vary across countries and over time; that over the short to medium run the resulting choices can widen divergence in patterns of governance across countries; but that, over the long run, the power of cumulative causation can lead to convergence.

Consider first the implications of differences across countries in the incentives and constraints that shape the decisions of policymakers. As we have explored throughout this book, a country's economic, social, and political institutions cannot be reengineered from scratch. At any moment, each country has a distinctive point of departure, with distinctive incentives and constraints, distinctive pathways of search and learning—and thus distinctive trajectories of change over the longer run. But while each country is distinctive, there are a few underlying patterns. This book has focused principally on two trajectories—dominant and competitive, each with a personalized and impersonal institutional variant. As we have explored in detail, the incentives and constraints are starkly different along the two trajectories and so, too, are the feasible ways forward.

In early stages along the dominant trajectory, the constraints on political leaders may be few; all too often, the result can be predation and continuing dysfunction. But on occasion leadership can emerge that is both developmentally oriented and has a firm hold on power. In such settings, top-down reform designs capable of leveraging robust principal–agent governance along the lines laid out in chapter 8 may have good prospects of getting results. The examples in chapter 4 of Korea and Ethiopia illustrate how this might work.

By contrast, in early stage personalized-competitive settings power often is fragmented, leaders are constrained, and public bureaucracies are weak. In these settings, maintaining political stability can be a challenge—and the deal-making through which it is sustained can fall way, way (way) short of any idealized notion of good governance. In these settings, the focus of reform efforts might better be on establishing "islands of effectiveness" within a broader sea of dysfunction by nurturing robust relationships among stakeholders who both enjoy influence and have a stake in achieving the targeted outcome. The examples in chapter 5 of Bangladesh and Zambia illustrate how seemingly modest beach-heads of dynamism can provide a platform for moving development forward.

Between these two contrasting ideal-type trajectories we find a variety of hybrid shades of gray. One hybrid type comprises dominant patrimonialism—where leaders have a sufficiently firm hold on power and enough commitment to move their country forward but in ways that fall far short of the ideal type of a developmental state, with corruption often endemic. Another comprises countries where the political rules of the game are competitive, but in practice one party dominates, at least for a period of time. The resulting pattern might resemble that of a dominant, developmental state (as in Georgia's performance between 2000 and 2010, as per chapter 7), or it might take on more of a dominant patrimonial flavor (as per South African governance under African National Congress leadership, detailed in chapter 6). But irrespective of the specifics of a country's institutional configuration—dominant, competitive, or some hybrid combination—the central point remains: that a country's distinctive political and institutional arrangements result in a distinctive set of incentives and constraints on decision making and thus distinctive trajectories of change.

The second step of the argument is that in the short to medium run, as countries develop, their institutional differences might widen. Here the underlying logic comes directly from Douglass North's analysis of "path dependence." As we have seen, each of the trajectories offer distinctive paths of growth—and, as North explored, this growth is likely to be accompanied by corresponding changes in policies, rules of the game, and organizational capabilities that reinforce the preexisting trajectory. Changes in policies and the institutional rules of the game evoke complementary investments in the capabilities of organizations that operate within that specific environment. And these organizations are likely, in turn, to generate pressure for a further round of supportive policy and institutional reforms. The result can be a cumulative process of change—one that can, over long periods of time, generate a very wide dispersion of patterns.[2]

But this brings us to the third step—namely the potential for cumulative causation to bring convergence over the longer run. As we explored in chapter 6, with continuing forward momentum—and with a pattern of growth that is inclusive—the private sector, civil society, and middle-class actors all are likely to strengthen. In turn, the growing strength of these actors can bring to the forefront a new set of institutional considerations. Actors who in earlier stages might have thrived on personalized arrangements might now seek something different—better public services, more contractual certainty, and greater personal freedom. These changes can provide a platform for addressing those institutional weaknesses where, in earlier stages of the process, the constraints on change were especially formidable. How this might play out is, again, different along the dominant and competitive trajectories.

Along the dominant trajectory, a central question concerns whether the greater complexity of social and economic organization will be accompanied by a strengthening of checks and balances institutions. In some settings

(Korea, for example), forward momentum provided a platform for successfully transforming the country into a sustainable democracy. In others, as in the Arab spring and the travails that followed, there may have been sufficient momentum to overthrow a hitherto dominant regime—but insufficient authority and capacity to subsequently put in place workable, open, checks and balances institutions. (Underlying these weaknesses may have been an insufficiently inclusive pattern of prior growth and hence perhaps an insufficiently strong middle class.) And, of course, there also are other countries where dominant development continues with little sign, at least on the surface, of any likely opening.

Along the competitive trajectory, the central long-run challenge often has to do with the quality of government. Dissatisfaction can grow with poor public services and with the corrupt abuse of political power for private purposes. At the same time, perceptions of the shared benefits of better public-sector capability might become strong enough to outweigh the gains from zero-sum competition among rivalrous groups. The late-nineteenth-century US example, discussed in chapter 6, illustrates how gains might be achieved incrementally and cumulatively, via both legislative reforms and skillful orchestration of new constituencies for change by reformers operating within the bureaucracy. And in *Jobs for the Boys*, Merilee Grindle documents how in the early 2000s democratic competition resulted in legislative reforms of both the Mexican and Chilean public administrations—though in both countries the process involved much less civic buy-in than in the century-earlier experience of the United States, and their impact remains uncertain.

Taken together, the three steps underscore that, as long as there is forward movement in some dimensions of the virtuous circle, it brings with it the possibility (though not the certainty) of gains in the others. Incremental, working-with-the-grain reforms thus offer an evolutionary path of progress, with the potential to cumulatively achieve progressively more far-reaching gains over time.

But working with the grain need not always be the right way forward. As we saw in chapter 7, in some settings the momentum of economic growth may be accompanied by a rise in corruption and a reversal in the quality of institutions. In these, the case can be strong for nongovernmental actors, for reformers within government, and perhaps for donors to take on a watchdog role—highlighting the reversals, and building coalitions to push back against signs of rising impunity. More fundamentally, in countries that have long been mired in stasis, dysfunction, and endemic exclusion, there may be little if any scope for working with the grain. In such settings, discontinuous policy and institutional reform—even discontinuous political change—may be necessary, indeed desirable.

Prioritizing and sequencing governance reform.   While virtuous circles create the opportunity for more far-reaching governance improvements over time, there is no automaticity to the process. It takes effort and leadership from political leaders, public officials, and civil society activists to sustain the momentum of institutional improvement. But if a maximalist "good governance" agenda is unhelpful what, concretely, does a working-with-the-grain approach imply as to how governance reforms might be prioritized and sequenced along each of the different trajectories?

Let us begin with reforms for improving public management. As we explored in depth in chapter 8, there is continuing controversy as to the right balance between efforts to strengthen the public management system as a whole, focusing on cross-cutting functions, and efforts that target specific results within specific sectors—including, at the limit, a focus on strengthening "islands of effectiveness" in a broader sea of dysfunction. Other things equal, a more integrated system is more desirable than one that is haphazard, fragmented. But other things are, of course, not equal. So in the spirit of strategic agnosticism, Table 12.1 (building on the earlier Table 8.2) suggests a more differentiated approach.

Along the dominant trajectory, "making government work" can indeed be the basis on which leaders championing development along the dominant trajectory assert their claim on power—and occasionally even mean it. In such settings, ambitious efforts to build public-sector capacity have the potential to yield steady improvements. Korea and Ethiopia (in chapter 4) and perhaps China, Rwanda, and Vietnam (as per the data in chapter 7) offer examples.

By contrast, in early-stage competitive settings leaders generally will not have uncontested authority to set and sustain a consistent vision over time, so the opportunities to strengthen public capacity are more limited. For this group of countries, gains in public management are likely to be achieved incrementally—building outward from sectoral and functional islands of effectiveness and spurred on, as development takes hold, by increasingly powerful private-sector and middle-class constituencies. In these settings, a preoccupation with comprehensive public management reform initiatives has a high risk of being counterproductive—distracting attention from more achievable goals, only to be abandoned before anything has actually been achieved.

If the standard agenda of public management reforms yields results only in the long run—and if long-run approaches are unlikely to gain traction in early-stage competitive settings—what actions can be taken to improve public services and provide development momentum in the nearer term, in both dominant and competitive settings? Table 12.1 highlights a variety of options from earlier chapters:

- Focus sectorally to get early results, without waiting for broader reforms of core public management systems. Note that a results focus is agnostic

Table 12.1 **Early-Stage Governance Reforms—Some Feasible Options**

	Public Management	*Multistakeholder*	*Other Checks and Balances*
Competitive	• Initiate merit-based management for some senior public service positions	• Incorporate stakeholders in governance of public-service provision • Strengthen "bottom-up" accountability of local governments	• Build strong, impartial electoral oversight arrangements • Provide legal platform for press freedom; support media capacity building; initiate right to information process
Dominant	• Initiate comprehensive public management reform		????
All	• Results-driven reform in a few priority sectors • Build small high-capacity units in central policy and budget agencies • Build internal financial controls	• Utilize participatory mechanisms for monitoring service provision • Consider "parallel" service provision initiatives • Utilize external anchors as commitment mechanisms	• Initiate capacity development for judiciary and other nonexecutive institutions of accountability

with respect to process. This can be especially crucial in early-stage settings where the most effective ways for leaders to deliver often can be to use their discretionary authority, bypassing whatever formal processes may be in place, and recruiting trusted associates who they are confident have the skills and commitment to deliver.[3]

• Give early priority to a few core systems that enable sector-level initiatives to move forward—policy processes for identifying a few key priorities and for getting resources to their champions, plus some initial steps in the ongoing long-term effort to put in place a robust system of financial controls.

• Initiate targeted efforts to introduce merit-based approaches to the management of a modest number of relatively senior civil service positions—thereby beginning to build a cadre of public officials with the skills, incentive, and commitment to sustain the development agenda over the longer term, through the vicissitudes of political changes, but without confronting directly the use by political leaders of patronage to reward allies and buy off potential opponents.

As a complementary way of moving rapidly to build momentum, the second column of Table 12.1 suggests a variety of options for engaging stakeholders in improving service provision, including:

- Participatory approaches to the governance and monitoring of service provision—especially crucial in early-stage competitive settings, where (as per chapters 8 and 9) involving stakeholders can help build a coalition capable of trumping predatory efforts to capture public purposes.
- "Parallel" arrangements for providing services—especially relevant in settings where public management capacity is weak (As chapter 9 explored, while such mechanisms often are criticized for undercutting efforts to build public-sector capacity, both the evidence and the logic of the argument are more ambiguous than the critics suggest.)
- Drawing in stakeholders from outside the country—via global and regional commitment mechanisms (along the lines of the Chad oil pipeline and other examples in chapter 10) as another way of filling the gap that comes from weak early-stage institutions.

Also included in the second column of Table 12.1 are efforts to strengthen the accountability of local governments; decentralization comprises a far-reaching set of potentially participatory governance reforms that need to be mentioned but an exploration of which goes way beyond the scope of this book.

Finally, Table 12.1 includes options for prioritizing and sequencing efforts to strengthen formal checks and balances arrangements. A principal goal of checks and balances reform is to provide credible commitment—assurance to citizens and firms that promises made by government (and restraints on arbitrary action more broadly) will be honored into the future. The long-run task is to enshrine commitments into laws, enforceable by an impartial judiciary and supported by other arms-length institutions of accountability (e.g., supreme audit agencies tasked with overseeing and reporting publicly on the quality of public spending). However, as chapter 6 explored, in many countries a capable judiciary may emerge quite late in the development process—only once contending elites conclude that it is in their interests to abide by impartial third-party dispute resolution, rather than try to impose their will directly.

For countries developing along the competitive trajectory, the early-stage reform priorities for strengthening checks and balances institutions are clear, though not necessarily easy to implement. As per the final column of Table 12.1, credible electoral competition can assure powerful groupings outside the circle of power that they have the potential to become insiders— it is fundamental to the stability of the system and needs priority attention from the first. Support for press freedom, for access to information, and media capacity building might also be useful early priorities, as signals of commitment to the type of political and civic discourse that must be nurtured if a country is to thrive along the competitive trajectory. But note that, even within the competitive group of countries, there is a need for differentiation. Reforms to foster openness will work best in settings where a baseline of political stability has been achieved. In more fragile settings, a determined commitment to openness runs the risk of bringing more contestation and conflict into the system than its weak institutions can bear.

One final question on the sequencing of checks and balances reform is highlighted (but not answered) in Table 12.1: How can countries developing along the dominant trajectory consolidate credibility over the long haul? This challenge goes to the heart of how their political regime is organized. In the near term, their principal source of credibility comes from consistent leadership— consistency in how the public sector performs, in the honoring of agreements, and in attention to the concerns of stakeholders (including private-sector stakeholders) outside the immediate inner circle of power. But leaders can change. One way of trying to sustain credibility is to do "more of the same, only better"—to strive (e.g., like Singapore) through continual improvement to be on the global cutting edge in providing a world-class business environment. The dilemma, though, is that this does not reckon with broader challenges of legitimacy. Whether, when, and to what extent countries along the dominant trajectory should proactively invest in checks and balances institutions is a fateful question that goes beyond the scope of this book. But it is one with which the countries themselves must continually wrestle, or else risk losing all.

Finding a good fit at microlevels.   Complementing reforms of governance systems, a variety of microlevel policy and institutional initiatives can help accelerate economic growth, improve public service provision, and alleviate poverty. At these microlevels, too, the choice arises as to which background policies, institutions, and political arrangements should be taken as given and worked around and which potentially are subject to change. Technocratic, "best practice," engineering approaches presuppose that everything can be modified. "Good fit" approaches explore how to work creatively with the prevailing policy, institutional, and political realities.

But "good fit" need not take as given the limitations of the background environment. Consider Figure 12.1, which characterizes a spectrum of reform options. Each point along the spectrum is a departure from "best practice." At one end is the option of adapting a reform agenda to align with the existing

Figure 12.1 **The Spectrum of Reform Space**

space for reform; at the other end is the option of engaging with stakeholders to expand the space for reform.

At every level of decision making, reformers (be they in government, civil society, or the donor community) must clarify how to position their engagement vis-à-vis this spectrum. While room for maneuver generally is likely to be limited vis-à-vis "big-G" reforms of a country's core governance arrangements, at more microlevels the scope potentially is larger along both trajectories to be proactive in working to ease constraints. In early-stage dominant countries, the goals of higher-level political leaders could lead them to facilitate initiatives that push against local power structures. In early-stage competitive countries, the configuration of power is likely to be quite fluid—affording ample opportunity for developmentally oriented actors to build alliances capable of warding off predators. Overall, less is at stake for political leaders at microlevels, so there potentially is greater scope for search and learning as to how to position a reform along the Figure 12.1 spectrum.

Table 12.2 summarizes six examples from a recent assessment of efforts within the World Bank to use political economy analysis to identify good-fit policy options.[4] The examples span three continents and a very broad range of sectors and policies—from electricity generation in Zambia, to food and fuel subsidies in Morocco, the allocation of mineral resource rents in Mongolia, agricultural investment in Ghana, and health, roads, and other local infrastructure in Papua New Guinea and the Philippines. In most of the countries, the proposed good-fit reforms drew from both ends of the Figure 12.1 spectrum.

Some of the left end of the spectrum proposals for feasible, politically responsive policy reforms did not stray far from the conventional wisdom; an example here is the proposal to accompany reforms of fuel subsidies in Morocco with the introduction of social programs to support the poorest. Other proposals were more heterodox—for example the proposal to go slow with broad-based reform of Zambia's electricity sector and instead work closely with mining companies to foster new investment in electricity generation. (Bangladesh's garment success—described in chapter 5 and organized around special purpose arrangements that finessed seemingly immovable institutional and political obstacles—comprises a further example of a left-end of the spectrum initiative.)

Table 12.2 **From Diagnosis to Action—Some Additional Examples**

Country and policy challenge	"Good Fit" Policy Proposals	
	Politically responsive design	*Information and multi-stakeholder approaches*
Morocco: Fiscal pressure to reform expensive food and fuel subsidies	Introduce social programs to support the poorest alongside subsidy reforms	Initiate communications campaign on who benefits from existing subsidies and what the costs are
Zambia: Below-cost pricing and underinvestment in electricity generation	Narrow the sectoral reform agenda; engage mining firms who have incentives to incur the costs of new investment	Communication campaign focused on low connectivity to electricity among poor and rural residents
Mongolia: Populist pressure to spend new mining revenues	Build capacity of nongovernmental actors to generate and communicate policy analysis on mining-sector-related policies and their economic impacts	
Ghana: Introduce commercialized agriculture	Create outgrower partnerships linking small and commercial farmers, and enhance mutual confidence on rules of game via multistakeholder consensus-building process around local benefits of incoming agriculture investment	
Papua New Guinea: Political capture of local infrastructure finance	Target grants to the lowest tier of local government	Provide citizen-friendly information on local infrastructure decisions
Philippines: Ad hoc, politically driven allocation of national funds for local health and roads	Specify very precise upfront, sector-specific, performance-based criteria as basis for targeting allocations	Provide comparable public information on performance across localities

Source: Case studies in Fritz, Levy, and Ort (2014).

Somewhat unexpected was the ubiquity of proposals to enhance transparency and participation along lines that paralleled the discussion of chapters 9 and 10. The studies were conducted independently of one another; and the authors brought very different analytical lenses to bear. Their convergence around informational and participatory initiatives as a way forward offers some encouragement that, while a move from "best practice" to "good fit" approaches opens up the range of options, it does not open it up so far as to undercut the potential for learning across countries and sectors.

The growing embrace of good fit and problem-driven, learning-oriented approaches at sectoral levels poses both an opportunity and a challenge for a new generation of work on governance-responsive policy and institutional reforms at microlevels. The opportunity arises from the extraordinary wide range of illustrative sectoral applications—a focus on "good fit" and on iterative learning has the potential to set in motion far-reaching changes in development practice. But therein lies the challenge. At microlevels, it is sectoral specialists who will need to take the lead in broadening the range of sectoral options. If this is to happen, it will require a willingness by these specialists to step out of familiar comfort zones— and be open to drawing on "softer" disciplines, letting go of some strong nostrums from their technical training, and learning how to select from the expanded menu of options in a way that better aligns design choices with specific country settings.

Entry Points for Public Entrepreneurs

The multilevel approach laid out in the previous section suggests ways forward for political leaders, policymakers, and practitioners tasked with the challenge of integrating governance into development strategy. But sometimes (perhaps most of the time), change does not happen only through formal, top-down channels—the role of public entrepreneurs is key. This section explores potential entry points for two types of public entrepreneurs—civic activists and public officials committed to finding ways to achieve development results from within an often dysfunctional system. The focus is not only on the "what" is to be done but also on the "how" and "by whom."

Strengthening public service.   As we have seen, especially in weak governance settings, senior public officials can have high levels of discretion. There has been intensive focus in the development discourse on the risks that officials will take advantage of this discretion for corrupt- self-seeking purposes. But less attention has been given to the development opportunity afforded by discretion— namely the potential to facilitate the emergence of "islands of effectiveness".

Discretion opens up the possibility for officials in positions of influence to act as public entrepreneurs: to devote themselves to the achievement of a specific public purpose; to give concreteness and direction to that purpose; and to nurture within their corner of government a team with the skills and commitment to achieve that purpose. Working closely with external stakeholders is key: By engaging stakeholders in processes of implementation and oversight, public entrepreneurs both can build the external alliances needed to fend off opposition, and can win a reputation for integrity—and thereby signal their commitment, even in seemingly unpropitious settings, to be civil servants in the fullest sense of the term.

To be sure, viewed from the conventional perspective of the role of bureaucracy, goal setting is the responsibility of the political leadership; it is for public officials to follow through, not to hubristically take for themselves a power that lies elsewhere. But such a dictum has little, if any, practical relevance in the many settings where the realities of politics fall way, way short of the textbook model and where the risks of stasis and political capture loom large. Indeed, as we saw in chapter 6, public entrepreneurship in the face of opposition from politicians was integral to the emergence of performance-oriented bureaucratic autonomy in the United States.

To successfully pursue public entrepreneurship within government requires a long-term commitment. It takes well over a decade to get real traction for some very specific public purpose—to define a clear, implementable set of tasks; to build the requisite internal capabilities and alliances; and to follow through with implementation to a point of sufficient critical mass to resist reversal once the first generation of champions move from the scene. Top-level political appointees and career-oriented public officials eager to move on to the next step in the ladder of prestige appointments rarely are likely to be in position long enough to follow through in this way. Successful public entrepreneurship thus requires a rare combination of sufficient ambition and skill to get to a position from where it is possible to make a difference—and then a sufficiently deep commitment to a specific purpose to resist the lure of greater prestige, and seemingly greater opportunity, in some other position.

Civic activism—A long view.   For civic activists, a critical challenge is to find solid ground between large, idealistic but unattainable visions on the one hand and an often dispiriting reality on the other. A key distinction is between settings where development is blocked and those where, for all the myriad challenges, there is sufficient momentum to keep the process moving forward. For the latter, the with-the-grain approach to development laid out in this book points to abundant opportunities for directing the energies of civic activism toward concrete, less crisis-driven initiatives—with a particular premium on activities where results potentially are observable in the time horizons in which activists and their supporter engage.

The first and most straightforward entry point is to focus activism on participatory efforts to improve the provision of public services. As emphasized earlier in this chapter, in many countries, the emergence of islands of effectiveness offers the most feasible way to get results—and the success of these islands depends crucially on the robustness of developmentally oriented multistakeholder coalitions. Leadership can come from committed public officials—but it can equally well come from civil society activists, perhaps via initiatives that function entirely outside of government, perhaps working to build alliances with partners within government from the outside in.

The benefits of focusing on the quality of public services potentially can go beyond specific gains in the targeted areas. Such a focus—especially where it incorporates participatory results monitoring—has the potential to be a powerful way of combating corruption by helping to hold providers accountable for how public resources are used, in the context of a positive discourse of partnership and poverty reduction. A focus on specific public actions also opens up the opportunity for public–private partnerships—for example, by orchestrating anticorruption initiatives around integrity pacts incorporating third-party monitoring of large-scale public procurement transactions.[5] There also may be some synergies between democracy advocates and champions of participatory service provision. As discussed in chapter 9, though the evidence remains mixed, there are at least some grounds for optimism that these kinds of bottom-up approaches can contribute somewhat to the cultivation of an ethos of active citizenship. There is much still to be learned—some of which is surely likely to be important to understanding better how democracies might consolidate over time.

A second promising entry point is to seek out targeted opportunities for leveraging globalized initiatives as institutional substitutes for weaknesses in country-level governance. Chapter 10 suggested a wide variety of ways in which a focus on the corporate governance practices of global firms might have an impact—perhaps through initiatives to rein in bribe-giving (corruption is, of course, a transaction that has a private as well as a public-sector dimension) or perhaps by targeting corporate practices vis-à-vis environmental protection, labor standards, and the extraction of natural resources. Shareholder activism, tightly managed global value chains, and global internet connectivity offer a powerful new generation of tools. Using trade regimes to set minimum standards for imports offers another lever—one that already is being used in the United States as a tool for helping to enforce environmental regulations in developing countries, protecting endangered species, and protecting the ozone layer via a ban on the importation of products manufactured with chloro-fluorocarbons.[6] Given these opportunities, for development activists from Northern countries in particular, advocacy for better governance might most usefully begin at home.

A third potential entry point comprises a reorientation of the approach to governance monitoring—one that focuses less on comparative ranking of countries and year-to-year changes in specific indicators and more on broad trends over time. Such an approach is not geared to getting immediate results; rather, it offers a way of focusing on big governance questions without becoming trapped in polarizing cycles of judgment and recrimination. Monitoring might focus on broad trends over time in the quality of a country's control of corruption—and be ready to sound the alarm in the face of evidence of any systematic weakening, which might be an early warning signal of a downward slide from, say, stability-enhancing patronage to predation. More broadly, the focus could be on trends over time across a range of governance dimensions—not only corruption but also, say, the quality of elections, quality of the rule of law, transparency, and the quality of government—providing a platform for nurturing constructive dialogue on the limits and risks implied by the lagging areas and how they might be addressed.

Leading ethically.   One final but fundamental point for public entrepreneurs emerges from this book's focus on governance and institutions—namely the central importance of leading ethically. While an ethical approach to leadership always is desirable, it has special relevance in weak governance settings. Why? Because where the rules of the game remain fluid, effective leadership is key to moving things forward—but the risks also are large of opportunistic, unethical leaders taking advantage of fluid rules to pursue narrowly personal goals. Personal ethics is the crucial difference-maker as to which of these radically different outcomes transpires in practice.

Ethical leadership is crucial along both the dominant and competitive trajectories—but the channels through which it makes a difference are different in each. In early-stage dominant settings there can quite often be a sense of momentum—but whether it brings dynamism or predation depends to an extraordinary degree on the example modeled (and enforced) by top political leadership. In early-stage competitive settings, the frontier challenge is not to transform government as a whole but is rather the more modest goal of building islands of effectiveness. But islands can take hold only where principals have sufficient confidence among one another to cooperate—and such cooperation is hugely facilitated where participants have a reputation for integrity. Always and everywhere, a commitment to integrity is a crucial buttress to the development process.

A Journey of Hope

The great development economist Albert Hirschman described the "fundamental bent" of his writing as being "to set the stage for conceptions of change to which the inventiveness of history and a 'passion for the possible' are admitted as vital actors."[7] The title of his 1971 book on development and Latin America—*A Bias for Hope*—captured the spirit of his endeavor.

Hope can come in different intonations. There is the drumbeat of exhortation, of a world on the march to some more perfect destination on the horizon. But hope can also come in a quieter pitch: softer voices, calming rather than raising the temperature, searching—encouraging deliberation, reflection, co-operation. The past half-century has witnessed historically unprecedented gains in development on both the economic and governance fronts. But for reasons this book has tried to explore, the institutional underpinnings of these gains remain fragile: Developmental leadership can all too easily turn predatory; democracies often can be less inclusive, less responsive, and more prone to violent confrontation than we might have hoped. Building sturdier foundations is a many-decades-long task.

In the later stages of his career, Hirschman turned his attention from trying to understand the processes of social and economic change to trying to understand how we thought and spoke about them—and how our framing often hindered our efforts to find ways forward. In his deceptively simple book, *The Rhetoric of Reaction*, he seemingly sets out to unearth the rhetorical devices that, over many centuries, have underlain critiques of reform. But then, toward the end, he confesses that his goal is more ambitious.[8] He suggests that

> *Reactionary theses . . . along with their progressive counterparts, [are] extreme statements in a series of imaginary, highly polarized debates. . . . There remains a long and difficult road to be traveled from the traditional internecine, intransigent discourse to a more "democracy-friendly" kind of dialogue. . . . My purpose is to move public discourse beyond extreme, intransigent postures of either kind, with the hope that in the process . . . participants engage in meaningful discussion, ready to modify initially held opinions in the light of other arguments and new information.*[9]

In its confident assertions that the full set of "good governance" reforms is necessary for development and that, without this full set, governance reform—and development more broadly—cannot succeed, the dominant discourse on governance offers a powerful example of the rhetoric of intransigence in action: If the only available actions and outcomes are "all" or "nothing" efforts at change will almost certainly fall short, leading to disillusion and despair.

In this book, I have sought to portray development as an evolutionary process—not as an engineering task of constructing some edifice on the basis of prespecified blueprints, but as a journey of exploration. The book has tried to identify some key challenges along the way, to offer some navigation charts for a variety of different routes, and to suggest some tactics that can perhaps facilitate forward movement. A vision of "good governance" is perhaps somewhat helpful as a north star that can help guide navigation, but it is no more than that. If the journey requires crossing a stormy sea, voyagers must navigate the heavy winds and the churning currents. Inevitably, the winds, the tides, the ocean will bring new, unanticipated, and sometimes seemingly intractable challenges. Our task is to bring our best effort to the search for ways forward. We can do no more than that, and should strive to do no less.

NOTES

Prelude

1. Larry Diamond, *The Spirit of Democracy* (New York: Times Books, 2008, p. 372).
2. Classic texts include Albert Hirschman, *The Strategy of Economic Development* (New Haven, CT: Yale University Press, 1957); Paul Rosenstein-Rodan, "Problems of Industrialization of Eastern and South-Eastern Europe," *Economic Journal*, Vol. 53, No. 210, 1943; W.W. Rostow, *The Stages of Economic Growth* (Cambridge: Cambridge University Press); and Fernando Henrique Cardoso and Enzo Faletto, *Dependency and Development in Latin America* (Berkeley: University of California Press, 1979).
3. Key contributions include Douglass North, John Wallis, and Barry Weingast, *Violence and Social Orders* (New York: Cambridge University Press, 2009); Francis Fukuyama, *The Origins of Political Order* (New York: Farrar, Straus and Giroux, 2012); and Daron Acemoglu and James Robinson, *Why Nations Fail* (New York: Crown Books, 2012).
4. The phrase is the title of Albert O. Hirschman, *A Bias for Hope* (New Haven, CT: Yale University Press, 1971).

Chapter 1

1. World Bank, "Zambia: Completion Report for 1999–2003 Country Assistance Strategy."
2. Douglass North, John Wallis, and Barry Weingast, *Violence and Social Orders* (New York: Cambridge University Press, 2009); Dani Rodrik, *One Economics, Many Recipes* (Princeton, NJ: Princeton University Press, 2008); Francis Fukuyama, *The Origins of Political Order* (New York: Farrar, Straus and Giroux, 2012); and Merilee Grindle, "Good Enough Governance: Poverty Reduction and Reform in Developing Countries," *Governance*, Vol. 17, No. 4 (October 2004): 525–548.
3. Bill Easterly's distinction between planners and searchers—with its "searcher hero" groping in the dark, drawing on tacit knowledge of the unique characteristics of specific locales—risks falling into this trap. Its preoccupation with what we don't know undercuts almost entirely the value of both specific technical expertise and on-the-ground experience across multiple countries. See William Easterly, *The White Man's Burden* (New York: Penguin Books, 2006).
4. Daron Acemoglu and James Robinson's narrative in their widely read book *Why Nations Fail* (New York: Crown Books, 2012) spans half a millennium. North, Wallis, and Weingast immodestly give *Violence and Social Orders,* the subtitle, "a conceptual framework for interpreting recorded human history." And in his book *The Origins of Social Order,* Francis Fukuyama locates the deep roots of contemporary governance challenges in biologically conditioned patterns of personalized reciprocal altruism, which trace back to our prehuman ancestors.

5. Readers familiar with the literatures on complexity theory and evolution will recognize the three propositions as familiar properties for many complex systems. For one example from a very different domain than economics, see Richard Dawkins' classic book on evolution, *The Blind Watchmaker*.

6. Douglass North's classic book *Institutions, Institutional Change and Economic Performance* (New York: Cambridge University Press, 1990) highlights through the lens of economic history how this "path dependence" explains why some societies and economies thrived while others stagnated. In a similar vein, Albert O. Hirschman's lifelong body of work underscores the role of leads and lags in social change and the consequent advantages for policymakers of seeking not to effect change simultaneously on all fronts but rather to invest in fostering creative imbalances. Albert O. Hirschman, *A Strategy of Economic Development* (New Haven, CT: Yale University Press, 1955); see also his *A Bias for Hope: Essays on Development and Latin America* (New Haven, CT: Yale University Press, 1971).

7. Brian Levy, "Democracy Support and Development Aid: The Case for Principled Agnosticism," *Journal of Democracy*, Vol. 21, No. 4, (October 2010): 27–34.

Chapter 2

1. Brian Levy and Sahr Kpundeh (eds.), *Building State Capacity in Africa* (Washington, DC: World Bank, 2004).

2. The fifteen comprised the full set of projects designed and managed (and for which information on progress was available) over the recent time periods by the group I was then managing, the World Bank's Africa Public Sector Reform and Capacity Building Unit.

3. For some recent examples of critiques of democratization along these lines, see Steven Levitsky and Lucan Way, *Competitive Authoritarianism* (New York: Cambridge University Press, 2010); and Fareed Zakaria, *Illiberal Democracy* (New York: W.W. Norton, 2007).

4. For the classic statement of this argument, see Samuel Huntington, *Political Order in Changing Societies* (New Haven, CT: Yale University Press, 1968); see also Zakaria (2007).

5. More precisely, according to Khan a political settlement emerges when (i) the distribution of benefits supported by its institutions is consistent with the distribution of power in society and (ii) the economic and political outcome of these institutions are sustainable over time. See Mushtaq Khan, "Political Settlements and the Governance of Growth-Enhancing Institutions," mimeo 2010. North, Wallis, and Weingast (2009) use the terminology of a "fragile limited access order" to explore a similar issue.

6. Eminent early institutionalists include Thorstein Veblen, John Commons, and Karl Marx.

7. Seminal contributions include Douglass North, *Structure and Change in Economic History* (New York: W.W. Norton, 1982); Douglass North, *Institutions, Institutional Change and Development Performance* (New York: Cambridge University Press, 1990); Elinor Ostrom, *Governing the Commons* (New York: Cambridge University Press, 1990); Elinor Ostrom, *Understanding Institutional Diversity* (New York: Cambridge University Press, 2005); Ronald Coase, "The Nature of the Firm," *Economica*, Vol. 4, No. 16 (November 1937); Ronald Coase, "The Problem of Social Cost," *Journal of Law and Economics*, Vol. 3; Oliver Williamson, *The Economic Institutions of Capitalism* (New York: The Free Press, 1985); and Oliver Williamson, "The New Institutional Economics: Taking Stock, Looking Ahead," *Journal of Economic Literature* (September 2000): 595–613.

8. For a general discussion of the distinction between form and function, see Dani Rodrik, *One Economics, Many Recipes* (Princeton, NJ: Princeton University Press, 2007).

9. For the results of the research project, see Brian Levy and Pablo Spiller (eds.), *Regulations, Institutions and Commitment* (New York: Cambridge University Press, 1997); and

Levy and Spiller, "The Institutional Foundations of Regulatory Commitment: A Comparative Analysis of Telecommunications Regulation," *Journal of Law, Economics and Organization,* Vol. 10, No. 2 (1994): 201–246.

10. As of 2013, the Levy-Spiller synthesis article continued to be listed one of the ten most widely cited articles ever published in the *Journal of Law, Economics and Organization.*

11. North, Wallis, and Weingast, *Violence and Social Orders.*

12. North, Wallis, and Weingast, *Violence and Social Orders,* pp. 32, 264–265.

13. Two important early contributions were Anne Krueger, "The Political Economy of the Rent-seeking Society," *American Economic Review,* Vol. 64 (June 1974): 291–303; Jagdish Bhagwati, "Directly Unproductive, Profit-seeking (DUP) Activities," *Journal of Political Economy,* Vol. 90 (October 1982): 988–1002.

14. Scholars focused on postcolonial Africa did much of the important early work. See, for example, Christopher Clapham, *Third World Politics: An Introduction* (Madison: University of Wisconsin Press, 1985); Peter Lewis, "From Pre-bendalism to Predation: The Political Economy of Decline in Nigeria," *Journal of Modern African Studies,* Vol. 34, No. 1 (1996): 79–103; Michael Bratton and Nicholas van de Walle, *Democratic Experiments in Africa* (Cambridge, UK: Cambridge University Press, 1997); Thandika Mkandawire, "Thinking About Developmental States in Africa." *Cambridge Journal of Economics,* Vol. 25, No. 3 (2001): 289–313.

15. Mushtaq Khan and K.S. Jomo, *Rents, Rent-seeking and Economic Development: Theory and Evidence in Asia* (New York: Cambridge University Press, 2000).

16. North, Wallis and Weingast, *Violence and Social Orders* (2009). Phil Keefer and Stuti Khemani, "Democracy, Public Expenditures and the Poor: Understanding Political Incentives for Providing Public Services," *World Bank Research Observer,* Vol. 20, No. 1 (2005) explore how the "currencies of politics" can be programmatic in some settings and clientelistic in others.

17. For a classic statement of this process of creative destruction, see Joseph Schumpeter, *Capitalism, Socialism and Democracy* (New York: Harper & Brothers, 1942).

18. The quote is from Edward Kennedy's eulogy at Robert Kennedy's funeral, after his assassination in 1968. Robert Kennedy used a variant of this quote, which he noted was from a play by George Bernard Shaw, in his speeches.

19. *Pirkei Avot* (Ethics of the Fathers), Avot 2:21; attributed to Rabbi Tarfon.

20. International Development Association, Country Assistance Strategy for Zambia, Washington, DC, March 18, 2008, pp. 19–22.

Chapter 3

1. The term "Washington Consensus" was coined by John Williamson. For an overview of the term's history, see John Williamson, "What Should the World Bank Think about the Washington Consensus?" *World Bank Research Observer,* Vol. 15, No. 2 (August 2000): 251–264.

2. For one careful analysis of the benefits and limitations of structural adjustment, see World Bank, *Can Africa Claim the 21st Century?* (New York: Oxford University Press for World Bank, 2000).

3. Dani Rodrik, "Goodbye Washington Consensus, Hello Washington Confusion," *Journal of Economic Literature,* Vol. 44, No. 4 (December 2006): 973–987.

4. For an in-depth examination, see Melanie Mitchell, *Complexity: A Guided Tour* (New York: Oxford University Press, 2011). For a highly readable early overview, see M. Mitchell Waldrop, *Complexity: The Emerging Science at the Edge of Order and Chaos* (New York: Simon & Schuster, 1993).

5. Daron Acemoglu and James Robinson's *Why Nations Fail* (New York: Crown Business, 2012) also makes much of virtuous circles between governance and growth; chapter 6 has much to say about their approach.

6. For an earlier version of the approach laid out here, see Brian Levy and Francis Fukuyama, "Development Strategies: Integrating Governance and Growth," World Bank Policy Research Working Paper 5196, October 2010. We developed the approach to development strategy laid out in that paper while team-teaching between 2005 and 2008 at Johns Hopkins University's School of Advanced International Studies.

7. For a classic exploration of the developmental state, see Peter Evans, Dietrich Rueschemeyer and Theda Skocpol (eds.), *Bringing the State Back In* (New York: Cambridge University Press, 1985). Also Atul Kohli, *State-Directed Development: Political Power and Industrialization in the Global Periphery* (New York: Cambridge University Press, 2004).

8. Ricardo Hausmann, Lant Pritchett, and Dani Rodrik, "Growth Accelerations," *Journal of Economic Growth*, Vol. 10 (2005). Quotations are from Dani Rodrik (ed.), *In Search of Prosperity: Analytic Narratives of Economic Growth* (Princeton, NJ: Princeton University Press, 2004), pp. 8–9, 17; and Dani Rodrik, A. Subramanian and F. Trebbi "Institutions Rule: The Primacy of Institutions over Geography and Integration in Economic Development," *Journal of Economic Growth*, Vol. 9, No. 2 (June 2004).

9. To underscore: Not all growth is created equal. Some types of growth (light manufactures production, for example) are much more supportive of than others (e.g., extractive industries) of a cumulative process of development, of ongoing economic dynamism, and of the emergence and strengthening of sustainable institutions.

10. This schema is adapted from Brian Levy and Francis Fukuyama, "Development Strategies: Integrating Governance and Growth," World Bank Staff Working Paper 5196, 2010. Francis Fukuyama uses a similar schema in his book *The Origins of Political Order* (New York: Farrar, Straus and Giroux, 2012).

11. On two-way causality, see Roberto Rigobon and Dani Rodrik, "Rule of Law, Democracy, Openness and Income: Estimating the Interrelationships," *Economics of Transition*, Vol. 13, No. 3 (2005): 533–564. Also Alberto Chang and Cesar Calderon, "Causality and Feedback Between Institutional Measures and Economic Growth," *Economics and Politics*, Vol. 12, No. 1 (2000): 69–81. Dani Rodrik, Arvind Subramanian, and Francesco Trebbi, "Institutions Rule: The Primacy of Institutions Over Geography and Integration in Economic Development," *Journal of Economic Growth*, Vol. 9, No. 2 (June 2004) demonstrate a causal relationship from rule of law to growth. Daron Acemoglu, Simon Johnson, and James Robinson, "The Colonial Origins of Comparative Development: An Empirical Investigation," *American Economic Review*, Vol. 91, No. 5 (2001): 1369–1401, demonstrate a similar relationship, using different exogenous measures for property rights.

12. As chapter 6 explores further, North, Wallis and Weingast (2009) highlight the cumulative interaction between stronger institutions and strengthened organizations that are built on this institutional platform and in turn press for further strengthening of the rules as the key driver of institutional development. While North (1990) emphasized "path dependence"—how institutions and organizations can "lock in" to more versus less economically efficient rules and capabilities, with profound impact for a country's long-term prospects—North, Wallis, and Weingast view the process as less deterministic, with more space for adaptation over time.

13. Key contributions to the modernization literature that assert this sequence include Samuel P Huntington, *Political Order in Changing Societies*; Seymour Martin Lipset. "Some Social Requisites of Democracy: Economic Development and Political Legitimacy," *American Political Science Review* Vol. 53 (1959): 69–105; and Fareed Zakaria, *The Future of Freedom: Illiberal Democracy at Home and Abroad.* For a more nuanced perspective, see Larry Diamond "Economic Development

and Democracy Reconsidered," *American Behavioral Scientist*, Vol. 15, Nos. 4–5 (1992): 450–499.

14. Adam Przeworski, Michael Alvarez, Jose A. Cheibub, and Fernando Limongi, *Democracy and Development: Political Institutions and Material Well-being in the World, 1950–1990* (New York: Cambridge University Press, 2000); Daron Acemoglu, Simon Johnson, James A. Robinson, and Pierre Yared, "Re-evaluating the Modernization Hypothesis," *Journal of Monetary Economics*, Vol. 56 (2009): 1043–1058, raise questions as to the robustness of the pattern suggested by Przeworski et al.

15. Dani Rodrik, *One Economics, Many Recipes* (Princeton, NJ: Princeton University Press, 2007), pp. 168–182.

16. For a detailed analysis, see Richard McGregor, *The Party: The Secret World of China's Communist Rulers* (New York: Harper Collins, 2010).

17. For a classic study of these interactions, based on the US experience, see James Q. Wilson, *Bureaucracy* (New York: Basic Books, 1989). For a systematic review across OECD countries which draws a similar conclusion, see Christopher Pollitt and Geert Bouckaert, *Public Management Reform: A Comparative Analysis* (Oxford: Oxford University Press, 2000). For a recent study that explores this issue comparatively across developed and developing countries, see Merilee Grindle, *Jobs for the Boys* (Cambridge, MA: Harvard University Press, 2013).

18. Ricardo Hausmann, Dani Rodrik and Andres Velasco, "Growth Diagnostics," in Narcis Serra and Joe Stiglitz (eds.), *The Washington Consensus Reconsidered: Towards a New Global Governance* (New York: Oxford University Press, 2008).

19. Thomas Carothers, "The End of the Transition Paradigm," *Journal of Democracy*, Vol. 13, No. 1 (2002).

Chapter 4

1. As per the literature on growth, this focus on investment is not so much because it increases the capital stock, but because more efficient ways of doing things are embodied in equipment, broadly defined. See J. Bradford de Long and Lawrence H. Summers, "Equipment Investment and Economic Growth," *Quarterly Journal of Economics*, Vol. 106, No. 2 (1991): 445–502.

2. For a report on this renewed interest, see "Special Report: State Capitalism," *The Economist*, January 21, 2012.

3. World Bank, *The East Asian Miracle* (New York: Oxford University Press for the World Bank, 1993); also Jeffrey Henderson, David Hulme, Richard Phillips and Eun Mee Kim, "Economic Governance and Poverty Reduction in South Korea," *Globalization and Poverty Report to the DFID*, 2002.

4. Gregory Henderson, *The Politics of the Vortex* (Cambridge, MA: Harvard University Press, 1968).

5. Leroy P. Jones and Il Sakong, *Business, Government and Entrepreneurship: The Korean Case* (Cambridge, MA: Harvard University Press for Harvard Institute for International Development, 1980), pp. 66–68.

6. For some recent analyses of Korea during the Park period which add some complexity to the story, even as its central features remain similar, see Byung-Kook Kim and Ezra Vogel (eds.), *The Park Chung Hee Era: The Transformation of South Korea* (Cambridge, MA: Harvard University Press, 2011); and Ha-Joon Chang, *The East Asian Development Experience* (London: Zed Books, 2007); also David Kang, *Crony Capitalism: Corruption and Development in South Korea and the Philippines* (New York: Cambridge University Press, 2002).

7. The discussion that follows is summarized from Jones and Sakong, pp. 101–104. See also Alice Amsden, *Asia's Next Giant: South Korea and Late Industrialization* (New York: Oxford University Press, 1992).

8. Jones and Sakong, p. 109.

9. It is also important to note, though, that continuing space for markets and entrepreneurship also was part of Korea's export success: wigs, a market developed wholly through private sector entrepreneurship, comprised one of Korea's leading export products in the 1960s.

10. Yung Whee Rhee, Bruce Ross-Larson, and Garry Pursell, *Korea's Competitive Edge: Managing the Entry into World Markets* (Washington, DC: Johns Hopkins University Press for World Bank, 1984).

11. Jones and Sakong, pp. 357–358.

12. For details, see World Bank, *Ethiopia: Accelerating Equitable Growth, A Country Memorandum*, April 2007, pp. 6–7.

13. Meles Zenawi, *African Development: Dead Ends, and New Beginnings,* Columbia University, mimeo, Section 17.1. Available at http://cgt.columbia.edu/files/conferences/Zenawi_Dead_Ends_and_New_Beginnings.pdf.

14. For an overview of Ethiopia's history, see Christopher Clapham, *Transformation and Continuity in Revolutionary Ethiopia* (Cambridge: Cambridge University Press, 1988).

15. David Korten, *Planned Change in a Traditional Society: Psychological Problems of Modernization in Ethiopia* (New York: Praeger, 1972).

16. For a detailed analysis of Ethiopia's political discourse during the Meles Zenawi years from a cultural and historical perspective, see Sarah Vaughan and K. Tronvoli, "The Culture of Power in Contemporary Ethiopian Political Life," *SIDA Studies Number 10,* Stockholm, Sweden.

17. Tim Kelsall and David Booth, "Developmental Patrimonialism?" Africa Power and Politics Series, Working Paper 9, July 2010, London, Overseas Development Institute. For a more comprehensive elaboration of the argument, see also Tim Kelsall, *Business, Politics and the State in Africa* (London: Zed Press, 2013).

18. For a discussion of the central role of equity in facilitating Korea's economic and governance successes, see Jong-Sung You, "Transition from an LAO to an OAO: The Case of South Korea," in North, Wallis, and Weingast, 2013.

19. For a detailed analysis of this pattern of mutuality, see Ed Campos and Hilton Root, *The Key to the East Asian Miracle: Making Shared Growth Credible* (Washington, DC: Brookings, 1996).

20. World Bank, "Ethiopia Public Finance Review 2010," Report 54,952-ET, p. 5; and World Bank, "Ethiopia Public Expenditure Review 2004: The Emerging Challenge," Report 29,338-ET, pp. 27–32.

21. Robert Chase, "Progress on Social Accountability through Ethiopia's Basic Services Program," Powerpoint presentation, World Bank, September 2011.

22. World Bank, *The East Asian Miracle* (Washington, DC: Oxford University Press for the World Bank, 1993). For an influential critique of this report, see Robert Wade, "Japan, the World Bank, and the Art of Paradigm Maintenance: The East Asian Miracle in Perspective," *New Left Review,* Vol. 217 (May–June, 1996).

23. The description of the upgrading of Ethiopia's leather sector is from a baseline assessment of the sector conducted by Development Alternatives Incorporated in 2011 for Ethiopia's Ministry of Industry. See also Tetsushi Sonobi, John Akoten, and Kejiro Otsuka, "An Exploration into the Successful Development of the Leather Shoe Industry in Ethiopia," *Review of Development Economics,* Vol. 13 (2009): 719–736.

24. Elissa Jobson, "Chinese Firm Steps Up Investment in Ethiopia with 'Shoe City, –'" *The Guardian,* Global Development, April 30, 2013; and Bewket Abebe, "Ethiopia: Taiwanese Shoe Company to Construct Three Factories in Ethiopia," *Addis Fortune,* September 22, 2013. See also Hinh Dinh, Vincent Palmade, Vandana Chandra, and Frances Cossar, *Light Manufacturing in Africa* (Washington, DC: Agence Francaise de Developpement and World Bank, 2012).

Chapter 5

1. Data are from World Bank Group, Country Assistance Strategy for the People's Republic of Bangladesh for the Period FY11–FY14, Washington, DC, July 30, 2010.

2. I am grateful to Mushtaq Khan for numerous conversations about Bangladesh's development dynamics, which have been very influential in shaping my views, though the views on Bangladesh presented here should not be attributed to him. An important written contribution by Khan on which I have drawn here is Mushtaq Khan, "Bangladesh: Economic Growth in a Fragile LAO," in Douglass North, John Wallis, Barry Weingast, and Stephen Webb (eds.), *In the Shadow of Violence—the Problem of Development in Limited Access Order Societies* (New York: Cambridge University Press, 2013).

3. For a useful overview of the turmoil surrounding Bangladesh's independence, see the articles in Mohammad Mohabbat Khan and John P. Thorp (eds.), *Bangladesh: Society, Politics and Bureaucracy* (Dhaka: Centre for Administrative Studies, 1984). For a broad overview of the country, see David Lewis, *Bangladesh: Politics, Economics and Civil Society* (New York: Cambridge University Press, 2011).

4. For details, see David Lewis, *Bangladesh*, chapter 5; also World Bank, *Economics and Governance of Nongovernmental Organizations in Bangladesh*, Bangladesh Development Series, Paper 11, 2004 Dhaka.

5. Details of the origin of Bangladesh's garments sector are from Yung Whee Rhee and Therese Belot, "Export Catalyst in Low-Income Countries," World Bank Industry and Energy Department Working Paper, Industry Series Paper 5, 1989; also Khan (2013).

6. For further details, see World Bank, *Bangladesh: Strategy for Sustained Growth*, June 26, 2007.

7. The role of remittances in Bangladeshi growth is much larger than commonly recognized. Consider the following contrast with garments. From a development perspective, the key contribution of garments exports comprises value added (i.e., the value of sales net of the cost of imports); for lower-income countries, with few intermediate inputs available locally, value added generally comprises about 30 percent of sales. Using this ratio as a rule of thumb, as of 2006 the value added to Bangladesh from its garments exports comprised $2.4 billion, about half the value of worker remittances.

8. Khan (2013) includes a detailed discussion on the multiple roles played by Bangladesh's association of garment exporters.

9. This section builds on Brian Levy "Seeking the Elusive Development Knife-Edge: Zambia and Mozambique—A Tale of Two Countries," in Douglass North, John Wallis, Barry Weingast, and Stephen Webb (eds.), *In the Shadow of Violence—The Problem of Development in Limited Access Order Societies* (New York: Cambridge University Press, 2013).

10. The dominant mining company was the South African based Anglo American Corporation; the second company was the Roan Selection Trust (45 percent of which was owned by American Metal Climax).

11. Indeed, the boundaries of Zambia emerged as something of a "residual." As the British empire pushed north from southern into central Africa, it found its imperial ambitions coming into conflict with those of Germany, seeking to move into central Africa from its colonies in the west (what is now Namibia) and the northeast (what is now Tanzania), those of Belgium (expanding its positions from the immediate north, in the Congo), and the Portuguese (to the west, from Angola, as well as Mozambique in the east). Zambia's borders were the residual result of successful diplomatic maneuvers by the British to halt the advances of their rivals on each of these fronts.

12. For a detailed review, see Lise Rakner, *Political and Economic Liberalization in Zambia: 1991–2001* (Uppsala: NAI, 2003).

13. The experience on the political front is not all bleak, with democratic contestation continuing to remain robust. Though President Chiluba won reelection in 1996 with over two-thirds of the vote, subsequent elections were more closely contested; the Movement for Multi-Party Democracy won elections in both 2001 and 2006, but its vote total hovered at or below 40 percent. There also has been alternation: the Movement for Multi-Party Democracy was voted out of office in 2011. Moreover, when President Chiluba sought to amend the constitution to run for a third term of office, he was rebuffed by sustained civic opposition.

14. The examples in the text are taken from Scott Taylor and Neo Simutanyi, "Governance and Political Economy Constraints to Development Priorities in Zambia: A Diagnostic," mimeo, July 2007.

15. David Tschirley and Stephen Kabwe, "The Cotton Sector of Zambia," World Bank Africa Region Working Paper Series No. 124, March 2009.

16. For details of the negotiation with the Anglo American Corporation, see Taylor, p. 78. For details of the deal with Vedanta, see Andrew Sardanis, *A Venture in Africa: The Challenges of African Business* (New York: Palgrave MacMillan), 2007.

17. Khan (2012).

18. As readers familiar with game theory will recognize, propositions along these lines comprise the standard logic of collective action: Elementary game theory reveals that, even as individual participants in an elite bargain have an incentive to renege on parts of the bargain, it can be in their collective interest to ensure that the bargain as a whole does not unravel; all lose if the society descends into conflict.

19. World Bank, Taming Leviathan: Reforming Governance in Bangladesh—An Institutional Review (Dhaka: March 2002).

20. "In the Name of the Father," *The Economist*, August 13, 2011, 42.

Chapter 6

1. Acemoglu and Robinson, *Why Nations Fail*, pp. 332–333.

2. Acemoglu and Robinson, *Why Nations Fail*, pp. 436, 444, 446, 450. It is worth noting that the policy implication quoted in the text does not follow directly from the underlying analytic logic. The logic is laid out as follows: "Major institutional change, the requisite for major economic change, takes place as a result of the interaction between existing institutions and critical junctures. Critical junctures are major events that disrupt the existing political and economic balance. . . . In the same way that the genes of two isolated populations of organisms will drift apart slowly because of random mutations, two otherwise similar societies will also drift apart institutionally—albeit, again slowly. . . . However, when a critical juncture arrives, these may be the small differences that matter in leading otherwise quite similar societies to diverge radically . . . the contingent path of history implies that it is difficult to know whether a particular interplay of critical junctures and existing institutional differences will lead toward more inclusive or extractive institutions" (pp. 431, 436–437).

3. It should be noted, though, that South Africa's 2010 percentile rank for rule of law, government effectiveness, and control of corruption all continued to be higher than the 2010 rankings for Brazil, Colombia, Mexico, Turkey, and Thailand (five countries with more or less similar per capita incomes and population sizes).

4. Seymour Lipset, "Some Social Prerequisites for Democracy: Economic Development and Political Legitimacy," *American Political Science Review*, Vol. 53 (1959): 69–105. Samuel P. Huntington, *Political Order in Changing Societies* (New Haven, CT: Yale University Press, 1968); Samuel P. Huntington, *The Third Wave: Democratization in the Late Twentieth Century* (Norman: University of Oklahoma Press, 1991); Barrington Moore, *The Social Origins of Dictatorship and Democracy* (Boston: Beacon Press, 1966); Daron Acemoglu and James Robinson, *The Economic Origins of Dictatorship and Democracy* (New York: Cambridge University Press, 2006).

5. Data are from S. Kim and Ju-Ho Lee, "Changing Facets of Higher Education in Korea: Market Competition and the Role of the State," *Higher Education*, Vol. 52 (2006): 557–587.

6. Dan O'Meara, *Volkskapitalisme: Class, Capital and Ideology in the Development of Afrikaner Nationalism, 1934–1948* (Cambridge: Cambridge University Press, 1983).

7. For an early statement of this argument, see Heribert Adam and Hermann Giliomee, *The Rise and Crisis of Afrikaner Power* (Cape Town: David Phillip, 1979).

8. For a comprehensive review, see World Bank, *Equity and Development*, World Development Report 2006 (Washington, DC: World Bank and Oxford University Press, 2005), especially pp. 101–144.

9. For both these points see You, in North, Wallis, Weingast, and Webb (2012).

10. Data are from World Bank, World Development Indicators. The measure is for 2005 dollars, in purchasing power parity.

11. Justin Visagie, "Is the Middle Class Becoming Better Off? Two Perspectives," *Econ3x3. org*, July 2013.

12. For an analysis of the political economy of South Africa's structural unemployment, see Nicoli Nattrass and Jeremy Seekings, *Class, Race, and Inequality in South Africa* (New Haven, CT: Yale University Press, 2008).

13. 2010 data are from that year's National Income and Expenditure Survey. Other data are from Murray Leibbrandt, Ingrid Woolard, Arden Finn & Jonathan Argent, "Trends in South African Income Distribution and Poverty Since the Fall of Apartheid", OECD Social, Employment and Migration Working Papers No. 101, 2010.

14. Southern and Eastern African Consortium for Monitoring Educational Quality; results are from SACMEQ III survey, conducted in 2007.

15. Seymour Martin Lipset, *Political Man: The Social Bases of Politics*, 2nd ed. (London: Heinemann, 1983), p. 64.

16. Francis Fukuyama, *The Origins of Political Order* (New York: Farrar, Straus and Giroux, 2012), pp. 42–43, 445.

17. Merilee Grindle, *Jobs for the Boys* (Cambridge, MA: Harvard University Press, 2012), p. 253. Grindle includes a tenth case, Spain, where there was "a long-term failure to advance change."

18. Samuel P. Huntington, *The Third Wave: Democratization in the Late Twentieth Century* (Norman: University of Oklahoma Press, 1991).

19. Its per capita income, measured in 1990 PPP$, was about $2,400 in 1870.

20. For details, see Ronald N. Johnson and Gary Libecap, *The Federal Civil Service System and the Problem of Bureaucracy* (Chicago: Chicago University Press, 1994); and Daniel P. Carpenter, *The Forging of Bureaucratic Autonomy: Reputations, Networks and Policy Innovation in Executive Agencies, 1862–1928* (Princeton, NJ: Princeton University Press, 2001).

21. Edmund Morris, *The Rise of Theodore Roosevelt* (New York: Random House, 1979), pp. 443–445.

22. For these and additional details, see Ronald N. Johnson and Gary Libecap, *The Federal Civil Service System and the Problem of Bureaucracy*; Daniel P. Carpenter, *The Forging of Bureaucratic Autonomy*.

23. Thomas Carothers, "The Rule of Law Revival," *Foreign Affairs*, March/April 1998, 95–106; Stephan Haggard, Andrew MacIntyre, and Lydia Tiede, "The Rule of Law and Economic Development," *Annual Review of Political Science*, Vol. 11 (2008): 205–234; Rachel Kleinfeld, *Advancing the Rule of Law Abroad: Next Generation Reform* (Washington, DC: Carnegie Endowment for International Peace, 2012).

24. The qualification is important—North, Wallis, and Weingast emphasize that their argument is not teleological; there is no inevitability to the process.

25. Douglass North, *Institutions, Institutional Change and Economic Performance* (New York: Cambridge University Press, 1990). Whereas North (1990) highlighted the potential of "path dependent" lock-in into either open-access or limited-access institutions, North,

Wallis, and Weingast explore how open-access institutions can emerge out of a limited access order.

26. This classic modernization argument has also been made by Fareed Zakaria, *The Future of Freedom: Illiberal Democracy at Home and Abroad* (New York: Norton, 2003) and by Steven Levitsky and Lucan Way, *Competitive Authoritarianism* (New York: Cambridge University Press, 2010).

27. This discussion of the relation between Korea's transition to democracy and the evolution of the rule of law draws on You (2013).

28. Francis Fukuyama, *The Origins of Political Order* (New York: Farrar, Straus, and Giroux, 2011), especially chapters 17, 18, and 27.

29. Daron Acemoglu, Simon Johnson, and James A. Robinson, "The Colonial Origins of Comparative Development: An Empirical Investigation," *American Economic Review,* Vol. 91 (2001): 1369–1401.

30. For useful overviews of the progressive movement, see Michael McGerr, *A Fierce Discontent: The Rise and Fall of the Progressive Movement in America, 1870–1920* (New York: Oxford University Press, 2003); and Richard Hofstadeter, *The Age of Reform* (New York: Random House, 1955).

31. It must be noted that a quarter century prior to the Progressive Era, conflict had indeed descended into the American Civil War. Perhaps the memory of recent disaster offers a further explanation of why the conflicts of the Progressive Era did not result in a systemic unravelling.

32. In their commitment to restraining executive authority, America's "founding fathers" were powerfully influenced by struggles against absolutism in seventeenth century England, and their perception that eighteenth-century England had again strayed from the anti-absolutist principles, especially vis-à-vis their colonies. See Alfred F. Young, "English Plebeian Culture and Eighteenth Century American Radicalism" in Margaret Jacob and James Jacob (eds.), *The Origins of Anglo-American Radicalism* (London: Allen & Unwin, 1984), quoted in John Meacham, *Thomas Jefferson: The Art of Power* (New York: Random House, 2012).

33. This is the reason why Kleinfeld (2012) sets as the purpose of rule of law reform the reshaping of the relationship between a state and its society. For a seminal contribution which made this point, see Barry Weingast, "Constitutions as Governance Structures: The Political Foundations of Secure Markets, *Journal of Institutional and Theoretical Economics*, Vol. 149 (1993): 286–311.

34. For insightful policy-oriented discussions of the resource curse, see Paul Collier's two books, *The Bottom Billion* (Oxford: Oxford University Press, 2007) and *The Plundered Planet* (Oxford: Oxford University Press, 2010).

Chapter 7

1. A classic statement of how elite bargains can underpin islands of effectiveness can be found in Stephen Haber, Armando Razo, and Noel Maurer, *The Politics of Property Rights* (Cambridge: Cambridge University Press, 2003).

2. Peter Evans and James E. Rauch, "Bureaucracy and Growth: A Cross-National Analysis of the Effects of 'Weberian' State Structures on Economic Growth," *American Sociological Review*, Vol. 64 (1999): 748–765. For a discussion of the limitations of an approach along these lines in terms of uncovering causality, see Marcus J. Kurtz and Andrew Schrank, "Growth and Governance: Models, Measures and Mechanisms," *The Journal of Politics*, Vol. 69, No. 2 (May 2007): 538–554.

3. A statistically more rigorous effort might proceed on multiple fronts. An initial step could be to estimate a predicted value of bureaucratic quality for each country, given the value of independent variables such as per capita income, natural resource abundance,

population size, and whether the political settlement is dominant or competitive. One hypothesis would be that the coefficient for dominance would be positive and significant. A second hypothesis would be that among the group of early-stage countries which were growing rapidly, there will be a subset whose bureaucratic quality exceeded its predicted value, and that, controlling for other variables, these were disproportionately likely to be characterized by dominant political settlements.

4. Key articles that demonstrate this result are Daron Acemoglu, Simon Johnson, and James A. Robinson, "The Colonial Origins of Comparative Development: An Empirical Investigation," *American Economic Review*, Vol. 91, No. 5 (December 2001): 1369–1401; and Dani Rodrik, Arvind Subramanian, and Francesco Trebbi, "Institutions Rule: The Primacy of Institutions over Geography and Integration in Economic Development," *Journal of Economic Growth*, Vol. 9, No. 2 (June 2004). For a wide-ranging review of the empirical literature on the relationship between the rule of law and economic development, see Stephan Haggard, Andrew MacIntyre, and Lydia Tiede, "The Rule of Law and Economic Development," *Annual Review of Political Science*, Vol. 11 (2008): 205–234.

5. Robert Barro, "Economic Growth in a Cross-Section of Countries," *Quarterly Journal of Economics*, Vol. 106 (1991): 407–433, finds a significant relationship using indicators of political instability as the independent variable. Stephen Knack and Philip Keefer, "Institutions and Economic Performance: Cross-Country Tests Using Alternative Institutional Measures," *Economics and Politics*, Vol. 7 (1995): 207–227, found that broader, subjective indicators of political risk had greater explanatory power. Paolo Mauro, "Corruption and Growth," *Quarterly Journal of Economics*, Vol. 110 (1998): 681–712, found that higher corruption was associated with lower investment and growth.

6. Daron Acemoglu, Simon Johnson, James A. Robinson, and Pierre Yared, "Income and Democracy," *American Economic Review*, Vol. 98, No. 3 (2008): 808–842; and Daron Acemoglu, Simon Johnson, James A. Robinson, and Pierre Yared, "Re-evaluating the Modernization Hypothesis," *Journal of Monetary Economics*, Vol. 56 (2009): 1043–1058, using a "fixed effects" methodology, find that increases in per capita income have no independent impact on the likelihood of democratization once country-specific effects are accounted for. Adam Przeworski, Michael Alvarez, Jose A. Cheibub, and Fernando Limongi, *Democracy and Development: Political Institutions and Material Well-being in the World, 1950–1990* (New York: Cambridge University Press, 2000); and Adam Przeworski and Fernando Limongi, "Modernization: Theory and Facts," *World Politics*, Vol. 49, No. 2 (1997): 155–183, find that, while transition to democracy appears to be a random event, uncorrelated with per capita income, the probability of a reversal declines as per capita income rises and, indeed, that above a threshold (which they peg at $6,000 per capita in 1990 $) no reversals have ever been observed. But the results of Acemoglu et. al. (2009) cast doubt on the empirical evidence vis-à-vis "non-reversals."

7. Note that, given the emphasis in chapter 6 on inclusive growth, per capita income is a crude measure, which arguably provides only a lower-bound estimate of the impact of inclusive growth on institutional change. Additional research that disaggregated income according to the composition of the underlying productive structure (for example, light manufactures versus natural resource extraction) would be especially useful.

8. Roberto Rigobon and Dani Rodrik, "Rule of Law, Democracy, Openness and Income: Estimating the Interrelationships," *Economics of Transition*, Vol. 13, No. 3 (2005): 533–564. Also Alberto Chong and Cesar Calderon, "Causality and Feedback Between Institutional Measures and Economic Growth," *Economics and Politics* Vol. 12, No. 1 (2000): 69–81. Ricardo Hausmann, Lant Pritchett and Dani Rodrik, "Growth

Accelerations," *Journal of Economic Growth*, Vol. 10 (2005): 303–329, show econometrically that while growth spurts are not associated with initial improvements in institutions, such improvements help explain why some spurts are sustained beyond an initial eight-year period.

9. Polity IV includes a composite measure of "democracy" which rates countries on a 0–10 scale, based on four subindicators: (i) *the competitiveness of political participation* - the extent to which alternative preferences for policy and leadership can be pursued in the political arena; (ii) *the competitiveness of executive recruitment,* - the extent to which prevailing modes of advancement give subordinates equal opportunities to become superordinates; (iii) *the openness of executive recruitment,* - the extent to which all the politically active population has, in principle, an opportunity to attain the chief executive position through a regularized process; and (iv) *constraints on the chief executive,* - the extent of institutionalized constraints on the power of the chief executive. For the purposes of this book, the "executive constraints" subindicator poses a dilemma. It measures the quality of checks and balances, and thus cuts across the analytical distinction in the book's typology between the vertical (dominant-competitive) and horizontal (personalized-impersonal) axes—the settings which are both dominant and impersonal (i.e., are in the "rule-by law" category in the typology) have stronger checks and balances than their dominant and personalized counterparts. Weighting "executive constraints" as heavily as Polity IV does for its democracy variable would confound the distinction between the two dimensions, but excluding it entirely would lose an important differentiator for the vertical axis. So it is used, but given less weight. As per Polity IV, country scores are calculated by giving a maximum of three points for competitiveness of political participation, a maximum of 2 points for competitiveness of executive recruitment, and a maximum of 1 point for openness of executive recruitment. Countries receive 1 point of their Policy IV executive constraints rating is 5, 6, or 7, and zero points if the Polity IV rating is between zero and 4. Aggregating the components in this way, countries which score 0–3 in the modified Polity IV scale are categorized as "dominant" (though note the seven exceptions in the note to Annex Table A2.1); countries that score 4 or 5 are categorized as "intermediate" and countries that score 6 or 7 are categorized as competitive. Polity IV country-by-country measures are available at http://systemicpeace.org/polity/polity4.htm. For details of how the measures are constructed, see Monty Marshall, Ted Gurr, and Keith Jaggers, "Polity IV Project: Political Regime Characteristics and Transitions, 1800–2012—User's Manual" (Vienna, VA: Center for Systemic Peace, 2013).

10. For details of the Worldwide Governance Indicators and their construction, see Daniel Kaufmann, Aart Kraay, and Massimo Mastruzzi, "The Worldwide Governance Indicators: Methodology and Analytical Issues," World Bank Policy Research Working Paper 5430, September 2010.

11. For one review of the variety of governance indicators, and their strengths and weaknesses, see Brian Levy, *Governance Reform: Bridging Monitoring and Action* (Washington, DC: World Bank, 2007). For a critical assessment of the WGIs, see Melissa Thomas, "What Do the Worldwide Governance Indicators Measure?" *European Journal of Development Research*, July 16, 2009.

12. The standard errors (not shown in this chapter's tables) are unique to each individual data point. As a very, very rough rule of thumb, differences between two measures of less than 0.30 (i.e., twice a standard error of 0.15 for each data point) are unlikely to meet the test of being statistically significantly different from zero with 90 percent probability.

13. As per the note to Table A2.1, seven countries (Ghana, Kenya, Lebanon, Lesotho, Peru, Sierra Leone, and Zambia) were either in conflict or rated dominant in 2000 but shifted to intermediate or competitive within one to two years.

Chapter 8

1. For this formal definition of institutions, see Douglass North, *Institutions, Institutional Change and Economic Performance* (New York: Cambridge University Press, 1990), p. 3.

2. Note that two rationales for the provision of public goods are captured in the general framing of the text: "public goods" narrowly defined, that is, those where not all benefits and costs are privately-appropriable, so social returns exceed private returns; and also goods (e.g., education) where inability to pay would result in shortfalls in the absence of public financing and/or provision.

3. Dani Rodrik, *One Economics, Many Recipes* (Princeton, NJ: Princeton University Press, 2007), pp. 15–16.

4. The classic statement is Max Weber, *Economy and Society* (Berlin: 1922). For an important effort to apply Weber's framework in a developing country context, see Peter Evans and James Rauch, "Bureaucracy and Growth: A Cross-National Analysis of the Effects of 'Weberian' State Structures on Economic Growth," *American Sociological Review*, Vol. 64, No. 5 (October 1999): 748–765.

5. For a review of these programs and their (mixed) effectiveness, see World Bank, *Public Sector Reform: What Works and Why?* (Washington, DC: World Bank Group, 2008). For a conceptually anchored critique, see Matt Andrews, *The Limits of Institutional Reform in Development* (New York: Cambridge University Press, 2013).

6. For an extended review of different approaches to public sector reform in developing countries, see Brian Levy, *Governance Reform: Bridging Monitoring and Action* (Washington, DC: World Bank, 2007).

7. C. Pollitt and G. Bouckaert, *Public Management Reform: A Comparative Analysis* (Oxford: Oxford University Press, 2000), pp. 184, 188–189. For a classic discussion of both the opportunities and challenges of reform in the United States context, see James Q. Wilson, *Bureaucracy: What Government Agencies Do and Why They Do it* (New York: Basic Books, 1989).

8. Alan Schick "Why Most Developing Countries Should Not Try New Zealand Reforms," *World Bank Research Observer*, Vol. 13 (1999): 123–131, highlights the preexisting platform as a necessary condition for new public management reforms.

9. Absenteeism data are from Nazmul Chaudhry et. al, Missing in Action: Teachers and Health Worker Absence in Developing Countries", Journal of Economic Perspectives, 2006, p.92. Expenditure tracking data are summarized in Barbara Bruns, Deon Filmer and Harry Patrinos, Making Schools Work (Washington, DC: The World Bank, 2011), p. 9. supply shortfalls data are from WDR 2004, p. 24.

10. When a subsequent reform pre-determined the rules by which allocations were to be made to schools, the share which reached schools rose to 90 percent (Das, 2005).

11. WDR 2004, p. 58.

12. For a useful synthesis of the new institutional economics, see Oliver Williamson, "The New Institutional Economics: Taking Stock, Looking Ahead," *Journal of Economic Literature* (September 2000): 595–613.

13. Although it must be noted that the 2004 report also gave extensive attention to the roles of private service providers and of competition.

14. Grindle, *Jobs for the Boys*, p. 255.

15. For a statement of this argument, see Barbara Geddes, *Politician's Dilemma: Building State Capacity in Latin America* (Berkeley: University of California Press, 1994).

16. Grindle, *Jobs for the Boys*, pp. 191–195. Barbara Geddes, *Politician's Dilemma: Building State Capacity in Latin America* (Berkeley: University of California Press, 1994) explored more broadly this relationship between democratization and civil service reform.

17. Grindle, *Jobs for the Boys*, p. 261.

18. Grindle, pp. 261, 32.

19. Vivek Srivastava and Marco Larizza, "Working with the Grain for Reforming the Public Service: A Live Example from Sierra Leone," *International Review of Administrative*

Sciences, 2013; and Gary Reid, "The Political Economy of Civil Service Reform in Albania," World Bank, mimeo 2005.

20. Grindle, p. 224.

21. World Bank, *Public Sector Reform: What Works and Why?* (Washington, DC: World Bank Group, 2008).

22. World Bank, 2008, plus International Monetary Fund, Fiscal Affairs Department, "IMF Technical Assistance Evaluation: Public Expenditure Management Reform in Anglophone African Countries," Washington, DC 2005.

23. For a detailed development of this point, see Brian Levy and Michael Walton, "Institutions, Incentives and Service Provision: Bringing Politics Back In," Working Paper 18, Effective States and Inclusive Development Research Program, University of Manchester, February 2013.

24. Elinor Ostrom, "Beyond Markets and States: Polycentric Governance of Complex Economic Systems," Nobel Prize Lecture, December 8, 2009.

25. Some scholars recently have begun to suggest that collective action should displace principal–agent approaches as the central way of organizing our thinking about the institutional underpinnings of development. For an extended discussion along these lines, see David Booth, *Development as a Collective Action Problem: Addressing the Real Challenges of African Governance* (London: Overseas Development Institute, 2012). Booth's book is a synthesis of five years of detailed empirical work conducted by the Africa Power and Politics Programme, housed in the Overseas Development Institute.

26. For syntheses of that work, see Elinor Ostrom, *Governing the Commons* (New York: Cambridge University Press, 1990).

27. Ostrom, *Governing the Commons,* p. 29.

28. For a detailed discussion of these empirical and experimental underpinnings of her work, see Ostrom, *Understanding Institutional Diversity* (2005).

29. Ostrom, *Understanding Institutional Diversity,* p. 259.

30. Predation goes beyond "free riding" in which a presumptive participant in a collective effort chooses to shirk on his obligations, but nonetheless enjoys a share of the benefits—while mutual monitoring often is a key way in which protagonists of collective action mitigate this risk, monitoring cannot deter impunity. And it also goes beyond corruption, in which a participant in a collective action effort pays (or accepts) a bribe to illegally over-ride an agreed-upon formal or informal rule, but (contra to predation) is vulnerable to detection and, if detected, is subject to sanction.

31. Ostrom, *Understanding Institutional Diversity,* p. 58.

32. For other explorations of an "islands of effectiveness" approach to development engagement, see David K. Leonard, "Where Are Pockets of Effective Agencies Likely in Weak Governance States, and Why? A Propositional Inventory," IDS Working Paper 306, June 2008; R.C. Crook, "Rethinking Civil Service Reform in Africa: 'Islands of Effectiveness' and Organizational Commitment," *Commonwealth and Comparative Politics,* Vol. 48, No. 4 (2010): 479–504. Also Brian Levy, "Can Islands of Effectiveness Thrive in Difficult Governance Settings? The Political Economy of Local-Level Collaborative Governance," World Bank Policy Research Working Paper 5842, October 2011.

33. For development and elaboration of this argument, see Brian Levy and Michael Walton, "Institutions, Incentives and Service Provision: Bringing Politics Back In," ESID Working Paper 18, Effective States and Inclusive Development Research Centre, University of Manchester, February 2013.

34. Matt Andrews, *The Limits of Institutional Reform* (New York: Cambridge University Press, 2013).

35. For some useful analyses, see Pollitt and Bouckaert, *Public Management Reform: A Comparative Analysis;* Francis Fukuyama, *Statebuilding* (Ithaca, NY: Cornell University Press, 2004); Matthew Andrews, *The Limits of Institutional Reform in Development* (New York: Cambridge University Press, 2013).

Chapter 9

1. Details of the Brazilian municipal audit and its consequences are from Claudio Ferraz and Frederico Finan, "Exposing Corrupt Politicians: The Effects of Brazil's Publicly Released Audits on Electoral Outcomes," *The Quarterly Journal of Economics* (May 2008): 703–745.

2. Ghazala Mansuri and Vijayendra Rao, *Localizing Development: Does Participation Work?* (Washington, DC: World Bank, 2013), p. 287.

3. Shantayanan Devarajan, Stuti Khemani, and Michael Walton, "Civil Socieety, Public Action and Accountability in Africa," World Bank Policy Research Working Paper 5733.

4. James Manor, "User Committees: A Potentially Damaging Second Wave of Decentralization?" *European Journal of Development Research*, Vol. 16, No. 1 (Spring 2004): 206.

5. Samuel Paul, *Holding the State to Account: Citizen Monitoring in Action* (Bangalore, India: Books for Change, 2002).

6. Martina Bjorkman and Jakob Svensson, "Power to the People: Evidence from a Randomized Field Experiment of a Community-Based Monitoring Project in Uganda," *Quarterly Journal of Economics*, Vol. 124, No. 2 (2009): 735–769; see also the comparative review of a large number of health studies in Mansuri and Rao, *Localizing Development*, pp. 200–213.

7. Merilee Grindle, *Despite the Odds: The Contentious Politics of Education Reform* (Princeton, NJ: Princeton University Press, 2004); and Robert R. Kaufman and Joan M. Nelson, *Crucial Needs, Weak Incentives: Social Sector Reform, Democratization and Globalization in Latin America* (Baltimore: Johns Hopkins University Press, 2004).

8. For details, see Bruns, Flimer, and Patrinos, pp. 42–47.

9. The individual studies are Ritva Reinikka and Jakob Svensson, "Local Capture: Evidence from a Central Government Transfer Program in Uganda," *Quarterly Journal of Economics*, Vol. 119, No. 2 (2004): 679–705; Reinikka and Svensson, "Fighting Corruption to Improve Schooling: Evidence from a Newspaper Campain in Uganda," *Journal of the European Economic Association*, Vol. 3, No. 2 (2005): 259–267; E. Jimenez and Y. Sawada, "Do Community-Managed Schools Work?" *World Bank Economic Review*, Vol. 13, No. 3 (1999): 415–441; E. Duflo, P. Dupas, and M. Kremer, "Peer Effects, Pupil-Teacher Ratios, and Teacher Incentives: Evidence from a Randomization Evaluation in Kenya" (2007) and "Additional Resources versus Organizational Changes in Education: Experimental Evidence in Kenya" (2009) both unpublished manuscripts, Abdul Latif Jameel Poverty Action Lab, Massachusetts Institute of Technology, Cambridge, MA; A. Banerjee, R. Banerji, E. Duflo, R. Glennerster, and S. Khemani, "Pitfalls of Participatory Programs: Evidence from a Randomized Evaluation in Education in India," 2008 Policy Research Working Paper 4584 (Washington, DC: World Bank); and P. Pandey, S. Goyal, and V. Sundararaman "Community Participation in Public Schools: Impact of Information Campaigns in Three Indian States" *Education Economics* Vol. 17, No. 3 (2009): 355–375.

10. For this interpretation, see Badru Bukenya, Sam Hickey, and Sophie King, "Understanding the Role of Context in Shaping Social Accountability Interventions: Towards an Evidence-Based Approach," Report commissioned by the World Bank's Social Accountability and Demand for Good Governance Team, June 2012. They, in turn, draw on Paul Hubbard, "Putting the Power of Transparency in Context: Information's Role in Reducing Corruption in Uganda's Education Sector," Center for Global Development Working Paper 136 (2007).

11. Merilee Grindle, *Despite the Odds: The Contentious Politics of Education Reform* (Princeton, NJ: Princeton University Press, 2004).

12. This description is adapted from Patrick Barron, Rachael Diprose, and Michael Woolcock, *Contesting Development: Participatory Projects and Local Conflict Dynamics in Indonesia* (New Haven, CT: Yale University Press, 2011); Susan Wong, "What Have Been

the Impacts of World Bank Community-Driven Development Programs?" World Bank Social Develoment Department, 2012; and Benjamin Olken "Monitoring Corruption: Evidence from a Field Experiment in Indonesia." *Journal of Political Economy* Vol. 115, No. 2, (April 2007): 200–249.

13. These results are from Wong (2012). For the specific results quoted in the text, see pp. 17–21; 27–28, 44.

14. For details, see John Voss, "Impact Evaluation of the Second Phase of the KDP," June 2008; Anthony Torres, "Economic Impact Analysis of KDP Inferasturcture Projects," January 2005, both available (together with many more documents) on the evaluations page of the PNPM web site, at http://www.pnpm-support.org/evaluations.

15. This discussion draws on the reviews of the literature by Wong (2012), pp. 21–27; and Mansuri and Rao (2012), pp. 121–136.

16. Barron, Diprose, and Woolcock, *Contesting Development*, p. 180.

17. Wong, pp. 31–34; Mansuri and Rao, pp. 249–250.

18. It must be noted, though, that set against these positive results a recent careful impact evaluation based on a large, Indonesia-wide sample survey found that, while KDP's internal participatory processes generally functioned well, there was no statistically significant difference between KDP and non-KDP villages in their broader patterns of civic participation. John Voss, "PNPM Rural Impact Evaluation", BAPPENAS, Government of Indonesia, April 2012.

19. This example is from Levy (2007), pp. 109–111. Norbert Schady, "The Political Economy of Expenditures by the Peruvian Social Fund (FONCODES), 1991–1995," *American Political Science Review*, Vol. 94, No. 2 (2000): 289–303, explored the details of FONCODES allocation during the Fujimori era.

20. See William Easterly, *The White Man's Burden* (New York: Penguin Books, 2006), chapter 1; and Matt Andrews, *The Limits of Institutional Reform* (New York: Cambridge University Press, 2013).

Chapter 10

1. For an in-depth theoretical and empirical analysis of the issues, see Brian Levy, Albert Berry, and Jeffrey B. Nugent, *Fulfilling the Export Potential of Small and Medium Firms* (Boston: Kluwer, 1999).

2. For an early statement of this distinction, see Michael Porter, *The Competitive Advantage of Nations* (New York: The Free Press, 1998).

3. This is a central issue addressed by the New Institutional Economics, in particular the work of Williamson (1975, 1985, 2000). For an early contribution that framed the issue as an "obsolescing bargain," see Raymond Vernon, *Sovereignty at Bay* (New York: Basic Books, 1973).

4. Sue Unsworth, *An Upside-Down View of Governance* (Sussex: IDS, 2010), which draws on A. Hampton, "Local Government and Investment Promotion in China" mimeo, 2006; and A. Patunru, N. McCulloch, and C. von Luebke, "A Tale of Two Cities: The Political Economy of the Investment Climate in Solo and Manado, Indonesia," IDS Working Paper 338, 2009.

5. Stephen Haber, Armando Razo, and Noel Maurer, *The Politics of Property Right* (New York: Cambridge University Press, 2003). Haber et. al's formulation focuses more narrowly on the role of third-party enforcers with the incentive and ability to deter government officials (notably including political leaders) from predation. A credible third-party enforcer is, of course, one mechanism of assuring a "trumping coalition"— but as we have already seen in chapters 8 and 9, it is not the only one. For a related approach, see Mary Hallward-Driemeier, Gita Khun-Jush, and Lant Pritchett, "Deals Versus Rules: Policy Implementation Uncertainty and Why Firms Hate It," World Bank Policy Research Working Paper 5321, 2010.

6. Haber et. al, 164.

7. For a useful overview, see Stephen Haber, Herbert Klein, Noel Maurer, and Kevin Middlebrook, *Mexico Since 1980* (New York: Cambridge University Press, 2008).

8. See Jiahua Che and Yingyi Qian, "Institutional Environment, Community Government, and Corporate Governance: Understanding China's Township-Village Enterprises," *Journal of Law, Economics and Organization*, Vol. 14, No. 1 (19980: 1–23.

9. Peter Evans, *Embedded Autonomy: States and Industrial Transformation* (Princeton, NJ: Princeton University Press, 1996). Peter Evans, Dieterich Rueschmeyer, and Theda Skocpol, *Bringing the State Back In* (New York: Cambridge University Press, 1985). See also Sunita Kikeri, Thomas Kenyon, and Vincent Palmade, *Reforming the Investment Climate: Lessons for Practitioners* (Washington, DC: World Bank, 2006); and Atul Kohli, *State-Directed Development* (New York: Cambridge University Press, 2004).

10. For a detailed analysis of Zambia's cotton sector, see David Tschirley and Stephen Kabwe, "The Cotton Sector of Zambia," World Bank Africa Region Working Paper 124, March 2009. Also David Tschirley, Colin Poulton, and Patrick Labaste (eds.), *Organization and Performance of Cotton Sectors in Africa* (Washington, DC: World Bank, 2009).

11. See for example "Cotton Farmers Riot in Zambia," *Wall Street Journal*, July 2, 2012.

12. For details, see Elinor Ostrom, *Understanding Institutional Diversity* (Princeton, NJ: Princeton University Press, 2005).

13. On the contrary, the one proactive initiative attempted by government in the sector—a scheme to provide input finance to farmers—served to undermine, rather than strengthen, the outgrower arrangements. The number of farmers actually provided with finance was miniscule, but the presence of the scheme (which was very weak in its own record-keeping) provided a convenient explanation when farmers who sold to independent buyers were asked how they had financed their inputs.

14. Clothing imports grew from $223 million in 2000 to over $1 billion by 2006, with China's share jumping from under 30 percent to over 80 percent. Textile imports (primarily fabric and overwhelmingly from China) increased dramatically, nearly threefold, between 1999 and 2006.

15. For details, see Mike Morris and Brian Levy, "The Limits of Co-operation in a Divided Society: The Political Economy of South Africa's Garment and Textile Industry," in Anthony Black (ed.) *Structural Unemployment in South Africa* (Cape Town: UCT Press, in press).

16. South Africa's ruling group is a de facto alliance, comprising the African National Congress (as the alliance 'umbrella') plus the Congress of South African Trade Unions (with the South African Clothing and Textiles Workers Union as a core member) and the South African Communist Party.

17. It must be noted, though, that a few years after the initial failure of the initiative, a new Minister of Trade and Industry (with the African National Congress now led by Jacob Zuma, not Thabo Mbeki), revisited garment-sector policy and implemented unilaterally many of the policies that initially had been designed via the Ministry's customized sector planning process.

18. For an influential contribution that gave a central role to global anchors as a way forward in difficult governance environments, see Paul Collier, *The Bottom Billion* (Oxford: Oxford University Press, 2007).

19. For an in-depth analysis that assesses comparatively eighteen specific globalized standards initiatives, see Brian Levy, "Innovations in Globalized Regulation: Opportunities and Challenges," World Bank Policy Research Working Paper 5841, 2011. For broad overviews, see David Vogel, "The Private Regulation of Global Corporate Conduct," Center for Responsible Business, University of California, Berkeley, 2006; David Vogel, *The Market for Virtue: The Potential and Limits of Corporate Social Responsibility*

(Washington, DC: Brookings Institution, 2005); John Ruggie, "Taking Embedded Liberalism Global: The Corporate Connection," Keynote paper for American Political Science Association Meeting, Boston, August 31, 2002; Simon Zadek, "The Logic of Collaborative Governance," Corporate Social Responsibility Initiative Working Paper 17, 2006, Kennedy School of Government, Harvard University. For an analysis of collaborative governance from a more intergovernmental perspective, see Anne-Marie Slaughter, *The New World Order* (Princeton, NJ: Princeton University Press, 2005).

20. In hake fishing, two companies, Sea Harvest and I&J, had long been dominant in the industry. In the 1980s, they accounted for close to 90 percent of the allocated right to fish; as of 2010 their share, while lower, remained in excess of 60 percent. Both companies embraced the South African government's push to foster black economic empowerment (BEE), thereby bringing politically influential actors into the ownership structure. For a detailed analysis, see Brian Levy, Alex de Jager, Brendan Meehan, and Tony Leiman, "Regulatory Efficacy in a Changing Political Environment: A Tale of Two South African Fisheries," Paper presented at World Bank Workshop on the Political Economy Of Fisheries, Washington, DC, April 12, 2012.

21. The Western Cape rock lobster fishery is a case in point. See Levy, de Jager, Meehan, and Leiman for a detailed analysis.

22. One of the two companies, Sea Harvest, was sold in 2009 in its entirety to a new Black Economic Empowerment (BEE) consortium, with 80 percent of the equity going to two BEE investment holding companies and 15 percent to management. The other, I&J, sponsored a BEE deal that transferred 20 percent of equity to a BEE consortium and 5 percent to employees.

23. Indeed, part of the institutional arrangements for managing sustainability involved ongoing monitoring by research vessels, with the contracts financed by government. For decades, the process of contracting had proceeded smoothly. However, in 2012, the relevant government ministry decided to put in place a new set of arrangements, involving new actors. A highly fraught process resulted—and as of 2013 the research vessels were (at least temporarily) inoperative.

24. Note that all oil and mining companies active in countries that have joined the EITI are obligated to provide this information, regardless of whether they themselves are formally affiliated (as supporters) with the EITI. Corporate supporters are not, however, required to provide this information for payments made in non-EITI countries.

25. World Bank Group, "The World Bank Group Program of Support for the Chad-Cameroon Petroleum Development and Pipeline Construction," Report 50315, November 2009, 25.

Chapter 11

1. For an in-depth analysis of how this dynamic played out within the World Bank, which parallels the discussion in the text, see Catherine Weaver, *Hypocrisy Trap: The World Bank and the Poverty of Reform* (Princeton, NJ: Princeton University Press, 2008).

2. A benchmarking study of 160 new World Bank operations which were approved for financing in 2008, found that 44 percent of them incorporated transparency and participation into their designs, at least to some extent. World Bank, "GAC in Projects Benchmarking and Learning Review," Washington, DC, 2009.

3. For an overview of these efforts, see Thomas Carothers and Diane de Gramont, *Development Aid Confronts Politics: The Almost Revolution* (Washington, DC: Carnegie Endowment for International Peace, 2013). For an in-depth assessment of World Bank efforts, see Verena Fritz, Brian Levy, and Rachel Ort, *Problem-Driven Political Economy Analysis: The World Bank's Experience* (Washington, DC: World Bank, 2014).

4. Matt Andrews, *The Limits of Institutional Reform in Development* (New York: Cambridge University Press, 2013). Also Lant Pritchett, Michael Woolcock, and Matt Andrews,

"Capability Traps? The Mechanisms of Persistent Implementation Failure," Center for Global Development Working Paper 234, 2010; and R. Ashworth, G. Boyne, and R. Delbridge, "Escape from the Iron Cage? Organizational Change and Isomorphic Pressures in the Public Sector," *Journal of Public Administration, Research and Theory*, Vol.19 (2007): 165–187.

5. In addition to the data sources described in chapter 7, other well-known "scorecards" include Transparency International's annual ranking of countries' levels of corruption, the World Bank's Doing Business indicators, and the Global Integrity Index.

6. Andrews, p. 34.

7. These include Matt Andrews, *The Limits of Institutional Reform in Development*, 2013; Sue Unsworth, *An Upside Down View of Governance* (2010); and David Booth and Diana Cammack, *Governance for Development in Africa: Solving Collective Action Problems* (London: Zed Books, 2013). All of these are in the spirit of the path-breaking earlier effort by Ricardo Hausmann, Dani Rodrik, and Andres Velasco, "Growth Diagnostics," in Narcis Serra and Joe Stiglitz (eds.), *The Washington Consensus Reconsidered: Towards a New Global Governance* (New York: Oxford University Press, 2008).

Chapter 12

1. North, *Institutions, Institutional Change and Economic Performance*. Oliver Willliamson, "The New Institutional Economics: Taking Stock, Looking Ahead," *Journal of Economic Literature*, Vol. 38 (September 2000): 595.

2. Douglass North, *Institutions, Institutional Change and Economic Performance* (New York: Cambridge University Press, 1990).

3. For this point, see Merilee Grindle, *Jobs for the Boys*.

4. Verena Fritz, Brian Levy, and Rachel Ort, *Problem-Driven Political Economy Analysis—The World Bank's Experience* (Washington, DC: World Bank Institute, 2014).

5. Integrity pacts were pioneered by the global nongovernmental organization Transparency International. For a review of the experience with these pacts, see Transparency International, *Integrity Pacts: The Concept, the Model, and the Present Applications: A Status Report as of December 31, 2002* (Berlin).

6. The Lacey Act bans the importation of products (including forest and fishery products) that have been extracted in ways that fail to meet a country's own regulatory standards. The Montreal Protocol is a global agreement not to import CFC-using products. For further details, see Brian Levy, "Innovations in Globalized Regulation," 2011.

7. Albert O. Hirschman, *A Bias for Hope* (New Haven, CT: Yale University Press, 1971), pp. 28, 37.

8. Indeed, having completed the book, Hirschman asked his publisher whether he could change the title of the book to *The Rhetoric of Instransigence* but was turned down. See Jeremy Adelman, *Worldly Philosopher: The Odyssey of Albert O. Hirschman* (Princeton, NJ: Princeton University Press, 2013), p. 632.

9. Albert Hirschman, *The Rhetoric of Reaction* (Cambridge: Harvard University Press, 1991), pp. 167–170.

BIBLIOGRAPHY

Acemoglu, Daron, Simon Johnson, and James Robinson. 2001. "The Colonial Origins of Comparative Development: An Empirical Investigation," *American Economic Review* 91(5): 1369–1401.

Acemoglu, Daron, Simon Johnson, James A. Robinson, and Pierre Yared. 2008. "Income and Democracy," *American Economic Review* 98(3): 808–842.

———. 2009. "Re-evaluating the Modernization Hypothesis," *Journal of Monetary Economics* 56: 1043–1058.

Acemoglu, Daron, and James A. Robinson. 2006. *The Economic Origins of Dictatorship and Democracy* (New York: Cambridge University Press).

———. 2012. *Why Nations Fail* (New York: Crown Books).

Adam, Heribert, and Hermann Giliomee. 1979. *The Rise and Crisis of Afrikaner Power* (Cape Town: David Phillip).

Adelman, Jeremy. 2013. *Worldly Philosopher: The Odyssey of Albert O. Hirschman* (Princeton, NJ: Princeton University Press).

Amsden, Alice. 1992. *Asia's Next Giant: South Korea and Late Industrialization* (New York: Oxford University Press).

Andrews, Matt. 2013. *The Limits of Institutional Reform in Development* (New York: Cambridge University Press).

Ashworth, R., G. Boyne, and R. Delbridge. 2007. "Escape from the Iron Cage? Organizational Change and Isomorphic Pressures in the Public Sector," *Journal of Public Administration, Research and Theory* 19: 165–187.

Banerjee, Abhijit, R. Banerji, E. Duflo, R. Glennerster, and S. Khemani. 2008. "Pitfalls of Participatory Programs: Evidence from a Randomized Evaluation in Education in India," Policy Research Working Paper 4584 (Washington, DC: World Bank).

Barro, Robert. 1991. "Economic Growth in a Cross-Section of Countries," *Quarterly Journal of Economics* 106: 407–433.

Barron, Patrick, Rachael Diprose, and Michael Woolcock. 2011. *Contesting Development: Participatory Projects and Local Conflict Dynamics in Indonesia* (New Haven, CT: Yale University Press).

Bates, Robert H., Avner Greif, Margaret Levi, Jean-Laurent Rosenthal, and Barry R. Weingast. 1998. *Analytic Narratives* (Princeton, NJ: Princeton University Press).

Bhagwati, Jagdish. 1982. "Directly Unproductive, Profit-seeking (DUP) Activities," *Journal of Political Economy* 90: 988–1002.

Bhorat, Haroon, Carlene van der Westhuizen, and T. Jacobs. 2009. "Income and Non-Income Inequality in Post-Apartheid South Africa," Development Policy Research Unit Working Paper, University of Cape Town.

Bjorkman, Martina, and Jakob Svensson. 2009. "Power to the People: Evidence from a Randomized Field Experiment of a Community-Based Monitoring Project in Uganda," *Quarterly Journal of Economics* 124(2): 735–769.

Booth, David. 2012. *Development as a Collective Action Problem: Addressing the Real Challenges of African Governance*, Synthesis Report of the Africa Power and Politics Programme, Overseas Development Institute (London).

Booth, David, and Diana Cammack. 2013. *Governance for Development in Africa: Solving Collective Action Problems* (London: Zed Books, 2013).

Bratton, Michael, and Nicholas van de Walle. 1997. *Democratic Experiments in Africa* (Cambridge: Cambridge University Press).

Bruns, Barbara, Deon Filmer, and Harry Patrinos. 2011. *Making Schools Work: New Evidence on Accountability Reforms* (Washington, DC: World Bank).

Bukenya, Badru, Sam Hickey, and Sophie King. 2012. "Understanding the Role of Context in Shaping Social Accountability Interventions: Towards an Evidence-Based Approach," Report commissioned by the World Bank's Social Accountability and Demand for Good Governance Team, June.

Campos, Ed, and Hilton Root. 1996. *The Key to the East Asian Miracle: Making Shared Growth Credible* (Washington, DC: Brookings).

Cardoso, Fernando Henrique, and Enzo Faletto. 1979. *Dependency and Development in Latin America* (Berkeley: University of California Press).

Carothers, T., 1998. "The Rule of Law Revival," *Foreign Affairs*, March/April 1998: 95–106.

———. 2002. "The End of the Transition Paradigm," *Journal of Democracy* 13(1): 5–21.

——— and de Gramont, D. 2013. *Development Aid Confronts Politics: The Almost Revolution* (Washington, DC: Carnegie Endowment).

Carpenter, Daniel P. 2001. *The Forging of Bureaucratic Autonomy: Reputations, Networks and Policy Innovation in Executive Agencies, 1862–1928* (Princeton, NJ: Princeton University Press).

Chang, Ha-Joon. 2007. *The East Asian Development Experience* (London: Zed Books).

Chase, Robert. 2011. "Progress on Social Accountability Through Ethiopia's Basic Services Program," Powerpoint presentation (Washington, DC: World Bank).

Chaudhry, Nazmul, Jeffrey Hammer, Michael Kremer, Karthik Muralidharan, and F. Halsey Rogers. 2006. "Missing in Action: Teachers and Health Worker Absence in Developing Countries," *Journal of Economic Perspectives* 20(1): 91–116.

Che, Jiahua, and Yingyi Qian. 1998. "Institutional Environment, Community Government, and Corporate Governance: Understanding China's Township-Village Enterprises," *Journal of Law, Economics and Organization* 14(1): 1–23.

Chong, Alberto, and Cesar Calderon. 2000. "Causality and Feedback Between Institutional Measures and Economic Growth," *Economics and Politics* 12(1): 69–81.

Clapham, Christopher. 1985. *Third World Politics: An Introduction* (Madison: University of Wisconsin Press).

Coase, Ronald. 1937. "The Nature of the Firm," *Economica* 4(16): 386–405.

———. 1960. "The Problem of Social Cost," *Journal of Law and Economics* 3: 1–44.

Collier, Paul. 2007. *The Bottom Billion* (Oxford: Oxford University Press).

———. 2010. *The Plundered Planet* (Oxford: Oxford University Press).

Crook, R.C. 2010. "Rethinking Civil Service Reform in Africa: 'Islands of Effectiveness' and Organizational Commitment," *Commonwealth and Comparative Politics* 48: 479–504.

Dawkins, Richard. 1986. *The Blind Watchmaker* (Essex: Longman Scientific & Technical).

De Long, J. Bradford, and Lawrence H. Summers. 1991. "Equipment Investment and Economic Growth," *Quarterly Journal of Economics* 106(2): 445–502.

Devarajan, Shantayanan, Stuti Khemani, and Michael Walton. 2011. "Civil Society, Public Action and Accountability in Africa," World Bank Policy Research Working Paper 5733 (Washington, DC: World Bank).

Diamond, Larry. 1992. "Economic Development and Democracy Reconsidered," *American Behavioral Scientist* 15(4–5): 450–499.

———. 2008. *The Spirit of Democracy* (New York: Times Books).

Dinh, Hinh, Vincent Palmade, Vandana Chandra, and Frances Cossar. 2012. *Light Manufacturing in Africa* (Washington, DC: Agence Francaise de Developpement and World Bank).

Duflo, Esther, P. Dupas, and M. Kremer. 2007. "Peer Effects, Pupil–Teacher Ratios, and Teacher Incentives: Evidence from a Randomization Evaluation in Kenya," Unpublished manuscript, Abdul Latif Jameel Poverty Action Lab, Massachusetts Institute of Technology, Cambridge, MA.

———. 2009. "Additional Resources Versus Organizational Changes in Education: Experimental Evidence in Kenya," Unpublished manuscript, Abdul Latif Jameel Poverty Action Lab, Massachusetts Institute of Technology, Cambridge, MA.

Easterly, William. 2001. *The Elusive Quest for Growth* (Cambridge, MA: MIT Press).

———. 2006. *The White Man's Burden* (New York: Penguin Books).

Evans, Peter. 1996. *Embedded Autonomy: States and Industrial Transformation* (Princeton, NJ: Princeton University Press).

Evans, Peter, and James E. Rauch. 1999. "Bureaucracy and Growth: A Cross-National Analysis of the Effects of 'Weberian' State Structures on Economic Growth," *American Sociological Review* 64: 748–765.

Evans, Peter, Dietrich Rueschemeyer, and Theda Skocpol (eds.). 1985. *Bringing the State Back In* (New York: Cambridge University Press).

Ferraz, Claudio, and Frederico Finan. 2008. "Exposing Corrupt Politicians: The Effects of Brazil's Publicly Released Audits on Electoral Outcomes," *Quarterly Journal of Economics* 123(2): 703–745.

Fritz, Verena, and Brian Levy. 2014. "Problem Driven Political Economy in Action: Overview and Synthesis of the Case Studies," in Verena Fritz, Brian Levy, and Rachel Ort (eds.), *Problem-Driven Political Economy Analysis: The World Bank's Experience* (Washington, DC: World Bank).

Fritz, Verena, Brian Levy, and Rachel Ort (eds.). 2014. *Problem-Driven Political Economy Analysis: The World Bank's Experience*. World Bank Directions in Development Series. (Washington, DC: World Bank).

Fukuyama, Francis. 2004. *Statebuilding* (Ithaca, NY: Cornell University Press).

———. 2012. *The Origins of Political Order* (New York: Farrar, Straus and Giroux).

Geddes, Barbara. 1994. *Politician's Dilemma: Building State Capacity in Latin America* (Berkeley: University of California Press).

George, Alexander L., and Andrew Bennett. 2005. *Case Studies and Theory Development in the Social Sciences* (Cambridge, MA: MIT Press).

Greif, Avner. 2005. *Institutions and the Path to the Modern Economy* (New York: Cambridge University Press).

Grindle, Merilee. 2004. *Despite the Odds: The Contentious Politics of Education Reform* (Princeton, NJ: Princeton University Press).

———. 2004. "Good Enough Governance: Poverty Reduction and Reform in Developing Countries," *Governance* 17(4): 525–548.

———. 2013. *Jobs for the Boys* (Cambridge, MA: Harvard University Press).

Haber, Stephen, Herbert Klein, Noel Maurer, and Kevin Middlebrook. 2008. *Mexico Since 1980* (New York: Cambridge University Press).

Haber, Stephen, Armando Razo, and Noel Maurer. 2003. *The Politics of Property Rights* (New York: Cambridge University Press).

Haggard, Stephan, Andrew MacIntyre, and Lydia Tiede. 2008. "The Rule of Law and Economic Development," *Annual Review of Political Science* 11: 205–234.

Hallward-Driemeier, Mary, Gita Khun-Jush, and Lant Pritchett 2010. "Deals Versus Rules: Policy Implementation Uncertainty and Why Firms Hate It," World Bank Policy Research Working Paper 5321 (Washington, DC: World Bank).

Hampton, A. 2006. "Local Government and Investment Promotion in China," mimeo, Institute of Development Studies, University of Sussex.

Hausmann, Ricardo, Lant Pritchett, and Dani Rodrik. 2005. "Growth Accelerations," *Journal of Economic Growth* 10: 303–329.

Hausmann, Ricardo, Dani Rodrik, and Andres Velasco. 2008. "Growth Diagnostics," in Narcis Serra and Joe Stiglitz (eds.), *The Washington Consensus Reconsidered: Towards a New Global Governance* (New York: Oxford University Press).

Henderson, Gregory. 1968. *The Politics of the Vortex* (Cambridge, MA: Harvard University Press).

Henderson, Jeffrey, David Hulme, Richard Phillips, and Eun Mee Kim. 2002. "Economic Governance and Poverty Reduction in South Korea," *Globalization and Poverty Report to the DFID* (London: Department for International Development).

Hirschman, Albert O. 1957. *A Strategy of Economic Development* (New Haven, CT: Yale University Press).

———. 1971. *A Bias for Hope: Essays on Development and Latin America* (New Haven, CT: Yale University Press).

———. 1991. *The Rhetoric of Reaction* (Cambridge, MA: Harvard University Press).

Hofstadter, Richard. 1955. *The Age of Reform* (New York: Random House).

Hubbard, Paul. 2007. "Putting the Power of Transparency in Context: Information's Role in Reducing Corruption in Uganda's Education Sector," Center for Global Development Working Paper 136 (Washington, DC: Center for Global Development).

Huntington, Samuel P. 1968. *Political Order in Changing Societies* (New Haven, CT: Yale University Press).

———. 1991. *The Third Wave: Democratization in the Late Twentieth Century* (Norman: University of Oklahoma Press).

International Monetary Fund. 2005. "IMF Technical Assistance Evaluation: Public Expenditure Management Reform in Anglophone African Countries" (Washington, DC: International Monetary Fund, Fiscal Affairs Department).

Jimenez, Emmanuel, and Y. Sawada. 1999. "Do Community-Managed Schools Work?" *World Bank Economic Review* 13(3): 415–441.

Jobson, Elissa 2013. "Chinese Firm Steps Up Investment in Ethiopia with 'Shoe City,'" *The Guardian*, April 30.

Johnson, Ronald N., and Gary Libecap. 1994. *The Federal Civil Service System and the Problem of Bureaucracy* (Chicago: Chicago University Press).

Jones, Leroy P., and Il Sakong. 1980. *Business, Government and Entrepreneurship: The Korean Case* (Cambridge, MA: Harvard University Press for Harvard Institute for International Development).

Kang, David. 2002. *Crony Capitalism: Corruption and Development in South Korea and the Philippines* (New York: Cambridge University Press, 2002).

Kaufmann, Daniel, Aart Kraay, and Massimo Mastruzzi. 2010. "The Worldwide Governance Indicators: Methodology and Analytical Issues," World Bank Policy Research Working Paper 5430 (Washington, DC: World Bank).

Kaufman, Robert R., and Joan M. Nelson. 2004. *Crucial Needs, Weak Incentives: Social Sector Reform, Democratization and Globalization in Latin America* (Baltimore: Johns Hopkins University Press).

Keefer, Phil, and Stuti Khemani. 2005. "Democracy, Public Expenditures and the Poor: Understanding Political Incentives for Providing Public Services," *World Bank Research Observer* 20(1): 1–27.

Kelsall, Tim. 2013. *Business, Politics and the State in Africa* (London: Zed Press).

Kelsall, Tim, and David Booth. 2010. "Developmental Patrimonialism?" Africa Power and Politics Series, Working Paper (London: Overseas Development Institute).

Khan, Mushtaq. 2010. "Political Settlements and the Governance of Growth-Enhancing Institutions," mimeo.

———. 2013. "Bangladesh: Economic Growth in a Fragile Limited Access Order," in Douglass North, John Wallis, Barry Weingast, and Stephen Webb (eds.), *In the Shadow of Violence—The Problem of Development in Limited Access Order Societies* (New York: Cambridge University Press).

Khan, Mushtaq, and K.S. Jomo. 2000. *Rents, Rent-seeking and Economic Development: Theory and Evidence in Asia* (Cambridge, MA: Cambridge University Press).

Khan, Mohammad Mohabbat, and John P. Thorp (eds.). 1984. *Bangladesh: Society, Politics and Bureaucracy* (Dhaka: Centre for Administrative Studies).

Kikeri, Sunita, Thomas Kenyon, and Vincent Palmade. 2006. *Reforming the Investment Climate: Lessons for Practitioners* (Washington, DC: World Bank).

Kim, Sunwoong, and Ju-Ho Lee. 2006. "Changing Facets of Higher Education in Korea: Market Competition and the Role of the State," *Higher Education* 52: 557–587.

Kim, Byung-Kook, and Ezra Vogel (eds.). 2011. *The Park Chung Hee Era: The Transformation of South Korea* (Cambridge, MA: Harvard University Press).

Kleinfeld, Rachel. 2012. *Advancing the Rule of Law Abroad: Next Generation Reform* (Washington, DC: Carnegie Endowment for International Peace).

Knack, Stephen, and Philip Keefer. 1995. "Institutions and Economic Performance: Cross-Country Tests Using Alternative Institutional Measures," *Economics and Politics* 7: 207–227.

Kohli, Atul. 2004. *State-Directed Development: Political Power and Industrialization in the Global Periphery* (New York: Cambridge University Press).

Korten, David. 1972. *Planned Change in a Traditional Society: Psychological Problems of Modernization in Ethiopia* (New York: Praeger).

Krueger, Anne. 1974. "The Political Economy of the Rent-seeking Society," *American Economic Review* 64: 291–303.

Kurtz, Marcus J. and Andrew Schrank (2007). "Growth and Governance: Models, Measures and Mechanisms", *The Journal of Politics*, Volume 69, Number 2, pp. 538–554

Leonard, David K. (2008). "Where are pockets of effective agencies likely in weak governance states, and why? A propositional inventory", IDS Working Paper number 306, June.

Levitsky, Steven, and Lucan Way 2010. *Competitive Authoritarianism* (New York: Cambridge University Press).

Leibbrandt, Murray, Ingrid Woolard, Arden Finn, & Jonathan Argent. 2010. "Trends in South African Income Distribution and Poverty Since the Fall of Apartheid", OECD Social, Employment and Migration Working Papers No. 1010.

Levy, Brian. 2007. *Governance Reform: Bridging Monitoring and Action* (Washington, DC: World Bank).

———. 2010a. "Democracy Support and Development Aid: The Case for Principled Agnosticism," *Journal of Democracy* 21(4): 27–34.

———. 2010b. "Development Trajectories: An Evolutionary Approach to Integrating Governance and Growth," Economic Premise Note #15, PREM Vice Presidency, World Bank, Washington, DC.

———. 2011a. "Can Islands of Effectiveness Thrive in Difficult Governance Settings? The Political Economy Of Local-Level Collaborative Governance" World Bank Policy Research Working Paper 5842. (Washington, DC: World Bank).

———. 2011b. "Innovations in Globalized Regulation: Opportunities and Challenges," World Bank Policy Research Working Paper 5841 (Washington, DC: World Bank).

———. 2011c. "Seeking the Elusive Development Knife-Edge: Zambia and Mozambique—A Tale of Two Countries," in Douglass North, John Wallis, Barry Weingast, and Stephen Webb (eds.), *In the Shadow of Violence—The Problem of Development in Limited Access Order Societies* (New York: Cambridge University Press, 2013).

Levy, Brian, Albert Berry, and Jeffrey B. Nugent. 1999. *Fulfilling the Export Potential of Small and Medium Firms* (Boston: Kluwer).

Levy, Brian, Alex de Jager, Brendan Meehan, and Tony Leiman. 2012. "Regulatory Efficacy in a Changing Political Environment: A Tale of Two South African Fisheries," Paper presented at World Bank Workshop on the Political Economy of Fisheries, Washington, DC, April 12.

Levy, Brian, and Francis Fukuyama. 2010. "Development Strategies: Bridging Governance and Growth," World Bank Policy Research Working Paper 5196 (Washington, DC: World Bank).

Levy, Brian, and Sahr Kpundeh. 2004. *Building State Capacity in Africa*. World Bank Institute Development Studies (Washington, DC: World Bank).

Levy, Brian, and Pablo Spiller. 1994. "The Institutional Foundations of Regulatory Commitment: A Comparative Analysis of Telecommunications Regulation," *Journal of Law, Economics and Organization* 10(2): 201–246.

———, and Pablo Spiller. 1997. *Regulations, Institutions and Commitment* (New York: Cambridge University Press).

Levy, Brian, and Michael Walton. 2013. "Institutions, Incentives and Service Provision: Bringing Politics Back In," Working Paper 18, Effective States and Inclusive Development Research Program, University of Manchester, February.

Lewis, Peter. 1996. "From Pre-bendalism to Predation: The Political Economy of Decline in Nigeria," *Journal of Modern African Studies* 34(1): 79–103.

Lewis, David. 2011. *Bangladesh: Politics, Economics and Civil Society* (New York: Cambridge University Press).

Lipset, Seymour Martin. 1959. "Some Social Requisites of Democracy: Economic Development and Political Legitimacy," *American Political Science Review* 53: 69–105.

———. 1983. *Political Man: The Social Bases of Politics*, 2d ed. (London: Heinemann).

Manor, James. 2004. "User Committees: A Potentially Damaging Second Wave of Decentralization?" *European Journal of Development Research* 16(1): 192–213.

Mansuri, Ghazala, and Vijayendra Rao. 2013. *Localizing Development: Does Participation Work?* (Washington, DC: World Bank).

Marshall, Monty, Ted Gurr, and Keith Jaggers. 2013. "Polity IV Project: Political Regime Characteristics and Transitions, 1800–2012—Users Manual" (Vienna, VA: Center for Systematic Peace).

Mauro, Paolo. 1998. "Corruption and Growth," *Quarterly Journal of Economics* 110: 681–712.

McGerr, Michael. 2003. *A Fierce Discontent: The Rise and Fall of the Progressive Movement in America, 1870–1920* (New York: Oxford University Press).

McGregor, Richard. 2010. *The Party: The Secret World of China's Communist Rulers* (New York: HarperCollins).

Meacham, John. 2012. *Thomas Jefferson: The Art of Power* (New York: Random House).

Mitchell, Melanie. 2011. *Complexity: A Guided Tour* (New York: Oxford University Press).

Mkandawire, Thandika. 2001. "Thinking About Developmental States in Africa," *Cambridge Journal of Economics* 25(3): 289–313.

Moore, Barrington. 1966. *The Social Origins of Dictatorship and Democracy* (Boston: Beacon Press).

Morris, Edmund. 1979. *The Rise of Theodore Roosevelt* (New York: Random House).

Morris, Mike, and Brian Levy. In press. "The Limits of Co-operation in a Divided Society: The Political Economy of South Africa's Garment and Textile Industry," in Anthony Black (ed.), *Structural Unemployment in South Africa* (Cape Town: UCT Press).

Nattrass, Nicoli, and Jeremy Seekings. 2008. *Class, Race and Inequality in South Africa* (New Haven, CT: Yale University Press).

North, Douglass C. 1982. *Structure and Change in Economic History* (New York: W.W. Norton).

———. 1990. *Institutions, Institutional Change and Economic Performance* (New York: Cambridge University Press).

North, Douglass C., John Wallis, and Barry Weingast. 2009. *Violence and Social Orders* (New York: Cambridge University Press).

North, Douglass C., John Wallis, Barry Weingast, and Stephen Webb (eds.). 2013. *In the Shadow of Violence—The Problem of Development in Limited Access Order Societies* (New York: Cambridge University Press).

North, Douglass C., and Barry Weingast. 1989. "Constitutions and Commitment: The Evolution of Institutions Governing Public Choice in 17th Century England," *Journal of Economic History* 49(4): 803–832.

Olken, Benjamin. 2007. "Monitoring Corruption: Evidence from a Field Experiment in Indonesia," *Journal of Political Economy* 115(2): 200–249.

O'Meara, Dan. 1983. *Volkskapitalisme: Class, Capital and Ideology in the Development of Afrikaner Nationalism, 1934–1948* (Cambridge: Cambridge University Press).

Ostrom, Elinor. 1990. *Governing the Commons* (New York: Cambridge University Press).

———. 2005. *Understanding Institutional Diversity.* (Princeton, NJ: Princeton University Press).

———. 2007. "A Diagnostic Approach for Going Beyond Panaceas," *PNAS: Proceedings of the National Academy of Sciences* (September 25): 15181–15187.

———. 2009. "Beyond Markets and States: Polycentric Governance of Complex Economic Systems," 2009 Nobel Prize Lecture, *American Economic Review* 100(3): 641–672.

Pandey, Priyanka, Sangeeta Goyal, and Venkatesh Sundararaman. 2009. "Community Participation in Public Schools: Impact of Information Campaigns in Three Indian States," *Education Economics* 17(3): 355–375.

Patunru, A., N. McCulloch, and C. von Luebke. 2009. "A Tale of Two Cities: The Political Economy of the Investment Climate in Solo and Manado, Indonesia," *IDS Working Papers* 338.

Paul, Samuel. 2002. *Holding the State to Account: Citizen Monitoring in Action* (Bangalore, India: Books for Change).

Pollitt, Christopher, and Geert Bouckaert. 2000. *Public Management Reform: A Comparative Analysis* (Oxford: Oxford University Press).

Porter, Michael. 1998. *The Competitive Advantage of Nations* (New York: The Free Press).

Pritchett, Lant, Michael Woolcock, and Matt Andrews. 2010. "Capability Traps? The Mechanisms of Persistent Implementation Failure," Center for Global Development Working Paper 234 (Washington, DC: Center for Global Development).

Przeworski, Adam, Michael Alvarez, Jose A. Cheibub, and Fernando Limongi. 2000. *Democracy and Development: Political Institutions and Material Well-being in the World, 1950–1990* (New York: Cambridge University Press).

Przeworski, Adam, and Fernando Limongi. 1997. "Modernization: Theory and Facts," *World Politics* 49(2): 155–183.

Rakner, Lise. 2003. *Political and Economic Liberalization in Zambia: 1991–2001* (Uppsala: NAI).

Reid, Gary. 2005. "The Political Economy of Civil Service Reform in Albania," mimeo, World Bank, Washington, DC.

Reinikka, Ritva, and Jakob Svensson. 2004. "Local Capture: Evidence from a Central Government Transfer Program in Uganda," *Quarterly Journal of Economics* 119(2): 679–705.

———. 2005. "Fighting Corruption to Improve Schooling: Evidence from a Newspaper Campaign in Uganda," *Journal of the European Economic Association* 3(2): 259–267.

Rhee, Yung Whee, and Therese Belot. 1989. "Export Catalyst in Low-Income Countries," World Bank Industry and Energy Department Working Paper 5, Industry Series.

Rhee, Yung-Whee, Bruce Ross-Larson, and Garry Pursell. 1984. *Korea's Competitive Edge: Managing the Entry into World Markets* (Washington, DC: Johns Hopkins University Press for World Bank).

Rigobon, Roberto, and Dani Rodrik. 2005. "Rule of Law, Democracy, Openness and Income: Estimating the Inter-Relationships," *Economics of Transition* 13(3): 533–564.

Rodrik, Dani (ed.) 2004. *In Search of Prosperity: Analytic Narratives of Economic Growth* (Princeton, NJ: Princeton University Press).

———. 2006. "Goodbye Washington Consensus, Hello Washington Confusion," *Journal of Economic Literature* 44(4): 973–987.

———. 2007. *One Economics, Many Recipes* (Princeton, NJ: Princeton University Press).

Rodrik, Dani, A. Subramanian, and F. Trebbi. 2004. "Institutions Rule: The Primacy of Institutions over Geography and Integration in Economic Development," *Journal of Economic Growth* 9(2): 131–165.

Rosenstein-Rodan, Paul. 1943. "Problems of Industrialisation of Eastern and South-Eastern Europe," *Economic Journal* 53(210): 202–211.

Rostow, Walt W. 1960. *The Stages of Economic Growth* (Cambridge: Cambridge University Press).

Ruggie, John Gerard. 2002. "Taking Embedded Liberalism Global: The Corporate Connection," Paper presented at the American Political Science Association Meeting, Boston, August.

Sardanis, Andrew. 2007. *A Venture in Africa: The Challenges of African Business* (New York: Palgrave MacMillan).

Schady, Norbert. 2000. "The Political Economy of Expenditures by the Peruvian Social Fund (FONCODES), 1991–1995," *American Political Science Review* 94(2): 289–303.

Schick, Alan. 1999. "Why Most Developing Countries Should Not Try New Zealand Reforms," *World Bank Research Observer* 13: 123–131.

Schumpeter, Joseph. 1942. *Capitalism, Socialism and Democracy* (New York: Harper & Brothers).

Slaughter, Anne-Marie. 2005. *The New World Order* (Princeton, NJ: Princeton University Press).

Sonobi, Tetsushi, John Akoten, and Kejiro Otsuka. 2009. "An Exploration into the Successful Development of the Leather Shoe Industry in Ethiopia," *Review of Development Economics* 13: 719–736.

Srivastava, Vivek, and Marco Larizza. 2013. "Working with the Grain for Reforming the Public Service: A Live Example from Sierra Leone," *International Review of Administrative Sciences* 79: 458–485.

Taylor, Scott, and Neo Simutanyi. 2007. "Governance and Political Economy Constraints to Development Priorities in Zambia: A Diagnostic," mimeo.

Thomas, Melissa. 2009. "What Do the Worldwide Governance Indicators Measure?" *European Journal of Development Research* 22: 31–54.

Tschirley, David, and Stephen Kabwe. 2009. "The Cotton Sector of Zambia," World Bank Africa Region Working Paper 124 (Washington, DC: World Bank).

Tschirley, David, Colin Poulton, and Patrick Labaste (eds.). 2009. *Organization and Performance of Cotton Sectors in Africa* (Washington, DC: World Bank).

Vaughan, Sarah, and K. Tronvoli. 2003. "The Culture of Power in Contemporary Ethiopian Political Life," *SIDA Studies No. 10*, Stockholm, Sweden.

Vernon, Raymond. 1973. *Sovereignty at Bay* (New York: Basic Books).

Visagie, Justin. 2013. "Is the Middle Class Becoming Better Off? Two Perspectives," *Econ3x3. org*, July.

Vogel, David. 2005. *The Market for Virtue: The Potential and Limits of Corporate Social Responsibility*. (Washington, DC: Brookings Institution).

———. 2006. "The Private Regulation of Global Corporate Conduct," Center for Responsible Business, University of California, Berkeley.

Wade, Robert. 1996. "Japan, the World Bank, and the Art of Paradigm Maintenance: The East Asian Miracle in Perspective," *New Left Review* 217: 3.

Waldrop, M. Mitchell. 1992. *Complexity: The Emerging Science at the Edge of Order and Chaos* (New York: Simon & Schuster).

Unsworth, Sue. 2009. *An Upside-Down View of Governance* (Brighton: Institute of Development Studies, University of Sussex).

Weaver, Catherine. 2008. *Hypocrisy Trap: The World Bank and the Poverty of Reform* (Princeton, NJ: Princeton University Press).

Weber, Max. 1922. *Economy and Society* (Berlin).

Weingast, Barry. 1993. "Constitutions as Governance Structures: The Political Foundations of Secure Markets," *Journal of Institutional and Theoretical Economics* 149: 286–311.

Williamson, John. 2000. "What Should the World Bank Think About the Washington Consensus?" *World Bank Research Observer* 15(2): 251–264.

Williamson, Oliver. 1985. *The Economic Institutions of Capitalism* (New York: The Free Press).

———. 2000. "The New Institutional Economics: Taking Stock, Looking Ahead," *Journal of Economic Literature* 38: 595–613.

Wilson, James Q. 1989. *Bureaucracy* (New York: Basic Books).

Wong, Susan. 2012. "What Have Been the Impacts of World Bank Community-Driven Development Programs?" (Washington, DC: World Bank Social Development Department).

World Bank. 1993. *The East Asian Miracle* (New York: Oxford University Press for the World Bank).

———. 2000. *Can Africa Claim the 21st Century?* (New York: Oxford University Press for World Bank).

———. 2002. *Taming Leviathan: Reforming Governance in Bangladesh—An Institutional Review* (Dhaka).

———. 2003. "Zambia: Completion Report for 1999–2003 Country Assistance Strategy." Washington, DC.

———. 2004. "Economics and Governance of Nongovernmental Organizations in Bangladesh," Bangladesh Development Series, Paper 11, Dhaka.

———. 2004. "Ethiopia Public Expenditure Review 2004: The Emerging Challenge," Report 29338-ET.

———. 2004. "Making Services Work for Poor People," World Development Report 2004 (Washington, DC: World Bank and Oxford University Press).

———. 2006. "Equity and Development," World Development Report 2006 (Washington, DC: World Bank and Oxford University Press).

———. 2007. "Ethiopia: Accelerating Equitable Growth, A Country Memorandum," Report 38662.

———. 2008. "Country Assistance Strategy for Zambia," International Development Association, Report 43352-ET.

———. 2008. *Public Sector Reform: What Works and Why?* (Washington, DC: World Bank).

———. 2009. "Governance and Anticorrruption in Projects: Benchmarking and Learning Review". Washington, DC.

———. 2009. "The World Bank Group Program of Support for the Chad-Cameroon Petroleum Development and Pipeline Construction," Report 50315, November.

———. 2010. "Country Assistance Strategy for the People's Republic of Bangladesh for the Period FY11-FY14," Report 54615-BD.

———. 2010. "Ethiopia Public Finance Review 2010," Report 54952-ET.

You, Jong-Sung. 2013. "Transition from a Limited to an Open Access Order: The Case of Korea," in Douglass North, John Wallis, Barry Weingast, and Stephen Webb (eds.), *In the Shadow of Violence—The Problem of Development in Limited Access Order Societies* (New York: Cambridge University Press).

Zadek, Simon. 2006. "The Logic of Collaborative Governance," Corporate Social Responsibility Initiative Working Paper 17, Kennedy School of Government, Harvard University.

Zakaria, Fareed. 2007. *Illiberal Democracy* (New York: W.W. Norton).

Zenawi, Meles. N.d. *African Development: Dead Ends, and New Beginnings,* Columbia University, http://cgt.columbia.edu/files/conferences/Zenawi_Dead_Ends_and_New_Beginnings.pdf.

INDEX